STRESSPROOF

To my wife, Gaby, and sons, Isaac and Joshua;
you are my world and greatest blessing.

STRESSPROOF

The Game Plan

RICHARD SUTTON

MACMILLAN

First published in 2021
by Pan Macmillan South Africa
Private Bag X19
Northlands 2116
Johannesburg
South Africa

www.panmacmillan.co.za

ISBN 978-1-77010-782-3
E-ISBN 978-1-77010-783-0

Editing by Jane Bowman
Proofreading by Claire Heckrath
Design and typesetting by Triple M Design, Johannesburg
Cover design by publicide
Author photograph by Jason Crouse

FSC www.fsc.org MIX Paper from responsible sources FSC® C022948

Printed by ***novus print***, a division of Novus Holdings

CONTENTS

PREFACE
Where it all started

In 1998, having recently returned from the United States (US) where I had completed a course under the tutelage of the leading authority on core training and athletic development, a medical supply company approached me to put together a talk on proprioception and core training. They had made a large investment in exercise balls and similar devices that, to their surprise, were not selling, and they were hoping that through a series of seminars they could create enough awareness to increase sales.

The equipment was readily available in the US and was being used in a therapeutic context by top teams and athletes. It was very familiar to me and so I was comfortable speaking about the area of focus and, in turn, promoting the equipment.

The company requested that I start with a pilot session with a small audience in a small town and gauge the response. I was nervous at the thought of public speaking but at the same time I was very excited. The opportunity to be paid for what I believed in and loved was inconceivable. But there was one small snag – I was petrified of group and public speaking and my track record of effectively communicating with more than two or three people at a time was unimpressive.

Looking back more than two decades, I recall how unprepared I was, with no slides prepared and no formal structure to the all-day session. But what I did have was passion and enthusiasm.

The organisers picked me up at 5.30am that day and we drove to a small physiotherapy practice two hours outside of Johannesburg. It was mid-July and brutally cold (by South African standards) and I hadn't slept the night before as my fears and insecurities had been all-consuming and irrational. My 2am self-dialogue questioned what I had signed up for and that maybe I should cancel it all. Fortunately, by 5am I felt calmer and reconciled to the event.

We arrived at the physiotherapy practice where a modest-sized room had been set up. A group of nine highly experienced physiotherapists had graciously given up their day to learn about the new and innovative philosophy of training and rehabilitation that I was eager to share with them. They were warm and welcoming and after a super strong cup of coffee (in hindsight, not the best idea as coffee increases our stress response) I was standing in front of the group. I was so nervous that I could hardly get my words out for the first hour, which was interrupted by the occasional and involuntary tremble of my hands and chatter of my teeth. The group remained patient and extremely tolerant and my nerves abated as I became immersed in the content and engagement with the group.

The next few hours passed in what felt like minutes and the workshop became effortless and enjoyable. It turned out to be a great success, despite the lack of polish on my part, no dazzling keynote presentation, no impressive stage, no dramatic lighting or music effects or a designer suit. It was just me and a group of deeply caring women sharing a passion for knowledge, health and helping others.

This soon turned into a nationwide tour where the groups got bigger, the content was accompanied by a manual and my communication style became (a little) more refined. I never lost those initial nerves or that feeling of being completely overwhelmed but I simply resigned myself to the fact that the first five minutes might not be as coherent as the rest of the session and realised that nerves are a good thing and, when used correctly, stress gives us superpowers.

I spoke at clinics and private groups around the country and I was asked to speak at leading universities locally and, later, internationally. My audiences had become predominantly post-graduate students and the content far more academic, expansive and heavily evidence-based. I soon discovered a pattern and regardless of the topic, location or size of the group, the question of stress always came up. People constantly asked: What can I do for my stress? How can I better manage my stress? How will this help me with my stress? These questions were well-founded and working in one of the highest stress environments (that of elite level, professional sport), I had provided these kinds of solutions for my clients for almost 15 years.

This sparked an idea within me and I started preliminary research for my book, *The Stress Code*. Two years in, I was approached by the wellness team from a successful bank. They wanted to inspire and motivate one of their most influential leadership teams with health knowledge and personal awareness. I hadn't spoken to a corporate team before but had always aspired to move into this space when I moved out of professional sport. In a briefing session, the wellness team stated that the said high-performing team was struggling with stress and they desperately wanted to provide them with additional tools for their health promotion. The brief was very broad and so I decided to cover a wide variety of health topics that included diet, exercise and trending health topics (at that time it was ketogenic diets).

I was extremely nervous going into the two-hour session. While I had become very comfortable speaking to students and scholars who spoke the same language and shared the same passion, this was different. Quoting impressive academic studies would be dull and boring for this audience and explanations of complex biological interactions and processes would have the group switching off. It was well out of the comfort zone that I had established from my 17 years of academic lecturing.

My nervousness about the event was not related to the size of the audience but rather that one of the wellness team members had taken a chance on me. I wasn't established in the corporate space and this group of leaders and decision makers would not be overly tolerant of 'average'. The stress of not wanting to let her down was actually a positive driver because I put in a tremendous amount of extra time and effort in constructing the session and practising my delivery.

Following what had become my now standard practice of an initial few minutes of stuttering and stumbling, the session went well and received good reviews rated by the group according to scales. Much like the athletes and academic groups, following the session I was inundated by questions pertaining to stress management. These leaders were so affected by stress that it was impacting their performance and their sense of self. That moment was the genesis of my career in organisational leadership and performance.

Following a few more years of research and experience in the corporate space, in 2018 I published my first book, *The Stress Code*. Providing important clarity into the benefits and dangers of stress, as well as a structured model in stress reduction and health promotion, this knowledge set is exceptionally powerful in self-management during difficult and challenging periods. As well as being vital in developing personal resilience, the focus of the book is on self-enhancement and personal well-being.

Two years later, I launched The Stress Code App, which builds heavily on this personal narrative, but adds the extra dimension of being able to measure both personal and organisational stress and resilience and provides a modelling for possible outcomes and necessary interventions.

Fast forward a few months and the result is the book you are holding, *Stressproof: The Game Plan*. Adding two important aspects to the journey in the realisation of potential, it places tremendous weight on the understanding of what drives stress within our lives and those closest to us, specifically relating to the current global landscape within the workplace.

Whether addressing a small group of physiotherapists back in 1998, the main lecture hall at Nanjing University in 2009 or a high-performing leadership team in 2015, I am asked the same question over and over again: How do we deal with stress?

INTRODUCTION

Human potential is nothing short of extraordinary and, in many respects, it is limitless. The ability to grow, learn, adapt and transform is inextricably linked to our sense of fulfilment and, ultimately, our happiness.

Potential can only be fully actualised under two basic conditions: good health and deep human connection. Although good health is often perceived as something that exists within the confines of our physical set, in reality, this is not the case. Instead, health can be viewed as the mergence and co-dependence of our physical, psychological and emotional well-being. This sophisticated unit relies on an ensemble of biological systems all being masterfully conducted.

The role of connectivity and meaningful relationships is equally important in the actualisation of human potential. Social bonds, care, protection, guidance, support and shared identity form the backdrop to self-actualisation by providing direction, safety and confidence in all that we are likely to experience during the course of our lives.

Yet, we live in an age where despite medical advancements assisting us in living longer, health is more elusive and fragile. Chronic diseases, physical pain and mental health are independently and collectively viewed as global health pandemics affecting the lives of a significant portion of the world's population. At the same time, the world is being overwhelmed by viruses and micro-organisms that have brought the planet to a virtual standstill.

The very fabric of human strength and resilience is corroding exponentially. The security and protection once offered by our family units and broader communities is disappearing and being replaced by consumerism, social media and devices that compete fiercely for our limited time and attention. We have become lonely, isolated and vulnerable.

It is our very intelligence, creativity, innovation and ingenuity that ultimately jeopardises our current potential and that of future generations.

Through the process of improving and raising our standard of living, our health is being jeopardised and undermined by chronic stress, rising air pollution, water contamination, a corrupted food chain, not to mention the proliferation of electromagnetic fields through our obsession to be 'connected'. Equally as impactful are the influences of growing hunger, rising poverty and social injustice.

Despite the challenges, the times we are living in also provide tremendous opportunities to those willing to be courageous. The opportunity to rewrite our current script and change the course of history lies in the hands of today's leaders.

For decades we've watched famed naturalist, David Attenborough, document the marvels of our living world. Throughout his life's work he has shown us the urgency with which we need to act in order to save our planet and the dire consequences on inaction. Yet, in many respects we haven't heeded the warnings, resulting in severe climate change with catastrophic consequences.

By the same token, businesses and their people are equally as vulnerable. The corrosion of human health, especially mental well-being and sweeping disconnection, threatens the global economy and the very social fabric of human existence.

If we want the world to change, we have to start uplifting the lives and well-being of people. It is the people who arrive at work every day, who have families that love and rely on them, whose health is dependent on organisational policy and its culture. By the same token, organisations' well-being and future depends on those people.

Business success is ultimately in the hands of its people, their capabilities, their potential and the time they are willing to invest. Leaders need to fully appreciate and realise this shared destiny and the immense responsibility that comes with it.

By shielding those people from chronic stress and strengthening support networks, leaders are able to reduce the prevalence of mental and physical health compromise brought on by fears, distrust, insecurities and conflicts, and also create an environment where productivity increases, innovation grows and creativity blossoms.

When human potential is realised, the probability of business success increases with it. Economic growth coupled with social responsibility can raise more people out of poverty, reduce inequality, give more people access to education and healthcare, slow population growth and, ultimately, save the planet.

Now more than ever, leadership transcends title and jurisdiction and is defined by selfless actions. Role models such as Martin Luther King Jr, Nelson Mandela, Oprah Winfrey, Ruth Bader Ginsberg and Siya Kolisi represent this ideal and the ability to influence society positively.

Drawing from extensive research and case studies, *Stressproof: The Game Plan* unpacks the current barriers that exist in the realisation of individual and team potential and many of the factors that may be limiting growth on an organisational level.

While this understanding is vitally important, practical and established solutions are of equal, if not greater, value. The answer to the question that scientists have been working to resolve for well over 70 years as to how to effectively manage the socio-economic burden of chronic stress, involves three interconnected, yet complementary parts.

The first phase entails the effective delivery of critical knowledge, relevant tools and vital resources to teams to help them to successfully cope with their growing challenges and the relentless demands of the new and evolving reality we are all living in.

The second step centres on buffering and shielding people from modifiable stresses brought on by the Fourth Industrial Revolution. Internal conflicts, reduced sense of worth and value, a fading voice in decision-making, prejudice, bias, lack of respect, absent support structures, insecurities and uncertainties need to be systematically reduced if not altogether removed.

The third step requires that existing potential be translated into extraordinary performance. This requires an entirely new brand of leadership. If we want something to change, *we* need to change first. The entire professional landscape, businesses' teams needs and expectations and the overall pace of life have changed exponentially. This means that leaders need to be faster and more confident in making decisions. At the same time, leaders have to show greater adaptability and be prepared to take greater ownership, not only within their sphere of influence but also of self. The modern leader is a change agent, who is prepared to fail in pursuit of the truth, a visionary who acknowledges the need to act decisively and proactively on issues such as diversity and inclusion, health, environmental issues, personal information security as well as national challenges.

However, beyond the expanded role of guardian and custodian, there is a responsibility to inspire. The greatest ideas, successes and accomplishments invariably stem from a place of inspiration. For this to happen, leaders will have to possess strong inner resources, be able to set the tone, be able to connect with people and lead them.

Self-care, self-belief, selflessness, empowerment, openness, optimism and follow through must be merged with focus, clear direction, expanded vision, empathy and humility.

Let us heed the warnings delivered by the world's leading health agencies pertaining to the growing fragility of human well-being. Let us learn from the failures in combating climate change and take a proactive stance in the protection of our people, their families, communities, businesses and livelihoods. In this way, not only will we promote greater organisational success, but also much-needed social change.

South Africa's 2019 winning World Cup rugby team is the actualisation of this broader vision. Every member of the squad was invested in personal health development and advancement, they were strongly connected and unified, they formed a single identity and were led by a coalition of Siya Kolisi and Rassie Erasmus, who were able to inspire the team fully. This not only promoted the realisation of individual and collective potential, but also the ultimate expression of performance excellence.

In the same way, businesses and their leaders can pull on these core levers that will uplift the lives of their people and also ensure the greatest possible opportunity for continued success and future growth.

1

THE CONUNDRUM

In an attempt to better understand the complexities of stress, several definitions of this physical and emotional state have been created and modified. But even with this repertoire of descriptions, stress is impossible to clearly define because it means different things to different people. At its core, stress is an emotional reaction to demanding circumstances.

The Oxford English Dictionary expounds on this definition and defines stress as:

> Stress [noun] a state of mental or emotional strain or tension resulting from adverse or demanding circumstances; [verb] subject to pressure or tension.

The stress response is by far the greatest example of the power of our emotional experiences over our physical set. When we get stressed, we are essentially reacting to threatening or disturbing situations that when properly deconstructed amount to the experience of fear in some shape or form. Fear of the unknown, fear of uncertainty, fear of change, fear of unemployment, the fear of not being skilled enough, and the subversive fear of not meeting

> Stress is an emotional reaction to demanding circumstances.

general societal expectations is pushing the stress response into overdrive in all of us. The biological shift in our bodies is the first line of defence in overcoming challenging situations and adapting to change. It is a tried and tested channel through which humankind has overcome all historic challenges and extreme adversity. This biological shift known as the stress response offers us protection from every manner of threat and challenges we are confronted with today.

STRESS – THE PERFORMANCE ADVANTAGE

When subjected to perceivably distressing circumstances, the first region of the brain to react is the amygdala, a collection of cells in the brain (one in each hemisphere) that play a primary role in decision-making and memory of emotional responses and processing. The amygdala instantaneously sends a distress signal to the brain's command centre, the hypothalamus. The hypothalamus then pushes the 'emergency button' and activates the nervous system to signal the adrenal glands to produce the hormones and neurochemicals, adrenaline and noradrenaline, also referred to as epinephrine and norepinephrine. Following a 300% to 500% surge in adrenaline, the body enters the 'performance zone'. Our sense of taste, smell and sight heighten and heart rate, respiration and blood pressure all increase. Energy reserves are liberated into the bloodstream, our immune system is launched into action and we produce hormones such as corticotrophin-releasing hormone (CRH), vasopressin and oxytocin, making us resistant to pain and even euphoric albeit briefly.

Incredibly, this is all initiated before the visual centres in the brain have had a chance to fully process what is happening. Within two to three minutes, the first wave (known as the sympathetic-adrenal-medullary [SAM] pathway) is in full gear and will be sustained for approximately an hour, depending on

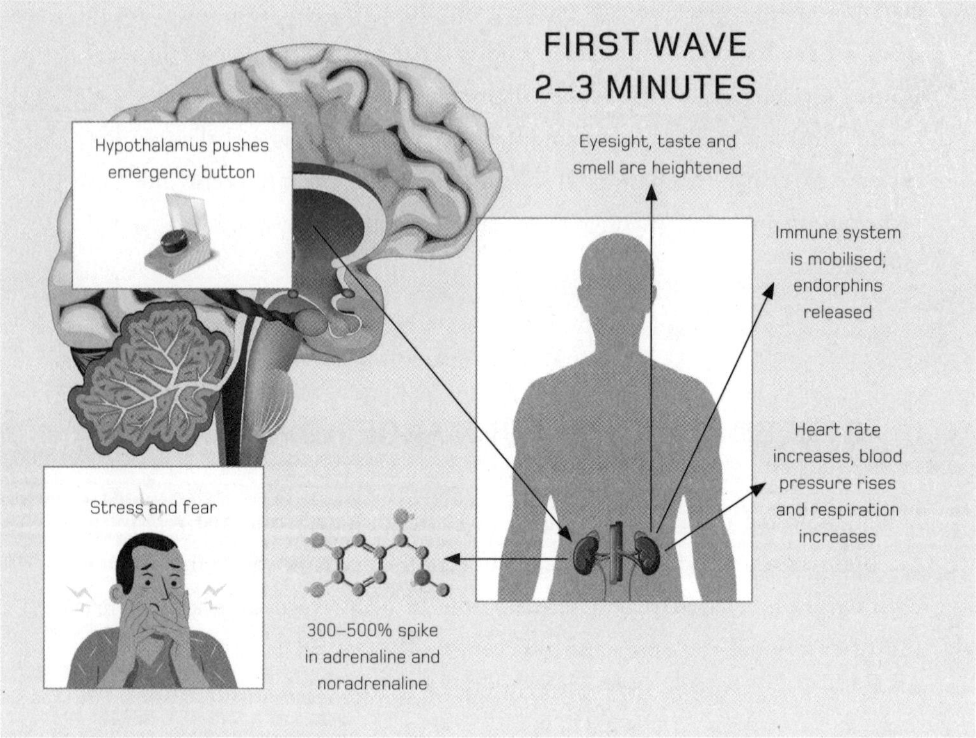

Sympathetic-adrenal-medullary (SAM) pathway

individual circumstances, genetics and environmental and situational factors.

During this biological shift, a second wave, with an equally powerful effect is initiated. This wave is referred to as the hypothalamic-pituitary-adrenal (HPA) axis.

The hypothalamus then produces several hormones that signal the 'master gland of the body' – the pituitary – to release the hormone adrenocorticotropic (ACTH), which stimulates the adrenal glands to secrete copious amounts of cortisol.

Cortisol is an exceptional hormone with a wide field of influence. Almost every single cell in the body has the ability to respond to this hormone's strong call to action and almost every cell contains the receptors for cortisol.

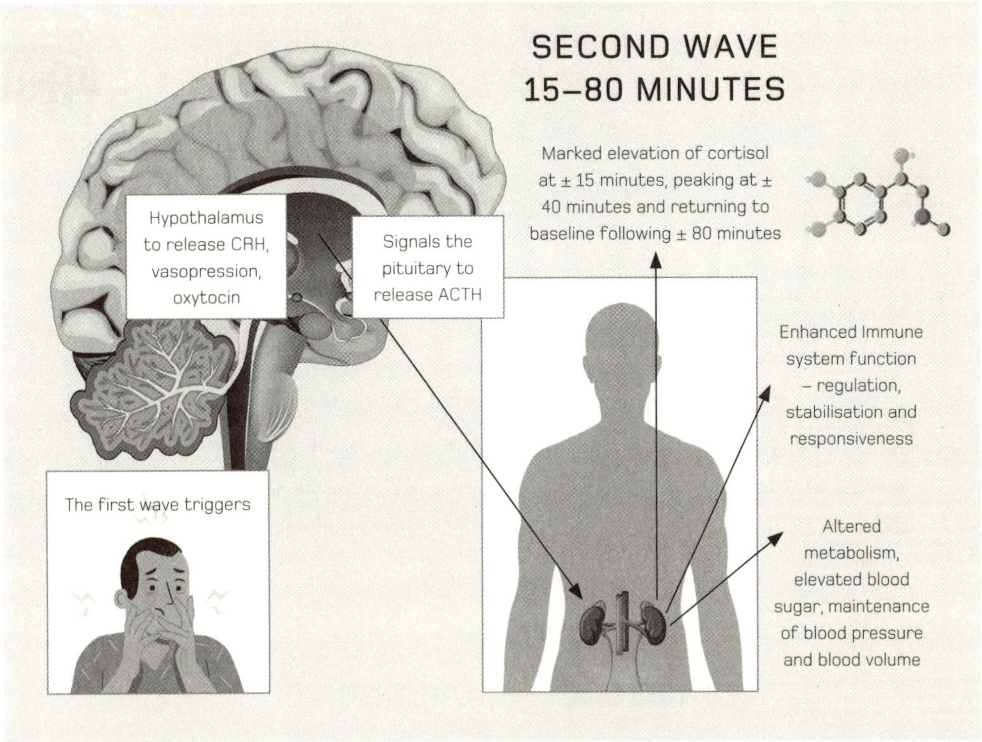

Hypothalamic-pituitary-adrenal (HPA) axis

Initially, and in the short term, cortisol has a very positive effect on our immune system. It improves regulation and responsiveness and stabilises the hyperactivity induced by the powerful adrenaline surge. It also influences our metabolism, elevates blood sugar and maintains blood pressure and blood volume.

When all these processes take place sporadically, stress can be energising and even health-promoting. These immense biological shifts help us cope with change (which is so important in our current climate), adapt better to all types of challenges and overcome even the most difficult of circumstances.

Based on these short-term adaptations, stress can be a great advantage in our lives and these stress-induced biological shifts are nothing short of

> Acute (short-term) stress gives us superpowers that include improved cognition, greater mental acuity, enhanced energy, heightened senses, pain resistance and improved immune function.

superpowers. They give us greater mental acuity, more energy, stronger immune defences, heightened senses and increased pain resistance and these tools help us thrive under a variety of conditions. Were it not for this upregulation of the nervous, cardiovascular, hormonal and immune systems, it is unlikely that we would have survived the challenges of our ancestral past.

But this gift of the stress axis is conditional. We cannot abuse it by activating it too frequently or for too long and should we break these rules, the very system that has protected us for thousands of years will become the system that compromises our well-being mentally, emotionally and physically.

A SYSTEM IN OVERDRIVE

Work and financial pressures, competing demands between our professional and personal lives, ongoing conflicts and relationship challenges, social isolation, feeling unappreciated and undervalued, unfairness and injustice, overwhelming uncertainty about the future and poor health, repeatedly activate the stress axis. Placed into overdrive, the stress response can do a complete about-turn and the system that once protected and helped us overcome the most hostile of circumstances, can transform into a response that ultimately destroys us.

The reason the stress response in overdrive can be so mentally and physically destructive is that in order to prime the body for action and heightened responsiveness, several systems have to be shut down or reorganised. The body simply can't run all systems, at full throttle, at once. One of the functions of the first wave is to direct blood flow away from the skin, as well as the digestive, urinary and reproductive systems.

The second wave of the stress response and its primary hormonal driver, cortisol, also further intensifies the disruption.

Scientists are of the opinion that the reason for this shift is because reproduction, excretion and food consumption are unlikely to help in any significant way during stressful encounters so these systems are shut down in favour of enhanced performance by the brain, the cardiovascular and the muscular systems. There is no denying that better mental acuity and heightened physical strength, superimposed on top of better endurance, surpasses the value of a meal or an intimate moment during a crisis, although some may disagree.

The net effect of this major redistribution of blood includes visible ageing of the skin, ongoing problems with the urinary and reproductive systems as well as significant digestive issues.

I'm sure there have been times during stressful periods in your life where you looked in the mirror and thought to yourself, 'I look so old'! I strongly believe that the sale of topical and ingestible collagen, the protein responsible for maintaining the structure and integrity of our skin, and other skin products, during the coronavirus pandemic, have been robust.

STRESS AND DIGESTIVE ISSUES

A review article in the *Journal of Physiology and Pharmacology*[1] describes a range of gastrointestinal disorders directly related to chronic stress. These include inflammatory bowel disease (IBD), irritable bowel syndrome (IBS), the onset of food intolerances, peptic ulcers and even reflux.

Moreover, the paper identified at least six reasons why our digestive systems become compromised in response to chronic stress exposure. These reasons include reduced movement within the entire digestive tract, heightened pain sensitivity, a decline in the secretion of digestive fluids and enzymes, reduced overall blood flow, increased intestinal permeability or 'leaky gut'.

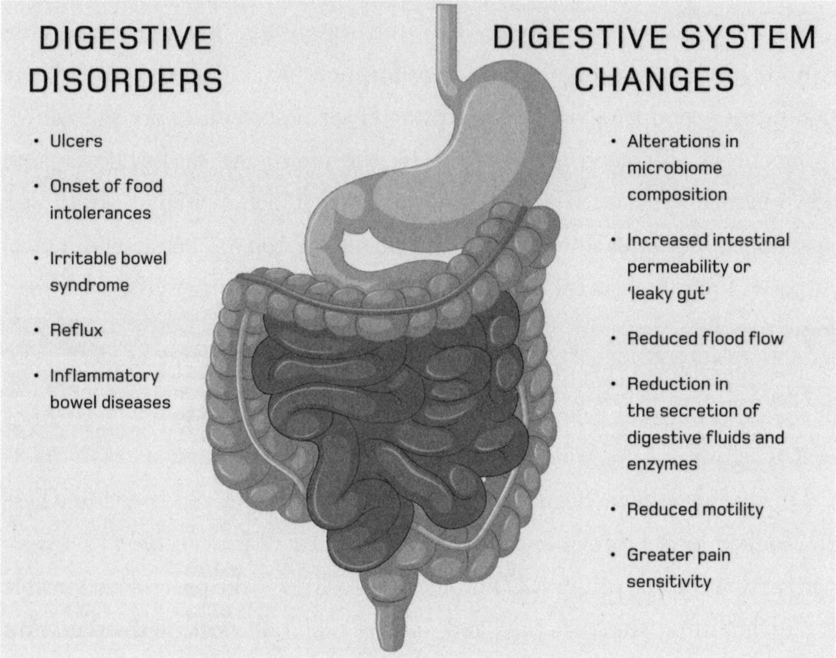

The collective impact of chronic stress on the digestive system

Considering the global prevalence of chronic stress it is little wonder that over 800 million people[2] around the world are effected by IBS alone. Moreover, the incidence of inflammatory bowel diseases such as Crohn's[3] and ulcerative colitis[4] has been rising steadily within newly industrialised nations. According to a 2017 review in *The Lancet*[5] there has been an 11% rise in the prevalence of Crohn's disease and almost a 15% rise in ulcerative colitis, since 1990. Of course there are numerous contributing factors such as dietary changes and some environmental factors such as a lack

Leaky gut is a condition in which the lining of the small intestine becomes damaged, causing undigested food particles, toxic waste products and bacteria to 'leak' through the intestines and flood the bloodstream.

of sleep, smoking and air pollution (specifically sulphur dioxide and nitric oxide), but it is fair to assume that chronic stress is central to the growing incidence of inflammatory bowel diseases.

STRESS AND OUR IMMUNE SYSTEM

As mentioned previously, adrenaline and noradrenaline call the immune system to action. According to researchers from Stanford University,[6] for a period of 2 to 30 minutes, immune cells are drawn from our bone marrow, spleen, lungs and lymph nodes into the bloodstream. This spectacular immune response involves neutrophils, helper T cells, cytolytic T cells and B cells and equips us to handle almost any threat that comes our way. Some of these regular threats include the need to heal damaged tissues, combating cancer cells and offering powerful protection from all sorts of viral, fungal and bacterial assaults on the body.

Once the second wave takes full effect and cortisol hits its full stride at about 30 to 40 minutes, many, if not most, of these immune cells are shuttled out of the bloodstream to possible sites of inflammation as well as to the skin, lining of the lungs, liver and urogenital tract. In essence, to the frontline of possible micro-organism threats.

Incredibly, the value of short-term stress is now recognised as a health advantage that can (and should) be harnessed for a range of specific outcomes that include speeding up recovery time from an injury or even combating the common cold.

> Acute stress triggers immune cells to be drawn from bone marrow, spleen, lungs and lymph nodes into the bloodstream to help us confront micro-organisms, repair damaged tissues and remove damaged or corrupted cells.

A good example of a controlled stress simulation is an ice-cold plunge. In the build-up to entering the water, your immune system kicks into full gear. As you approach the water's edge not only do you have second thoughts, but your heart begins to pound, your palms begin to sweat, your breathing rate increases and finally there is the 500% surge of adrenaline that floods the body upon entering the water. Once out of the water, you feel invigorated and energised and clear and calm as the stress axis begins its wind-down. This is the stress axis at its best.

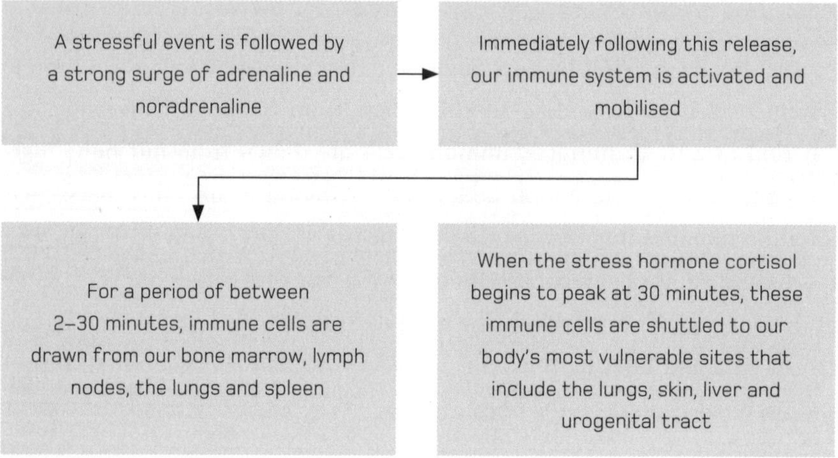

Under siege

Chronic stress is vastly different in its influence and its effect on our health and well-being and is essentially stress that persists for several hours a day, for weeks, months or even years on end. It is notorious for its destructive influence on several biological systems, especially the immune system.

Surprisingly, cortisol, which under acute stress promotes better functionality of our immune system, does a 180-degree turn when we are chronically stressed. Raised cortisol for days or weeks on end results in a marked suppression of a host of immune functions, ranging from overall reduced activity to lower production of all-important cells. On its own, this shift increases our susceptibility to seasonal colds and flu as well as a host of other infections. There are also several additional immune shifts triggered by chronic cortisol exposure and that add further complexity to an already precarious situation.

A study published in *Frontiers in Neuroendocrinology*[7] showed that chronic stress, or even exposure to cortisone-based medication, results in a dramatic and rapid ageing of our immune cells. This further reduces the immune system's ability to protect us from day-to-day threats and causes wide-scale confusion or dysregulation in the body and even significant dysfunction or immunopathology. The research article points out that this dramatic immune shift may be associated with suppressed anti-tumour immunity and the increased susceptibility to the emergence and progression of various types of cancer.

> Chronic stress can result in immune system suppression (reduced immune cell production and activity) and ageing, reducing its effectiveness to combat potential threats.

Knowing all this, we need to ask to what extent chronic stress is contributing to the global cancer epidemic, which is now ranked as the second largest cause of premature deaths globally (behind cardiovascular disease) that is costing the world economy well over $1.2 trillion every year. And whether the steep rise in chronic stress is contributing towards the 28% increase in the incidence of cancer cases seen in the last decade.[8]

Linking autoimmune conditions to chronic stress

To further add to the dire effects of chronic stress, chronically raised cortisol can trigger several immune-mediated inflammatory diseases such as asthma, allergies and sinusitis and potentially life-threatening autoimmune disorders such as multiple sclerosis (MS), Hashimoto's disease and rheumatoid arthritis. This disturbing finding is off the back of discoveries made by psychology professor, Sheldon Cohen,[9]

> When we are heavily stressed for extended periods, our cells can become resistant to the modulating effects of cortisol, resulting in raised inflammation and even increasing the risk of developing autoimmune conditions in those who are predisposed.

and his team from Carnegie Mellon University in the US. Cohen's research shows that the sustained elevation of cortisol creates a resistance of cells and tissues to its actions. In other words, under normal circumstances, cortisol effectively controls inflammation in the body, but when stressed for several weeks, months or years on end, our immune cells can fail to respond to the normal regulatory actions of cortisol resulting in a trail of immune-mediated casualties.

In 2018 a team of Scandinavian researchers published an extensive study on the association of stress-related disorders and their relationship to autoimmune diseases.[10] The study was done on a massive scale and involved 1 297 756 people over a period of more than three decades. The researchers divided the participants into three groups:

- Group one: 106 464 individuals previously diagnosed with any stress-related disorder such as post-traumatic stress disorder (PTSD), anxiety, etc
- Group two: 1 064 640 healthy, matched controls
- Group three: 126 652 siblings of those individuals who were diagnosed with a stress disorder so as to establish possible genetic influences in the development of potential autoimmune diseases

> Suffering from a stress-related disorder such as anxiety or PTSD significantly increases the risk of developing an autoimmune disease.

What the researchers found was that when compared to the other two groups, those individuals who had been diagnosed with a stress or mental health disorder, were at a 36% higher risk of developing an autoimmune disease, regardless of family and health history.

The study also revealed that since 1980, with every advancing decade, the risk of stress-induced autoimmune disease development has steadily increased and is showing no sign of slowing down. What was most striking about the research data was that it showed that the younger you are when you develop a stress condition, the higher your risk of developing an autoimmune disease. This means that current events such as COVID-19 and future trends such as the advancement of the Fourth Industrial Revolution, are likely to have a destabilising impact on the health and well-being of our youth. More research is underway to establish the underlying reason for this unexpected occurrence.

To illustrate this further: if you are approximately 50 years old and subject to significant stress which unfolds in either generalised anxiety disorder (GAD), obsessive-compulsive disorder (OCD) or even major depression, you will have a 23% higher risk of developing an autoimmune disease in the coming years. Consider that if you are in your 20s and experience the same events (ie stress) and outcomes (common mental health disorders), you will have a 48% higher risk of developing an autoimmune condition. That is more than double than a person in their 50s.

One of the biggest challenges we are currently facing throughout the developed world is that stress levels are reported to be highest in the younger generations. According to the American Psychological Association, 91% of individuals between the ages of 18–21 report experiencing either physical or psychological symptoms of stress within a month.

> 91% of those under the age of 21 report experiencing either physical or emotional symptoms of stress within a month.

Perfectionism may be destroying our youth

Numerous theories have emerged as to why stress has become so prevalent in the Millennial generation (those born between 1977 and 1994) and the Generation Zs (those born between 1995 and 2012). One theory that is gaining momentum is the growing obsession with perfectionism.

From the 1980s, the ideological model of neoliberal governance that emphasises the value of free-market competition within developed nations, has emphasised competitive individualism. This message has been strongly adopted by the younger generations who have done their utmost to perfect themselves and their lifestyles. Early in 2020, English researchers published an extensive meta-analysis on the rising trend in perfectionism[11] involving over 41 000 individuals from the US, Canada and the United Kingdom (UK).

The review looked at students who had completed the Multidimensional Perfectionism Scale, devised by researchers Paul Hewitt and Gordon Flett in 1991. This assessment focuses on three aspects of perfectionism that include self-oriented, other-oriented and socially prescribed. The data was collected between 1989 and 2016, providing almost three decades of detailed information.

The results of the study revealed that all three areas of perfectionism have increased during this time. These trends were neither influenced by gender nor inter-country differences.

According to the authors: 'Overall, in order of magnitude of the observed increase, the findings indicate that recent generations of young people perceive that others are more demanding of them, are more demanding of others, and are more demanding of themselves.'

The study also points out that the rates of depression, anxiety, eating disorders, loneliness and body dysmorphia are at record highs among the youth and it attributes the rise in perfectionism to the rise in pathopsychology.

Trying to live up to a construct of this nature, at this time in human history, is not only practically impossible within the chaos and volatility, but it can tip many over the edge of the proverbial cliff. It adds additional feelings of failure and only compounds the current experience of a lack of control and uncertainty. Moreover, it also creates self-doubt and low self-esteem, corroding self-worth and perceived value in society. Surely the world is saturated enough with stress and fear.

While today's youth may believe that the coronavirus is not their concern due to the fact that their risk of mortality is extremely low, a subversive threat looms within this group. The threat is immune system compromise and chronic diseases.

Based on the influence of chronic stresses on our immune behaviours, specifically triggering inflammatory and autoimmune diseases, the world might be on the brink of yet another health challenge. Based on this body of research, this scenario is becoming increasingly more likely.

> Perfectionists can reduce their stress and the risk of developing physical health issues by being more emotionally and psychologically agile, adaptable, supportive and forgiving of themselves and others.

The inability of the immune system to respond to the effects of cortisol is not the only reason for the strong association between chronic stress and autoimmune conditions. It appears that this is only one piece of a very complex puzzle.

Recent research published in *Biological Psychiatry*[12] has identified at least four major changes in immune system regulation that increase the risk of developing autoimmune diseases in response to chronic stress and/or extreme lifetime trauma.[13] These influences are beyond the scope of this book.

Autoimmune diseases – once the exception, now the norm

The science is certainly convincing, but nothing drives the message home more than experiencing it first-hand with the countless patients from diverse backgrounds that I have seen over a period of two decades.

Several years ago, a young woman came to see me for various chronic health issues she was experiencing. Despite the fact that she was only in her late 20s, her condition was highly complex with several interconnected parts, generally only seen in older individuals with multiple and compounding life traumas.

Her case was challenging as nothing was as it appeared. For example, her responsiveness to treatment was unpredictable and overall patterns were hard to establish. The more I worked with her, the clearer it became that the solution would perhaps come from a deeper understanding of her past.

From a young age, my client always wanted to be a lawyer. Her grandfather was a respected attorney and her family held the profession in very high regard. This ambition was further fuelled by hit TV series such as *Ally McBeal* and *Suits*. These shows portray the legal profession as exciting and glamorous with problem-solving, interesting cases, work variety and lots of lunches and dinners in tailored designer clothes forming the base of many of these popular legal shows.

One aspect of the legal industry that *is* accurately portrayed in these series is that the legal profession requires intellect, cognitive firepower and loads of wit. Fortunately, my client was extremely gifted and had an abundance of all the traits required.

After finishing high school, she enrolled in one of South Africa's premier universities and proceeded to harness her powerful intellect, completing her Bachelor of Commerce cum laude. From there, she embarked on her Bachelor of Law degree, where once again she completed her studies cum laude.

When she reminisced about her studies and her time at university, she had a big smile on her face and a twinkle in her eye. She fondly remarked that they were some of the best years of her life that included passionate philosophical debates, an environment of rich cultural diversity all cemented by strong interpersonal relationships.

Being a top-performing student with ample charm and charisma, it wasn't long before leading law firms started approaching her to recruit her to their respective organisations. At the time, one particular firm had established itself as the premier institution, where only the best of the best were given an opportunity to form part of their performance-driven team. This energetic hub was the ultimate environment for any high achiever to be placed. It should come as no surprise that she was wooed by the firm and offered a position to complete her articles there. Her dream was materialising, her life just beginning.

In addition, this ambitious but inexperienced 24-year-old woman was assigned to work with the firm's top performers in the mergers and acquisitions space.

Equipped with robust health, youth and enthusiasm, the first few weeks at the firm were, by her account, nothing short of incredible. She felt valued, respected and admired and in her mind, she was poised to be the next hot-shot recruit and was going to change the world.

Like all wooing phases though, hers began to draw to a close, exposing a very different reality. The keen interest she was shown during recruitment faded and the realisation that she was at the bottom of the organisational structure soon hit home. Her voice soon faded away in any attempts to communicate, her opinion was not welcome and any decisions pertaining to her professional and personal life were no longer within her jurisdiction.

Working on weekends was the norm, late nights at the office were expected and her social and support structure began to disintegrate and ultimately disappear. The high demands of the job, extremely long working hours, together with the fact that there was little to no support in her life, caused her significant stress. Tears were a daily occurrence.

Acute stress (ie stress for short intervals of time) will do little to impact your health, but over several months a different picture emerges.

This experience was not unique, as all the new candidates started to break down from the relentless stress and compounding pressures. The first sign of this inevitable breakdown was frequent and intense headaches and body pain. This further evolved into significant digestive issues. Numerous doctor's visits and copious amounts of medication became routine. Despite the debilitating physical pain from various sources, she soldiered on. However, this set of symptoms was merely the precursor for what was to come. After a year, anxious episodes became more frequent and depression set in. The days became harder to navigate and being productive became ever more challenging. In an attempt to turn it around, she moved teams on more than one occasion in the three or so years she worked for the firm. Her thinking was that it was merely circumstantial and perhaps the type of legal practice, and maybe even the team, and that she was the exception and not the norm.

In reality, this isn't the case. What this young woman was learning was that she had chosen one of the most stressful professions and she was ill-equipped to cope with the new and relentless demands.

According to the Health and Safety Executive (HSE), a UK government agency responsible for the encouragement, regulation and enforcement of workplace health, safety and welfare and for research into occupational risks in Great Britain, the prevalence rate of self-reported work-related stress, depression or anxiety in the legal profession is almost 200% higher than 'typical' occupations.

As the days passed, her health became more and more compromised. Within this period, after having an extensive blood panel done, it was discovered that she had Hashimoto's thyroiditis. Hashimoto's is a disorder in which the thyroid gland is gradually destroyed. Medical experts cite a combination of genetic predisposition and environmental factors (ie chronic stress) as the triggers for developing this condition.

Soon after her diagnosis, following several all-nighters, she physically collapsed in the office. Her body threw in the towel. The chronic stress had taken its toll and left her cognitively, emotionally and physically broken. She was forced to resign and her dream was shattered and stress was the protagonist. Following her departure from the firm, she spent three months in bed trying to recover from this period of her life. Unfortunately, the toll on her immune system was more permanent as it was later discovered that she had developed two additional autoimmune diseases, which she would have to manage for the rest of her life.

Sadly, this story is not a unique or exceptional event, but one that plays out on a daily basis among many young rising stars and highlights the impact that chronic stress has on immune functionality, especially in those with genetic vulnerabilities. What can be extrapolated from my patient's narrative is that stress can crush dreams if it is not managed effectively. This scenario did not have to play out the way it did and with proper stress-management knowledge and tools, as well as a resilience template, the side effects could have been averted.

Fortunately, given a deeper understanding of my patient's background and her inherent weaknesses, through extensive biomedical evaluation that involved genetic, metabolic and food allergy testing, we were able to implement a course of action that transformed her health. The action steps included dietary changes, nutritional supplements, regular exercise, psychotherapy and visceral osteopathy.

This story ends on an even greater high. Not only did my client overcome her significant health challenges, but she also returned to the law profession. Only this time she was armed with self-awareness and knowledge on health management – a trait that all great leaders have. She was able to carve out a unique space for herself within the legal profession and is now regarded as the authority within her chosen specialty. She currently works for a leading American law firm.

WHAT CHRONIC STRESS DOES TO THE HUMAN BRAIN

One of the greatest concerns that scientists have raised in recent years is the impact that chronic stress is having on the human brain. According to the World Health Organization (WHO), one in four people will be effected by a mental or neurological disorder at some point in their lives.[14] All indicators suggest that chronic stress may be one of the stronger influences behind this global health challenge (yes, another one). It has been well established that cumulative adversity and chronic stress are unquestionably associated with a higher risk of developing a broad range of psychiatric disorders including anxiety, addiction and depression.

> One in four people will be affected by a mental or neurological disorder at some point in their lives.

In 2012 researchers from the departments of Psychiatry and Neurology

Cumulative life stress is associated with reduced size and function in at least seven areas of the brain. These regions are responsible for cognition, self-awareness, self-control, motivation and coordination.

at Yale University published a study[15] that investigated the impact of repeated life traumas and stress on the structural make-up of the brain.

The study involved 103 healthy participants, with no prior history of mental health diseases, between the ages of 18 and 48. The entire group completed a 140-item interview, which assessed challenging life events and chronic subjective stress. The subjects then all underwent comprehensive MRI scans.

The research team found that cumulative adversity over a lifetime was associated with atrophy in some of the most important functional regions of the brain. In fact, as many as seven highly influential areas such as the frontopolar cortex, ventromedial and orbitofrontal cortex, gyrus rectus, inferior frontal gyrus, anterior cingulate, caudate, and subgenual cingulate, showed morphological changes in response to chronic stress. These regions are collectively responsible for higher functions, complex intellectual behaviour, self-awareness, self-control, coordination and even motivation.

Two additional ideas were highlighted in this study. The first is that reduced brain size was directly proportionate to the degree of chronic stress and not necessarily related to the perceived intensity of adverse experiences. What this means is that protracted and relentless stress, as opposed to merely the scale of challenges faced, results in the most profound adaptations seen in the brain.

Prolonged stress, as opposed to the magnitude of a stressful event, is associated with reduced brain volume. Lower brain volume has been linked to anxiety, depression and cognitive decline.

The other important connection that the scientists were able to make was that the decrease in brain mass induced by chronic stress correlated to cognitive decline, anxiety, depression, addiction, as well as a host of other neurological conditions. This finding explains the relationship between the feeling of uncertainty and corresponding mental health compromise.

Supporting this association, Dutch researchers published an extensive meta-analysis on the relationship between brain volume and depression.[16] The review involved 64 studies, 2 418 patients with depressive disorder and 1 974 healthy individuals. The groundbreaking analysis revealed that in those individuals diagnosed with depression there were 'large' volume reductions in areas of the brain such as the anterior cingulate, orbitofrontal and prefrontal cortex responsible for important cognitive processes, emotional regulation, social behaviour and reward. Regions such as the hippocampus, the putamen and caudate nucleus involved in movement, procedural and associative learning as well as memory, also showed 'moderate' reductions in volume.

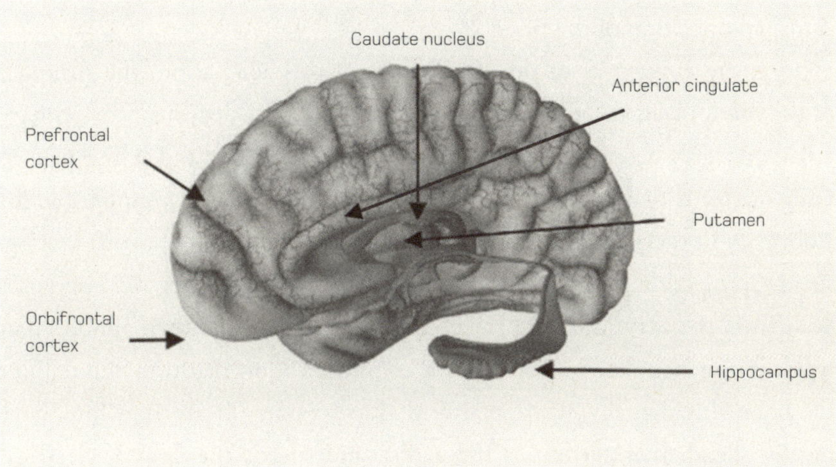

The very regions of the brain that show volume reductions in those suffering from depression are the same areas that atrophy in response to chronic stress. The problem is that this can become a self-perpetuating cycle in that stress reduces brain volume, which increases your predisposition towards the development of emotional disorders, that in turn increases your susceptibility to stress.

Although the relationship between emotional disorders and reduced regional brain size is a relatively recent finding, scientists have known for some time that chronic stress negatively affects grey matter volume and have identified several mechanisms through which this occurs. These include a loss of neurons, compromised connections between cells and a reduction in the development of new brain cells known as neurogenesis.

Altered structure, reduced function

Recent discoveries by neuroscientist, Daniela Kaufer, and her team at the University of California (UC) have revealed yet another way in which chronically raised cortisol and stress negatively influences the brain. Kaufer discovered that raised cortisol results in stem cell malfunction, altering the actual composition of the brain.[17]

To create context as to the significance of this adaptation, the structure of the brain needs to be understood. The brain is divided into two primary cell types: grey matter and support cells known as glia and white matter. Grey matter is densely packed with nerve cell bodies and is responsible for storing and processing information. White matter consists of axons (a long, slender projection of a nerve cell that typically conducts electrical impulses away from the nerve cell body) that collectively form a network of fibres that interconnect neurons and establish a communication platform throughout the brain. Incidentally, white matter derives its name from the white, fatty myelin sheath that surrounds the axons, and speeds the flow of electrical signals between neurons and brain region.

The study focused on the region of the brain known as the hippocampus. The hippocampus regulates memory and emotion and plays a key role in a variety of emotional disorders. Part of the reason for focusing on this region of the brain is the fact that changes in hippocampal composition increase vulnerability to and progression of many mental illnesses that have become so prevalent today.

Moreover, this powerful memory and emotional centre is populated with vast reserves of neural (nerve) stem cells, which grow and multiply throughout adult life offering protection from acute stress as well as states of fear, anxiety and depression. These stem cells typically transform into grey matter, however this is not the case during periods of chronic stress. What the researchers discovered is that these all-important stem cells malfunction in the presence of chronically raised cortisol. Instead of developing into new neurons, they transformed into cells that produce white matter, altering the delicate composition of this vital regulatory region of the brain.

Kaufer points out that a greater production of myelin-producing cells could create hyper-connectivity between the hippocampus and the stress and fear epicentre of the brain – the amygdala.

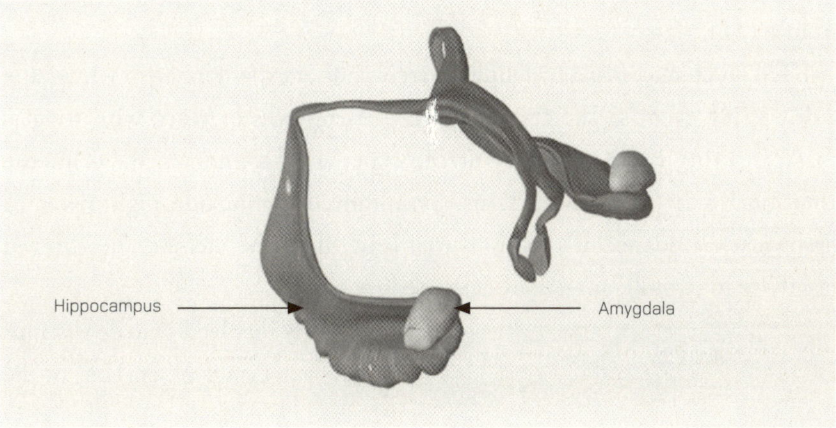

With these two centres better connected, fear responses are not only quicker, but also significantly more amplified. Additionally, the hippocampus and the region of the brain that moderates our stress responses (the prefrontal cortex) become increasingly less connected, impairing our ability to shut down the stress axis itself.

Chronically elevated cortisol heightens connectivity between the brain's emotional centres. This can create the propensity for hyper-emotional responses to demanding circumstances.

Essentially, the emotional centres enable each other, inciting irrational responses, and the 'voice of reason' gets completely cut out of the loop.

We have all been in that situation where prolonged stress makes us hyper-emotional, irrational and even the slightest upset triggers disproportionate reactions and emotional outbursts. During these periods, logic, rational thinking and calculated responses don't exist. In the short or medium term, these compositional changes may be harmless, but in the long term the implications are extremely significant. Research shows that alterations in white matter tracts and myelin formation are present in numerous mental disorders, including PTSD.[18]

In 2015 a research paper was published in *Frontiers in Behavioral Neuroscience*[19] on brain alternations in a group of 19 individuals suffering from PTSD.

PTSD is characterised by failure to recover after experiencing or witnessing a distressing event/s. The condition may last months or years, with triggers that can bring back memories of the experience accompanied by intense emotional and physical reactions. Symptoms may include nightmares or flashbacks, avoidance of situations that bring back the memory, heightened reactivity to stimuli, anxiety or depressed mood.

> The neurological signature of PTSD is increased white matter (myelin) concentrations in the memory and emotional centre of the brain, the hippocampus.

The study involved 38 male veterans with an average age of 43. Half of the group had been diagnosed with PTSD and the other 19 were trauma-exposed veterans without PTSD. Supporting previous studies, the researchers found that those individuals with PTSD had significantly more white matter in the hippocampus than the control group. What's more is that the scientists also found a positive correlation between the degree of compositional shift and PTSD and depression severity. Simply put, the greater the degree of change in the hippocampus, the worse the symptoms within the group suffering from PTSD.

The impact of chronic stress on the nervous system

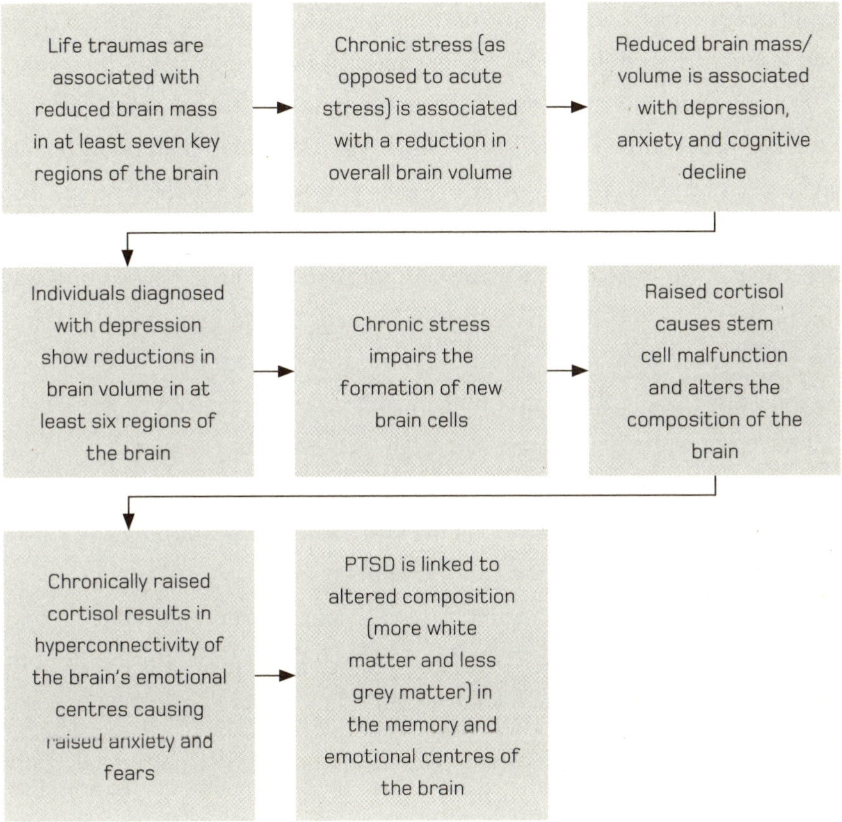

STRESS – THE GREATEST LEADERSHIP CHALLENGE OF OUR TIME

Chronic stress is not only a challenge for each and every one of us on a personal level, but it also poses an enormous challenge for businesses, especially in light of recent global events and the current socio-economic trajectory. Acute or episodic stress can be immeasurably valuable in overcoming challenges and obstacles as it creates numerous positive biological shifts that provide us with more energy, clarity, motivation, creativity and urgency, which ultimately facilitates our 'best performance' on the job, for example. But there is a stress 'sweet spot'. I found this to be very apparent in the area of high-level sport.

For two decades I sat on the sidelines watching the athletes and teams that I worked with compete against the world's best. In terms of their performance and success on the field or court, there were two certainties. The first was that if the players were not a little stressed or nervous, their performance would never live up to expectations or be close to their potential. The second was that if they were too stressed and over-aroused, or had been worried about the event for a protracted period of time, they would most likely have a disappointing result. The same holds true for all businesses and professionals.

However, while businesses and high achievers can capitalise on the numerous positive effects of short-term stress, if it is not held on a very tight leash, stress can turn out to be highly destructive, undermining the entire framework of the organisation and its members.

Chronic stress results in compromised mental health, immune system dysregulation as well as a rapid decline in physical integrity. This can lead to increased absenteeism in the workplace and higher rates of presenteeism, the practice of going to work despite illness, injury, anxiety, often resulting in reduced productivity and reduced employee engagement and inspiration. But this is merely the beginning of what stress can do in the workplace. On the ground, you can expect fragmented relationships, a disintegration of trust, emotional volatility, reduced agility, little to no creativity, disappearance of passion and a decline in overall professional commitment. No business can afford this reality, especially during the current climate.

Leaders, managers and decision makers need to consider the following in order to overcome and thrive amid the current challenges we are facing:

- How can we, as an organisation, create an environment where stress does not overwhelm our employees and contract workers?

- How can the business and its leadership create a safe zone where only the necessary work-related stresses (ie high demands and long working hours) are present at levels that create a positive 'push' without having a destructive influence?
- Knowing that productivity, innovation and creativity is underpinned by employee health, how can we enhance the health and well-being of our teams?
- Knowing that the future of many of our employees lacks any degree of certainty, how can we as leadership assist in lessening their fears?
- Knowing how many lives and livelihoods are dependent upon us, are we personally doing enough to promote our own health and resilience in these uncertain times?

However, before any of these action steps can be initiated, it is important to fully understand what the primary causes of stress are in the first place.

2

WHY NOW?

Long before the global coronavirus pandemic, the world was burdened with a stress crisis of immense proportions. Despite remarkable technological advancements and high levels of overall prosperity, literacy, personal freedom, greater life expectancy and access to knowledge, stress levels have been consistently rising. Research shows that global prosperity in 2016 (as measured by GDP per capita) was higher than at any point before in recorded history.[1]

Results published by the Maddison Project Database[2] on 169 countries from the years 1870 to 2016, shows that in 1870 the global GDP per capita was estimated to be approximately $1 263 per year (this is accounting for inflation and all other relevant factors). By comparison, in 2016, the average GDP per capita was $14 574 per year.

An obvious assumption is that this growth in wealth and the standard of living would be confined to a handful of industrialised economies. Of course, strong regional disparities do exist, but the project clearly points out that economic prosperity in every region of the world is greater now than ever before.

There are several sound measures that show the world to be on a positive trajectory within the context of human growth and development, which brings into question why we are currently confronted with this seemingly disproportionate stress crisis.

Probably the most accurate measure of societal integrity is The Human Development Index (HDI). The HDI data is regularly published by the United Nations Development Programme and measures three key dimensions of human development including life expectancy, access to education and a decent standard of living. Human development from 1980 to 2017 shows a steady rise throughout the world.[3] Added to this is the fact that the world is going through a relatively stable period in the context of war and conflict. With the exception of the Middle East, major conflicts are currently at a 75-year low.

Lastly, despite dramatic climate change, agricultural yields are some of the highest ever seen in recorded history, in every region of the world.

I could provide many more examples of positive human developments and successes, but on the surface, there appears to be a paradox in the current state of the world and the ever-growing societal burden of chronic stress.

> While at face value it appears that we are in a better place now than at any previous points in human history, with greater life expectancy, prosperity, literacy, basic freedoms and access to knowledge, there are clear indications of a societal fragility. Stress, mental illness, chronic diseases, suicide rates and drug and alcohol abuse are growing exponentially in many of the world's developed nations.

Scratch a little beneath the surface and you will see that we are in the process of undergoing the most profound shift ever experienced in human existence, which has now been dramatically amplified and accelerated by the coronavirus pandemic. From a business standpoint, every industry is changing – and rapidly. Disruption is evident in all areas of business from demand, production, consumption, transportation, as well as delivery systems.

From a societal aspect, how we relate to others, the way we work, how we learn, the manner in which we communicate and even the way we socialise is transforming. What's most overwhelming is the scale, speed and depth of these changes. It is like nothing we have seen in human history.

The root cause of the global stress epidemic that has governments and health agencies scrambling is rapid and exponential change. Uncertainty, fear and a lack of control, whether on a conscious or unconscious level, underpin every facet of our lives and drive chronic stress, compromised health and ultimately the reduced actualisation of potential.

EVERYTHING IS CHANGING

It seems that in a very short space of time, and with a nudge from a virus, we transitioned into a new era in human history – the Fourth Industrial Revolution. This shift is bringing with it transformation and complexity on a scale that is completely unprecedented. Unlike its predecessors, this revolution is not confined to mechanisation, mass production or mere automation – in fact, the Fourth Industrial Revolution appears devoid of limitations or delineation. It is a time in human history where the living world, the abstract and the tangible, all amalgamate into a unified existence.

When I was growing up, if you wanted to see a lion, you went to the zoo or a national park and spent hours observing this majestic animal at a fair distance. My three-year-old son, however, has a very different understanding of a lion. When he asks to see a lion, we don't need to plan an expensive trip, we simply google '3D lion' and in a few seconds, an augmented reality of a 3D-version of a lion pops up.

No one can predict the effect that altered reality will have on broader humanity, where virtual worlds and experiences are steadily replacing tangible perceptions of our environment. But what economists are certain of, is that it is going to have a monumental effect on trade, investment, consumption and employment.

A fair assumption is that with rapid technological advancement comes robust economic growth and prosperity. This potential certainly exists but according to the World Economic Forum (WEF), this has not materialised and may even be negatively impacting global economics in some way.

In the years preceding the 2008 financial crisis, or the Great Recession, the world economy was growing at a rate of almost 5% a year.[4] This robust growth created new employment, increased wealth, caused a reduction in poverty and was associated with a steady decline in hunger prevalence. However, unlike previous recessions where economies rebounded, following the 2008 financial crisis, the world economy was unable to find its feet again despite capital injections of over $10 trillion by central banks. Much of the sustained downturn was believed to be as a consequence of several converging factors that included excess debt, capital misallocation, an ageing global population as well as a dramatic decline in productivity. In 2020 the world economy took an enormous blow and according to the International Monetary Fund (IMF) global GDP is set to be at negative growth of 3%.[5]

The issue with a prolonged period of reduced or limited growth is that fewer people will be lifted out of poverty and overall development will be sluggish (if not come to a complete standstill). This means that the years of progress towards reducing hunger, poverty and inequality are rapidly being reversed, more so with the advent of the coronavirus pandemic.

POVERTY AND HUNGER ARE INCREASING

According to the 'Global Competitiveness Report 2019: How to end a lost decade of productivity growth',[6] extreme poverty is now impacting nearly half of the world's population. And what's more is that not even steady employment can protect against poverty. For example, of the 3.3 billion people who are currently employed around the world, the vast majority are living off only $5.50 (R90) a day and are struggling to meet the most basic of needs.

The vast majority of the world's working population live off approximately R90 per day.

Moreover, after 16 years of steady decline, global hunger levels have once again increased and now affect more than 826 million people or 11% of the world's population.

Hunger is a critical issue in South Africa and is a reflection of the political and economic upheavals seen in recent years. The UN Food and Agriculture Organization[7] doesn't draw data prior to 2000 but their report shows that hunger in South Africa is at a 20-year high, impacting 3.6 million people or 6.2% of the population. The events of 2020 have only worsened this situation with figures expected to rise dramatically.

In South Africa, the combined effect of the political and economic upheavals over the last eight years, together with the coronavirus, has resulted in millions of people unable to consume enough food to meet basic energy requirements.

Sadly, it is always the most vulnerable members of society who become the greatest casualties of any crisis. In the case of the coronavirus it is the elderly and those with existing health issues, but when it comes to hunger and poverty, it is children who are being impacted the most.

Hunger and malnutrition impact mental health and emotional stability later on in life

In South Africa, the number of children younger than five years of age who are stunted (significantly shorter and smaller than the average for their age) as a consequence of poor nutrition and/or repeated infection, has increased steadily since 2008. Data from UNICEF[8] shows that in 2016, over 27% of children under five have been physically compromised due to malnutrition.

Since 2008, almost 1 in 3 children in South Africa are physically, cognitively and emotionally affected by undernourishment.

Consider that while the physical effects of malnutrition and poverty are more defined (muscle wasting, stunted growth, frequent illnesses) the cognitive and emotional impacts are equally, if not more, impactful and are likely to have lifelong effects. Poverty and undernourishment in early life has an enormous impact on cognition, mood and behaviour.

Despite strongly empathising with the circumstances, it might not seem clear what the significance of this is within the context of organisational stress and performance. South African (and emerging market) leaders and decision makers need to consider that the current mental health landscape within the business has already been profoundly influenced by this societal injustice, as many of your employees come from impoverished and disadvantaged backgrounds. Moreover, leaders will be required to future-proof the well-being of their teams, especially considering that the prevalence of mental health compromise in employees due to early life circumstances, is likely to grow due to the current set of socio-economic factors occurring simultaneously throughout the world.

In order for a company or economy to thrive, it needs its most valuable resource – its people – to be engaged, inspired and living up to their intrinsic potential. Good health is not only a requirement but a fundamental prerequisite. Overcoming the compounded challenges brought on by the combined effects of the coronavirus pandemic and the Fourth Industrial Revolution, will require that every business (regardless of location, size or sector) have a proactive plan to assist its people in their wellness and personal growth. Reactive measures, ie prescribing time off for depression and burnout or receiving counselling following an emotional breakdown, is simply not enough.

I treated a patient several years ago who was in his late 30s and extremely successful and physically fit. His greatest assets were his intellect and compassion, conversely, by his admission, his weaknesses included extreme emotional volatility and a tendency towards self-destructive behaviours that were aptly identified and described as self-sabotage. His childhood was turbulent, and I asked him where he grew up and he responded with a list of countries, cities and suburbs that seemed endless. Clearly there was no stability in his childhood, but as the conversation unfolded it became apparent that that was merely the tip of the iceberg. He explained that his nomadic childhood was partially due to the fact that his family could seldom afford rent, let alone buy their own home. Basic groceries were a luxury and he described his adolescent diet consisting of white bread, margarine, processed cheese, various types of jam and some of the more affordable sweets and chocolates.

From the age of 13, school attendance became near impossible as he had to work most evenings to contribute towards supporting himself and his family. Due to relationship conflicts and ongoing struggles, he left home at 17 years old and through sheer grit and determination found a way to get a proper education, that he self-funded, built a successful career and became a respected member of his community.

Despite having become successful and things seemingly ending well, the client came to see me because he had not lived up to his potential on so many levels. We spent a tremendous amount of time together and as I got to know him better, I came to realise that he was incredibly intelligent, in a somewhat unconventional way, and could somehow master whatever he chose to do, through sheer persistence and drive.

But he was undoubtedly his own worst enemy. His emotional volatility had destroyed many of his close personal and professional relationships. His intense moods would affect co-workers and from time to time he would withdraw for days on end.

While the challenges of his childhood had given him the power of determination, the will to be successful and the courage to take on any challenge, it also came at a price. Whether it was the psychological and emotional trauma of his childhood or the years of malnutrition and undernourishment in this formative period I wasn't quite sure of initially, but I knew he was capable of achieving and what he had done thus far was incongruent. He had a full range of extra gears and he knew it and so did I, so the challenge was how we were going to augment his potential at this fairly late stage in his life.

To establish a base of understanding and insight into how the experiences of his past could have impacted him, I performed several genetic tests pertaining to behaviour, cognition and health. These panels are available through DNAlysis in South Africa and DNA Life in the rest of world. The tests assess a range of genes central to the promotion of physical and mental well-being.

My interest centred on determining his biological regulation of stress responses, the production, transportation and uptake of molecules like serotonin, dopamine and brain-derived neurotrophic factor (BDNF) – all molecules involved in emotional regulation, cognition, learning and IQ.

The findings told the complete story. As it turned out, the undernutrition he had experienced as a child was central to his emotional volatility and self-destructive tendencies. He had several genetic variants that influence emotional and mood regulation (ie methylation,[9] neurotrophin production,[10] GSK3ß[11] and serotonin[12] metabolism) which meant that nutritional deficiencies during his core developmental years were able to manifest as emotional and behavioural compromise as an adult. Despite his high level of self-awareness and willingness to address the scenario, he had been unable to make headway up to this point in his life.

Based on the genetic information and the results from additional metabolic tests, I was able to put together a targeted and highly individualised approach to address many of his physiological challenges that fundamentally form the basis of psychological resilience. Nutritional supplements supporting areas in need, specific exercise protocols, further dietary changes as well as activities that helped to modulate stress responses, like swimming, yoga, meditation and time in nature, formed the basis of his new resilience plan.

Several years later, he has lived up to his fullest potential, although who's to say there isn't even more to come. Many of his self-destructive habits have disappeared, his mood stability has dramatically improved and his career and personal achievements have hit unprecedented highs. He is no longer just a respected member of his community but is known and respected in his industry throughout the world.

My client's circumstances all came down to the basic biological function of molecules. Hormones, neurochemicals, neuropeptides and proteins govern our reality, and ultimately our potential in life. The more we are able to support this delicate and complex ecosystem, the greater our coping mechanisms, intellect, learning potential, creativity, sociability and overall health will be. Undernourishment and poverty are devastating from a societal and organisational perspective as nutrition is central to the effective regulation of this delicate biological balance. Not only does the social injustice of hunger and undernourishment affect the present, it also affects the future and the potential that lies ahead for each and every person afflicted.

> Each and every one of us has the potential to make a profound difference in the world.

With strong aspirations, drive and determination, intrinsic potential can be realised, despite past limitations. Governments, leaders and businesses have a responsibility to nurture and develop their people through strong organisational health promotion initiatives and personal development and leadership programmes. Many studies have clearly shown the impact that poverty and malnutrition have on mental health and wellness.

THE SCIENCE

In 2017 researchers from the London School of Economics and the University College of London, published a study on the impact of malnutrition during pregnancy on mental health outcomes in offspring later in life.[13] The study used data from the Dutch famine, which was a consequence of food-supply chains being cut off during the later stages of the Second World War between November 1944 and May 1945. During this six-month period, average calorie intake ranged from a mere 1 000 to 500 kcal/day.

What the researchers found when analysing the children conceived during the famine, was a significantly higher prevalence of mental health issues later in life, compared to those children of the same age who were from regions of Holland unaffected by the dire food shortages. Several other studies on the Dutch famine and health outcomes supported these findings and two studies revealed a high prevalence of antisocial behaviour in those conceived in the famine as well as a very high occurrence of schizophrenia.[14]

Maternal malnutrition at conception and during pregnancy is associated with mental health compromise and an increased prevalence of antisocial behaviour in children.

Consider that this period of severe food shortage was only six months whereas many of those who live in impoverished communities in South Africa, and throughout the world, experience hunger and malnutrition for years, if not decades.

Several studies have looked into more protracted undernutrition and the long-term impact of those affected. One such study was published in 2016 by a team of researchers from the School of Public Health at Capital Medical University in Beijing in China. The study aimed to identify the long-term effects of the Chinese famine of 1958 to 1961 on cognitive function and mental well-being later in life.[15] Up until this study, the influence of undernutrition during pregnancy, or in childhood, on cognitive functioning (as opposed to behavioural outcomes) in late adulthood, had not been examined.

The study involved 1 366 adults born between 1950 and 1964. The participants were divided into five groups to assess whether a child's age during a period of limited food supply will have an influence on long-term cognitive development. The five groups included those that were foetal-exposed, early childhood-exposed (1–3 years old during the famine), mid childhood-exposed (4–6 years old during the famine), late childhood-exposed (7–9 years old during the famine) and non-exposed.

In order to ensure an accurate picture of the post-famine landscape, the Chinese team used numerous, widely recognised, cognitive assessment protocols including the Mini-Mental State Examination (MMSE),[16] the Montreal Cognitive Assessment (MoCA)[17] and the Stroop Color and Word Test.[18]

The outcome of this study has exceptional relevance to all leaders and decision makers. The results showed that undernutrition in utero and during

> Poor nutrition during early childhood is associated with reduced attention, focus and impulse control later in life.

childhood is associated with not only an overall reduction in cognitive functionality, but also a decline in specific executive functions such as attention and focus as well as reduced impulse control.

In emerging economies like South Africa, each and every business needs to consider employee background and life experiences and future-proof their employees by providing tools and resources that support cognitive and emotional health. This would include health education, continued education platforms, healthy meal amenities and, in some instances, exercise facilities.

Future-proofing requires the following action steps:

The process of future-proofing

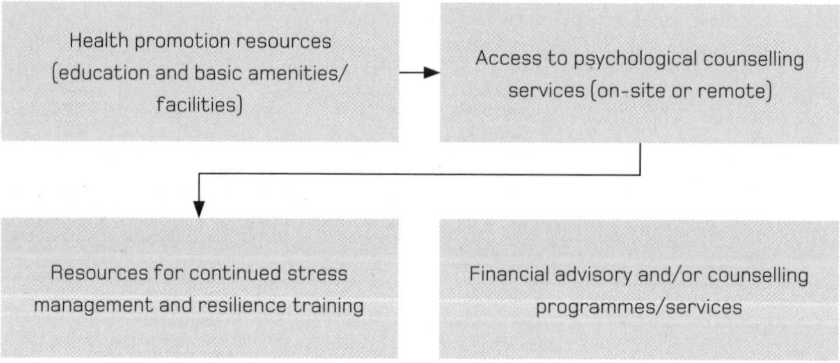

THE ALL-CONSUMING STRESS OF FINANCIAL PRESSURE

In 2015 Jim Goh from Harvard Business School and Jeffrey Pfeffer and Stefanos A. Zenios from the Stanford Graduate School of Business published one of the most impactful reviews on stress in the workplace and health outcomes.[19] The meta-analysis initially began with 741 studies but was rigorously filtered down to 228. Of these studies, none of them involved less than 1 000 participants and half of the studies followed these large groups over extended periods of time. From this, Goh and his team were able to analyse the effects of 10 different workplace (and life) stressors on four health outcomes: physical, mental, chronic disease diagnosis and premature mortality. The rationale was to allow policymakers to weigh the magnitude of each stressor's effects.

> Ongoing financial pressures increase the risk of developing mental health issues such as anxiety and depression by 90%.

According to Goh: 'Our objective was to analyse work stressors that affect people's psychological and physical health and that can be reasonably addressed by either public policy or managerial interventions'.

The review was able to accurately quantify the risk and health impact of many stresses, including dire financial challenges.

According to Goh, the stress of financial strain increases the risk of developing self-reported mental health issues by 90%, self-reported physical health issues by 70% and the risk of premature death by well over 40%.

In light of these figures, consider the devastating effects the coronavirus pandemic has had on households throughout the world. At the end of June 2020, McKinsey & Company released a report entitled 'A Global View of Financial Life During COVID-19'.[20] The authors tracked consumer sentiments across 30 countries and the paper provided the following insights:

- 20% to 60% of people who make financial decisions for their household, fear losing their jobs;
- Throughout the world, household financial decision makers feel that their country's economies are weak. This feeling was most pronounced in South Africa and Italy, where 73% and 64%, respectively, of respondents, assessed the economy as weak;

- More than two-thirds of household financial decision makers in countries such as the UK, Germany, Spain, Italy, South Africa and Russia believe that the economic impact will last well over a year, further amplifying existing financial insecurity and strain;
- Well over 70% of South Africans reported a drop in earnings and reduction in savings. Moreover, at the time of the report, the vast majority of South African households were only able to survive on existing savings for a period of less than four months.

It has become a vicious cycle where a global health pandemic has resulted in a global economic crisis, which is now materialising in a mental health emergency.

Sadly, in many less socialised countries around the world, financial hardships are also strongly linked to yet another major stress – an inability to afford basic healthcare. In a country like South Africa where the population exceeds 59 million people, only 2.8 million are able to afford membership to Discovery Health, the country's largest and most recognised medical scheme.

The paradox is that the stress of not having medical aid or access to adequate medical care is associated with a 120% higher risk of being diagnosed with a chronic disease.

Challenge #1

Limited/slow economic growth and rising poverty

Stress associations

Financial strain, limited access to proper medical care, unemployment

Negative health associations

Mental health and physical health compromise, chronic disease diagnosis as well as premature mortality

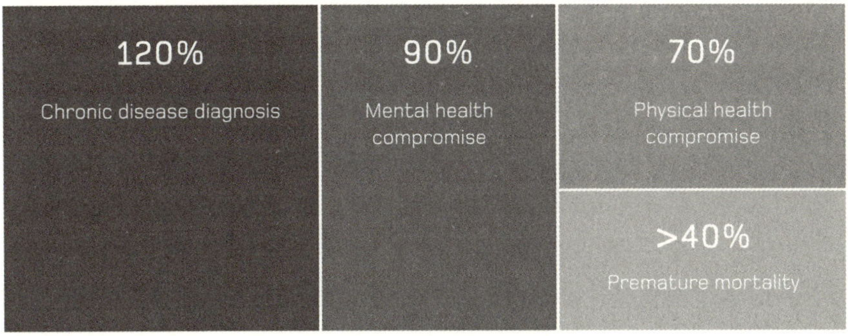

Poverty and financial stress impact risk

PRODUCTIVITY – A DISAPPEARING ACT

Productivity is the most important determinant of long-term growth and rising living standards and is central to a thriving global economy. Yet many, if not most, businesses are struggling with this key performance metric.

In theory, business growth should be well-served by the rapid advancements in technology and innovation. After all, technology can, and should, translate into greater organisational efficiencies, promoting growth opportunities and ultimately the creation of new wealth. But the last decade reveals a very different picture.

Productivity, whether measured by labour productivity or total factor productivity has been on the decline, or at best remained stagnant, for some time. Labour productivity measures the hourly output of a country's economy and charts the amount of real GDP produced by an hour of labour. It is largely driven by investment in capital, technological progress and human capital development. Total factor productivity (TFP) is a measure of productivity calculated by dividing economy-wide total production by the weighted average of inputs from labour and capital. It represents growth in real output which is in excess of the growth in inputs.

Economists and financial analysts are perplexed by the fact that there is a failure of innovation to translate to higher levels of productivity across the globe. Moreover, no clear or definitive explanation for this phenomenon has been identified.

What this means, in simple terms, is that the amount that is produced for every hour of work is barely increasing in some countries and falling in others, putting a brake on living standards in the developed world and dramatically slowing down the rate of improvement in the emerging economies.

Although this does sound counter-intuitive, reflect on your average day at work or at home (although, in many cases, during COVID-19, they were often the same). Many of us would find it extremely difficult to live without high-speed internet, our smartphones glued to our hands and the diverse array of communication portals such as Zoom, Microsoft Teams, WhatsApp, Instagram, Facebook, Gmail and email. We can connect to information and people anywhere in the world in a matter of seconds. We assume that this state of hyper-connectedness translates into incredible efficiencies, but it doesn't. The reason why is because every time you are interrupted during a meaningful task it does two things: first, it dramatically increases the likelihood of making errors and secondly, it shifts you away from your thinking.

A research paper published in the *Journal of Experimental Psychology* found that an interruption of four seconds or more during a task, increases the error rate on resumption of the task by 300%.[21]

> When we are interrupted for a period of four seconds or longer, it increases the likelihood of making errors by over 300%.

Equally as concerning within the context of productivity, is that answering a call, quickly responding to your messages, scrolling through your Instagram feed or having an impromptu chat with a colleague, increases stress responses, frustration, time pressure and overall effort when resuming your activity. According to researchers from the University of California and Humboldt University in Germany, when we are interrupted during a task, it will take most people at least 23 minutes to return to the original activity.[22]

I can personally identify with both the error factor and the struggle to regain focus. During the sustained worldwide lockdowns, working at home became a reality for almost four billion people. The first few weeks were something of a novelty for many people; no traffic or wasted time in the car, more autonomy and spending more time with family, were some of the perks. But as my boys (who were two and three years old at the time) discovered that Dad, the food, beverage and entertainment director, was home and available for activities 24/7, it became increasingly more challenging for me to work effectively.

Every few minutes, I was interrupted by a smiley face or a tug on my sleeve for participation in a game, show, sporting activity or snack assembly. At some point, the TV or iPad was the only solution to keep them occupied for a chunk of time, but that came at a price. If they were watching TV, every five to 10 minutes I would be called to change the channel. If I didn't respond in good time, their calls would become louder and more frequent. They would not stop until their needs were met, but they often didn't even know what they wanted, which resulted in me being called back to attend to them further. The price of my home-working arrangement was that I had to reread documents countless times and creating new talks and projects took considerably longer. This was further amplified and compounded by the stream of calls, emails and messages that accompany remote working conditions and the overnight change in the professional landscape. While I was still producing the same amount of work, the days were three to four hours longer due to the frequent interruptions.

As the weeks passed, I felt more and more depleted, fatigued and began picking up small niggles in my training. Burnout was officially setting in. For many, the opportunity to simply extend the day is not possible due to overall work volume, time restrictions, family commitments and so on. In this instance, the direct consequence of frequent distractions and

> Despite technological advancements, there has been a steady decline in productivity within developed economies over the last 50 years.

interruptions is reduced output (productivity) and the overwhelming feeling that you are constantly falling behind.

A 2017 report done by the IMF, 'Gone with the Headwinds: Global Productivity'[23] provides a detailed overview of the steady decline in productivity over the last 50 years within developed economies. It also suggests that over the medium term, productivity growth prospects are highly uncertain and, at very best, may return to the levels seen in the mid-1990s, which weren't very high. This said, in light of the coronavirus pandemic, these conservative projections might still be overly optimistic.

The 'high-performance' culture

With productivity on a downward or static trajectory, this means companies wishing to grow and increase their competitiveness through increased output and efficiencies will be faced with a huge stumbling block. The corporate 'push' for greatness will invariably play out in many instances as it unfolds with a model that demands more of existing employees, creates higher and often unrealistic professional expectations, sets bigger, almost unattainable targets, all under the so-called 'high-performance' culture.

While this model can be successful in the short term, the limitations in human capabilities will always begin to unfold. Without proper management, the 'high-performance' environment transforms into one of liability and subsequent collapse of the workforce, regardless of their level within the organisation. These environments are typically associated with a very high prevalence of mental and physical health issues.

> Without proper management, high-performance environments can result in significant mental and physical strain within the workforce.

Having spent the better part of two decades working at the top level of professional and international sport, with successful Olympic teams, numerous national teams, elite individual athletes, I've realised that pushing harder doesn't necessarily translate into better outcomes. The popular notion that because I work harder than you, I will be more successful, is fundamentally flawed and completely outdated as a performance model. Certainly, when a team, group or individual is apathetic and lethargic, working harder *would* translate to improved outcomes, but not in environments where athletes (or professionals) are already highly driven, self-motivated and ambitious. Hard work is certainly a key ingredient in successful outcomes, but it is innovation, adaptability and intuition that have the greatest potential to create success on the field, mat or on the court.

It appears that this fundamental principle holds true for the Fourth Industrial Revolution, whether on a governmental, business or individual level. Those who are more creative in their offerings, more innovative in their approach and show greater agility, will benefit the most under the new set of economic and social conditions. Merely pushing harder, working longer and cutting expenditure further does not ensure a position at the table going forward.

> Success in these difficult and challenging times is largely dependent on innovation, adaptability and intuition.

These sentiments are strongly echoed by Klaus Schwab, the founder and executive chairman of the World Economic Forum (WEF) who believes that only those companies that adopt entirely new economic and organisational structures will be able to capitalise on the immense value that exists within the Fourth Industrial Revolution. He also asserts that the competitiveness rules are vastly different when compared to all previous periods of change. According to Schwab: 'To remain competitive, both companies and countries must be at the frontier of innovation in all its forms, which means that strategies which primarily focus on reducing costs will be less effective than those which are based on offering products and services in more innovative ways'.

> Both the WEF and IMF believe that increased productivity and economic success can only be achieved by being at the forefront of innovation as well as by strengthening education and training efforts.

Not surprisingly, the IMF shares the same views on sustainable growth and increased productivity. They are of the opinion that attention must be given to strengthening innovation, education and training policies.

Extreme cost-cutting, radical restructuring and indiscriminate retrenchments have resulted in fewer people fulfilling the same operational roles. This has culminated in excessive demands being placed on remaining employees. Moreover, when combined with a low level of discretion, ie no voice or decision-making latitude, as is often the case, results in a significant level of job strain that will corrode and undermine health in the future on a level that is unimaginable. Yet this scenario is already playing out in almost every business throughout the world.

Stress associated with chronically high demands, increases the risk of developing mental health compromise by about 60%, physical health issues by almost 50%[24] and is a primary driver of burnout (something I personally experienced during the lockdown). Also, this increased risk in physical and mental health compromise is based solely on high demands and to the exclusion of other stresses (an unrealistic and improbable scenario).

Seldom do stresses occur in isolation. High demands are often accompanied by long working hours and increased conflicts between the demands of your personal and professional lives. When you begin to put all these stresses and their negative health associations together, the picture can be frightening.

The implosion of the 'high-performance' model

In 2019 I was approached by a leading financial institution to assist them in managing their growing stress and employee wellness challenges.

The organisation was the ultimate showcase for the 'high-performance' model and the bank always strived to be the 'best of the best' in a highly competitive market. In 2019 the South African financial system was ranked 19th in the world, scoring 83 out of a possible 100 on the WEF's Global Competitiveness Index. Banking and finance are, by far, South Africa's most successful sectors.

At my first meeting, I could feel the intensity and energy in the room. This can be a good thing in some situations, but in this instance it felt frenetic and like a short circuit was affecting everyone in the room. It reminded me of some of the experiences I had in my career in professional tennis. The build-up to a Grand Slam event like Wimbledon sees several hundred of the top male and female players come together to compete for much-needed ranking points and, of course, vast sums of prize money. The week before the tournament is exciting and frenzied, and the nervous tension in the air is almost unendurable, even by standards of the top-ranked players. Fear, uncertainty, self-doubt and individual insecurities seem to grow exponentially throughout the week, not just for the players themselves but also among their teams of coaches, managers, trainers, therapists and family members.

Young aspiring players, as well as older athletes trying to make a final push in their careers, turn up their training to full throttle. Incidentally this is not the best strategy as it can result in undue fatigue and/or injury just before the tournament.

Everyone is looking at what the competition is doing (without being noticed), trying to gain a competitive advantage by incorporating drills and often peculiar techniques into their final pre-tournament programme. I got caught up in this on more than one occasion and looking back at some of the drills we all adopted at the Grand Slams, I can only laugh as they would be considered absurd or ridiculous. One of these drills involved a trainer or coach instructing a player to run around his or her tennis racket 10 times and then rush to the net to catch a ball. The 'theory' was that it simulated disorientation and dizziness and trained the player to run and catch under extreme circumstances. There was certainly no basis for their application in tennis, or any sport. It was about looking the part; the perfect mask to disguise fear, self-doubt and insecurity. Something we can all identify with.

Grand Slams are unlike the other elite tennis events of the year such as ATP or WTA events which are typically limited to a handful of the highest-ranked players. In my experience, the more accomplished players have a tremendous self-assuredness and intrinsic belief in themselves and are fully prepared by the time they arrive at an event. They won't be trying funky drills, changing treatment techniques or training too hard. Remarkably, despite the fact that they are competing against rivals of comparative skills and abilities from day one, the environment is always remarkably calm and serene.

The meeting that day at the bank felt like the frenzied build-up to a Grand Slam. The wellness team pointed out many of the challenges they were being confronted with within the organisation. Burnout, poor mental health and even staff retention were growing concerns despite having one of the best wellness programmes in the country. As we started to unpack the details within this 'high-performance' culture, it became clear how the model had imploded, not at the outset, but over a period of a few years. Coffee breaks taken away from your desk were viewed as apathetic, workdays shorter than 12 hours were frowned upon and the weekends … well, they were a fantasy. There was no respite. An additional strain was that co-workers were purposefully vetted against each other in order to 'bring out the best' in the them. The competition was fierce.

While mental health of staff members, burnout and resignation trends provide a good indication of the professional landscape, for stakeholders the truest measure of the bank's success, or alternatively its challenges, is The Banker Top 1000 rankings. Over the last few years, local economic circumstances such as a recession and decline in economic growth pulled most South African banks down in the international rankings, with few exceptions.

The question leadership was asking its teams on the ground was why the 'high-performance' environment was unable to anticipate the effects of the macroeconomic shifts, to the extent that forward-thinking strategies could have been put in place that would have offset some of the financial losses, together with the decline in the international banking rankings?

This may seem overly critical, even in a sector that is notoriously intolerant. The reason for this condemnation of performance was because not all South African banks had dropped in global rankings. If fact, a fairly young, highly innovative and agile competitor was able to move up the rankings and gain the prestigious title of *Forbes'* Best Bank in South Africa in the same year.

In subsequent meetings, the dynamic wellness team felt that employees needed to be motivated and given the tools to help them cope better with the increasing demands placed on them. We decided that the wellness intervention would kick off with a talk at the bank's central offices with a core group of approximately 500 employees. Additionally, live feeds were set up to different offices within South Africa and Europe. The message was to be one of personal empowerment through the provision of effective stress-management tools. My goal was to weave this into a story that would connect the audience to the content over a three-hour period.

Speaking to such a large audience was a great opportunity for me to assess the current stress and resilience environment at the bank. Just prior to the session, the majority of the group downloaded The Stress Code app, the app I had recently created, and engaged in the stress and resilience self-assessments.

> The Stress Code app is a tool that I developed over a two-year period that assists organisations in measuring and managing stress and resilience. The intention of using a technology platform was to make it accessible to all employees and create a real-time window into organisational stress and potential.

The answers as to how and to what extent the 'high-performance' culture had impacted employees' health and well-being would be accessible within a few minutes. On completion, the data was captured and sorted in terms of relevance.

That evening, on a flight to the Netherlands for a speaking engagement the following day, I went through the results of the self-assessments. The data confirmed what scientists and performance coaches know all too well and that is that the 'always-on' model is failing to achieve the desired productivity and success outcomes. Moreover, the casualties from pushing for greater productivity were clearly visible. Over 6% of the institution's key employees were at risk of resignation. Additionally, 71% of employees were experiencing burnout and 50% were at risk of developing a chronic disease (aside from those that already had one). However, the biggest casualty in the push for greater productivity was compromised mental health. Of the bank's employees, 44% were either experiencing a common mental health disorder or were predisposed to one in the near future.

In a highly competitive market such as the financial sector, where the stakes are so high, the talent within the organisation need to be at their best. There is no doubt that the platform for exceptional performance is optimal health! Burnout, exhaustion, emotional fragility and physical strain create no productivity and performance advantages whatsoever and will always detract from achieving the desired goals on a personal or organisational level. Take a moment to reflect on times when you were productive, creative and inspired; they probably coincided with high levels of personal wellness, health and vitality.

> The changes felt as a consequence of the Fourth Industrial Revolution can offer exceptional opportunities for growth and success. But the rules of engagement are vastly different. You have to think creatively, trust your intuition and above all, be innovative. Merely pushing yourself or your team harder is simply not enough to be successful.

The Fourth Industrial Revolution can be a stage for unimaginable success, but this new era favours innovation, intuition and creativity; three characteristics that are scarce, if not altogether absent, in a state of stress, burnout and exhaustion.

The situation at the bank was a clear example of the implosion of the 'high-performance' model when not effectively measured and/or managed. For whatever reason (perhaps budget constraints, differences in viewpoints, the enormity of the challenge, etc), the HR team never proceeded further with the illuminated and defined issues.

There are several ways to promote greater productivity in an organisation that are not associated with a decline in the wellness potential of the entire organisation. All of which I have implemented at some stage in my career, on different levels, suited to the specific industry.

Action steps and measures to create greater efficiencies

1. Place a significant emphasis on the development of skills within the business →
2. Show a strong commitment to employee education and further training →
3. Adopt technology where possible to augment innovation →
4. Promote and encourage employee health and well-being →
5. Create an inspired workforce and leadership →
6. Create organisational priorities

Challenge #2
Low productivity

Stress associations

High demands, long working hours, work-family conflict, job and employment insecurity

Negative health associations

Burnout, mental health and physical health compromise, chronic disease diagnosis and premature mortality

±60%	±55%	±52%	± 22%
Mental health compromise	Chronic disease diagnosis	Physical health compromise	Premature death from all causes

The collective risk of ongoing high demands and long working hours

THE LABOUR MARKET – IS EMPLOYMENT BECOMING A LUXURY ITEM?

As the Fourth Industrial Revolution gains more momentum, new technologies have, and will continue, to change the nature of work in every industry and occupation. Automation and capital are substituting labour so it is not a question of if, but to what extent and over what period of time. The global recalibration of businesses has impacted employment growth, a trend that has been visible for over a decade and one that has been exacerbated by the pandemic.

The failure to achieve sustainable and inclusive growth and decent work for everyone, places the world in a precarious and potentially volatile socio-economic position as unemployment is strongly associated with social unrest. After several years of relative calm, social unrest around the world began to rise, affecting seven out of 11 regions of the world including Europe, North Africa and Asia, coinciding with the decline in employment growth.[25]

Social unrest is measured by the Internal Labour Organization (ILO) Social Unrest Index, which tracks the frequency of manifestations of social unrest and includes protests and demonstrations (anti-government, climate change, sustainable economic development, etc).

The global labour market suffered a huge blow following the outbreak of COVID-19. In March 2020 many countries around the world were in enforced national lockdowns (with varying degrees of stringency) and three months later, 93% of the world's working population were living in countries with workplace closure measures still in force.[26]

According to the ILO, working-hour losses from April to June of 2020 reached a level of 14% worldwide or the equivalent of 400 million full-time jobs. Bear in mind that unemployment doesn't factor in labour underutilisation. The mismatch between labour supply and demand extends well beyond the 188 million unemployed people across the world in 2019. An additional

165 million people are in employment but need additional work in order to properly support their families. Also, about 120 million people are not officially classified as unemployed, but are only marginally attached to the labour market and could potentially be unemployed at any moment. Frighteningly, more than 470 million people worldwide lack adequate access to paid work.

The ongoing and escalating combination of a greater number of people in need of employment and less available jobs has been a historic source of conflict in many countries throughout the world, highlighted even more by the waves of xenophobic violence experienced in South Africa.

At its core, experts attribute the aggression that is expressed towards foreign nationals as a consequence of threatened livelihoods and ongoing economic struggles. In March 2019, the seriousness of the circumstances on the ground led the South African government to launch a National Action Plan in order to combat racism, racial discrimination, xenophobia and related intolerance. Invariably, the roots of social unrest, increased protectionism and political instability often lie in high unemployment, poverty and inequality.

Pushing harder to stay in the race

Life in the developed world appears to have changed overnight from an almost predictable life trajectory that routinely began with basic schooling, progressed to higher education and was then followed by a career at the company of your choice, and culminated in starting and growing a family with the ability to balance life and work. The TV shows and movies many of us grew up with in the late 80s, 90s and early 2000s portray this aspirational life journey extremely well.

Things are vastly different today. We can all attest to the fact that the landscape is far more uncertain and unpredictable than it ever was before. Basic schooling, possible university or college (if you are in a strong financial position or willing to take on significant debt), applying for whatever job is available and hoping for the best is the new template. Unlike in many previous generations, you have to earn your right to work, outshining fierce competition and the biggest adversary of them all – redundancy due to technology and automation.

A privileged person (ie able to receive 15 years or more of formal education), who is highly motivated, with a strong support infrastructure of friends and family, will be able to navigate their way through life's newest obstacle course and hopefully find themselves successfully on the other end, but of course this comes at a cost.

Teenagers pushing themselves to achieve the necessary grades to be accepted for their chosen degree, at their desired university and even their career of choice, results in significant stress exposure at a developmental period in their lives where strong physical and emotional vulnerabilities exist. Once they have completed their education, the likelihood of arriving at their professional destination in a state of compromised health and burnout is extremely high, or even a forgone conclusion.

Now consider that successful companies seek to hire only the 'best of the best' and will go to great lengths to hand-pick their future talent. Although this additional pressure has been well anticipated and modelled in terms of outcomes by the rising stars, the consequences of pushing the physiological and psychological limits for years on end hasn't. Not only is this felt on an individual level, but also on an organisational and societal one.

While a handful of people are born with exceptional ability and a multitude of talents, most of us only develop skills through extremely hard work, repetition and tremendous personal sacrifice.

In the future, many companies may need to ask to what extent has the journey to excellence impacted their new recruits. After all, the relentless pressure, years of limited sleep, hundreds of hours of extra lessons and days that typically lasted 14 hours will have impacted the newcomer. For some outliers, this 'pressure cooker' creates strength and resilience that is extraordinary, but for most it can create fragility in long-term health and well-being.

Employee retention, presenteeism, burnout, mental wellness and chronic diseases are the greatest challenges that businesses face throughout the world. Radical shifts in the labour market and the relentless pressure placed on individuals to outperform their intrinsic capabilities, not to mention their contemporaries, is a major contributing factor in the promotion and creation of this compromised organisational health set.

Earnings not aligned with basic living expenses

Another growing challenge confronting the global labour market, whether as a direct or indirect consequence of the Fourth Industrial Revolution is difficult to say, is the inability of employees to meet their basic living expenses.

According to the ILO, 3.3 billion people around the world were employed in 2018. Following the coronavirus, these figures are likely to be radically different, at least in the short term. But even with employment, the majority of the world's workforce experiences a lack of material well-being, economic security, future opportunities, let alone any scope for personal development.[27]

A further statistic tells us that prior to the pandemic, over 1 in 4 workers in low- and middle-income countries are living in extreme poverty, existing off of an average of only R44 per day ($2.50).

We are fully cognisant of the impact of financial pressures and employment insecurity on stress and health outcomes, but the feelings most of us associated with the announcement of the lockdown is a tiny fraction of what millions of people feel like every day.

The moment lockdown was announced, the question many of us would have asked was, 'What are we going to do?' Work as we knew it had come to an abrupt end – with no timeline to work towards. On a personal and professional level, consulting with groups and individuals and running workshops is my career, and one based on direct human interaction and engagement. In a single moment that was gone. The vast majority of the world's population felt the same sense of uncertainty and anxiety and as the days unfolded, for millions of people around the world, that anxiety increased, sleep patterns were affected and the future was unclear.

The impact of the pandemic has dramatically amplified what millions of people living in poverty, who are unemployed or marginally attached to the workforce, feel like on a daily basis. The feeling of utter desperation is a daily struggle and the basic need of food and shelter is one that is often not met.

For this reason, financial strain and economic uncertainty can be considered one of the primary contributors to the growing stress and mental health crisis that we are confronted with today.

Corroded self-worth and personal value

Limited employment opportunities and financial hardships are strongly associated with an equally impactful and menacing stress known as an effort-reward imbalance. Crucial to all social relationships is a sense of reciprocity. One-sided relationships have been shown to be a significant source of stress and associated illness.

The effort-reward balance is perceived and measured in three different ways in the workplace. These include fair financial compensation, appreciation for the value that we hold in the professional environment and, equally importantly, the opportunity for professional growth and advancement.

> We are currently in the midst of a global effort-reward imbalance. This is characterised by the feeling of being undervalued and underappreciated. Limited professional and personal growth opportunities are all compounded by the fact that the majority of the world's workforce is not earning enough to cover basic living expenses.

Today, expectation has replaced appreciation, not only in the workplace, but in almost every sphere of our lives. Added to this is the fact that the majority of the world's workforce has limited material well-being and almost no scope for future advancements, and it becomes evidently clear that an effort-reward imbalance exists of global proportions. The negative impact of an effort-reward imbalance in human stress and health outcomes was first described and validated by German researchers as far back as 1986.[28]

In 2005 a team of researchers from Holland published an extensive meta-analysis on the relationship between an effort-reward imbalance and its impact on health.[29] The study reviewed 45 high-quality research papers investigating the effects of professional environments in which efforts were consistently high, ie relentless demands and responsibilities, and where rewards were perceivably low, ie poor remuneration, being undervalued, little to no job security and limited future advancement opportunities.

It has been known for decades that strong negative emotions such as those experienced with an effort-reward imbalance can trigger the stress axis,[30] leading to biological shifts that may result in significant mental and physical health compromise. The question is how and to what extent is this impacting the majority of the world's 3.3 billion employees, many of which are struggling to meet basic living expenses. The Dutch review found that those individuals who frequently reported high efforts, together with low rewards, were almost nine times more likely to experience physical health issues such as cardiovascular disease. Moreover, the prevalence of premature death was also higher in these employees.

> An effort-reward imbalance increases the likelihood of developing an array of physical health issues by almost 900% and depressive symptoms by 49%.

The analysis also found a higher association between an effort-reward imbalance and negative behaviours such alcohol abuse and the onset of smoking. Almost all of the studies in the analysis found that an ongoing effort-reward imbalance is strongly associated with reduced employee well-being and an increased risk of developing depression and physical pain. This is relevant considering that mental health, as well as musculoskeletal disorders, rank firmly in the top five causes of lost years of life due to disability.

Further linking an effort-reward imbalance to depression, in 2017 Danish researchers published a review involving eight studies that included almost 85 000 employees.[31] The aim of the extensive analysis was to determine whether employees exposed to an effort-reward imbalance at work have a higher prevalence of depression than non-exposed workforces. The results of the analysis showed that an effort-reward imbalance was associated with a 49% greater risk of developing depressive symptoms in those exposed. This outcome is extremely insightful as the researchers went to great lengths to weigh the outcomes by the quality of the study as well as by the type of effort-reward imbalance, ie monetary gratification, career opportunities, esteem, respect and job security.

I have been on the receiving end of an effort-reward imbalance several times in my career and it was extremely stressful. I worked for a high-performing sports team that had held the top position in the world at several junctures over the previous decade. The team had a strong work ethic and a reputation for always hiring the best practitioners and specialists in their respective fields. They were also known to be ruthless and highly intolerant of incompetence, and had the highest staff turnover rate in the sport. Notwithstanding, to be able to work for the franchise would be the ultimate career achievement and if you were fortunate enough to be approached by management and made an offer, there was no way you would turn down the opportunity. The experience and prestige of working with a team of their calibre would be a career milestone and they paid almost twice the established market rate, adding clothing deals and other perks and personal luxuries.

The entire team operated with clinical efficiency in everything they did. Within 90 minutes of them presenting me with an offer and the corresponding submission of my CV, I was hired. I postponed all the projects I was working on for the once in a lifetime opportunity and five days later was on a plane to Europe, ready to assume my responsibilities, fuelled with passion, excitement, and unwavering commitment to the project.

I started work as soon as I arrived and soon realised that the team had many stars who all enjoyed public attention and being in the limelight and were fairly absorbed in the promotion of their individual brands. This created a real disconnect and fairly strained relationships within the group. I coped fairly easily with the relationship peculiarities, as it was something I was used to in professional sport, but what really derailed me was the overt lack of appreciation for the effort and level of commitment I was showing for their well-being and advancement of their careers. Despite overt successes that ensued in the coming months, there was never any acknowledgment of my role in their journey and no verbal expression of appreciation. The culture was one of expectation and disregard of people's worth and value. And the reason for that was because I was being paid well by industry standards and therefore any form of appreciation or recognition of my role appeared to be unnecessary. This is a scenario all too familiar in too many businesses and one that most people have experienced in their professional and/or personal lives.

I managed fairly well for the first six months of the contract using a lot of self-dialogue and keeping myself physically and mentally healthy through regular exercise, a good diet and taking nutritional supplements. But as time went on, I started to feel more and more down and low moods became a common occurrence. I stopped sleeping and started wishing the time away. It was crazy to consider that I had been working towards this point in my career and now that I was there, I didn't want to be there. The irony was that I loved my role, the work, and respected the athletes but the stress had marred the entire experience for me. My self-worth, self-esteem and confidence all took a knock and while I managed to see out my contract, I chose not to renew it and took another position where the environment was far more positive and rewarding, despite a cut in salary. The lesson for me was that no matter how mentally, emotionally and physically strong you are, an effort-reward imbalance can derail you as it

> An effort-reward imbalance is so profoundly impactful on business success that leaders need to take extraordinary measures to provide a safe space in this regard.

is a deep-rooted stress that pierces your psyche like few others.

Leaders and decision makers within organisations need to be mindful of the immense impact an effort-reward imbalance can have on their employees. In light of this growing societal challenge, future-proofing will require policies and even cultural shifts that work to reduce this imbalance. This is especially important in the current climate as businesses themselves are struggling for survival and require full and absolute engagement of their workforces.

Businesses struggling to stay in the game

Sweeping changes in the marketplace, increased global competitiveness and the after-effects of the pandemic, means that companies are in the fight of their lives just to stay in business, let alone provide desperately needed employment.

A social media post sent during the lockdown by Vusi Thembekwayo, a prominent business leader and investment authority was extremely telling for the business community. Widely regarded as a visionary and highly respected by the business community, this CEO has always been measured and diplomatic in his public communication forums. Part of this eloquence stems from his adjunct career as a prolific, highly sought-after professional speaker with incredible communication skills.

His post was honest, raw and emotional and showed him walking through an empty office space, moving from room to room describing the lives of those affected by the business's closure. He went on to hold political decision makers accountable for the loss of jobs and the collapse of the economy in recent years. His empathy was brutally authentic and his tone showed his anger and frustration for those who have no voice. This scenario, where a business no longer has the reserves to fight and stay afloat, is playing out every minute of every day throughout world.

The magnitude of this global volatility in business can be seen by tracking changes in the S&P 500 Index, one of the most commonly followed equity indices and considered by many to be one of the best representations of the

US stock market. The S&P acts as a snapshot that exposes which companies and industries are the largest in the economy at any given time.

According to a report by Innosight,[32] a leading management consultancy firm, in 1964 the average tenure of companies on the S&P was 33 years. In 2016 it was only 24 years and within the next seven years it will be less than 12 years (at a stretch).

> At least 50% of the companies currently listed on the S&P 500 will be replaced within the next 10 years. Those most at risk are in financial services, healthcare, travel, energy and property sectors.

The report[33] also issued a strong warning to corporate leadership to embrace transformation, as what works today is unlikely to be effective in the near future. Innosight asserts that half of the companies on the S&P will be replaced in the next 10 years and the sectors that are most likely to experience the greatest degree of turbulence and volatility in the coming years are financial services, healthcare, energy, travel and property.

The new challenges we all face

Almost overnight, the world has become far more challenging, stressful and complex. For young families, as well as the more vulnerable members of society (ie the elderly, disabled, special needs, disadvantaged), it is an especially difficult time. It is a daunting prospect that this may be just the beginning of a long and substantial recalibration affecting both our personal and professional lives. It is clear that the relationship between the opportunity for employment, and the availability of labour to businesses throughout the world, is likely to be profoundly altered due to several converging factors.

One of the defining characteristics of humankind is the capacity to develop and use tools that reduce the burden of laborious tasks. For decades, mechanisation has profoundly influenced every sector within the global economy including mining, agriculture, manufacturing and transport.

The historic introduction of automation has followed a somewhat linear path, allowing enough time for new professions and activities to sprout up and for people to gradually develop additional and relevant skills. With the appropriate education and training, we remained strongly valued for the roles we played within society and were able to offer benefit to the people around us.

For example, if you were a fishmonger, you would be a specialist knowing everything about the seasonality of catches, differences in species, transportation, markers of freshness and even the best way to prepare the catch of the day. Boats, catching methods, transportation, cleaning and storage facilities would improve year on year, but very much at a speed where you were able to keep up with developments and retain a position as a respected authority and run a profitable business.

What creates such a high degree of uncertainty going forward is that the magnitude of growth, together with the speed of change in the Fourth Industrial Era, has not been linear, but instead, exponential. Moreover, the extreme depth and breadth of change is vast and unsettling, even for the most rational among us.

Numerous thriving professions have all but vanished within recent years. Professional recruitment has been replaced by LinkedIn, travel agents by user-friendly travel sites, shop assistants by online shopping platforms, the fishmonger by large multinational retailers and the list goes on. The most stressful aspect of this replacement of professions is the speed of the transition. Literally, a vibrant and lucrative profession today can be gone tomorrow.

It seems almost inevitable, and in some ways understandable, that the more repetitive and routine low-skilled activities will be replaced through innovation, but it is concerning as to what the fate will be of fields that are highly cerebral and non-routine such as medicine, law and the even the financial sector.

Our current skills are on the endangered list

In 2013 a team of researchers from Oxford University published a landmark paper entitled 'The Future of Employment'.[34] The article sought to develop a deeper understanding of the evolving global economy and examined many common occupations and how susceptible they were to computerisation. Technology and innovation has played a role in the advancement of many highly valued fields. We can clearly see these advancements in fields such as medicine. Recent developments include online medical records, improvements in pharmaceuticals as well as better and broader testing measures. The almost linear technology adoption trajectory then shifted to an exponential one in 2019. Robotic surgery, wireless brain sensors, 3D printing, artificial organs and significant expansions in gene-based medicine, including precision medicine and gene-editing, now allows practitioners far greater scope to improve and even save the lives of their patients.

Despite these monumental advancements, doctors and specialists are at the centre of the profession; you cannot replace expert clinical reasoning and life-determining decisions by any form of technology or artificial intelligence. Right? However, Carl Benedikt Frey and Michael Osborne, co-authors of the 'The Future of Employment' see the future of medicine somewhat differently. They point out that complex pattern recognition was already being used successfully seven years ago to diagnose and develop treatment plans for cancer patients. The recalibration of the medical profession can clearly be seen by the growth in the telehealth market, currently valued at $113 billion annually. Telehealth enables patients to download an app and have access to specialist advice at a fraction of the price, without the wait and repeat visits. What does this mean to the thousands of passionate doctors and specialists that have dedicated over a decade of their lives, if not more, to studying in the service of others? Will there be fewer opportunities within the field? Will the nature and scope of practice change? Only time will tell.

The legal sector is also likely to experience upheaval due to sophisticated algorithms that have started taking over a number of tasks historically performed by paralegals and commercial and intellectual property lawyers. McKinsey currently estimates that 22% of a lawyer's job and 35% of a paralegal's job can already be automated.

> 47% of US jobs may not exist within the next 10 years due to technological advancements and digitisation.

According to an experiment conducted by LawGeex, pioneers in contract review automation, AI has officially overtaken lawyers in speed and accuracy in spotting risks in everyday contracts.[35] Dubbed as the 'ultimate showdown', 20 highly experienced lawyers took on AI in a critical review of five non-disclosure agreements. Law professors from Duke University, Stanford and the University of Southern California vetted the research methodology. Three litres of coffee later, the best-performing lawyer had an accuracy of 94% and the worst-performing 67%. The overall average was 85% and the average time taken to complete the task was 92 minutes. By contrast, LawGeex took a total of 26 seconds with a 94% accuracy level. The question is whether AI will turn the legal industry on its head in the future.

The primary intention of Frey and Osborne's paper was certainly not to promote widespread panic and fear, but rather to address and quantify the potential effects of technological developments on the 702 common professions included in the study to enable future-proofing against the impending changes. Using a novel methodology, they were able to differentiate between high, medium and low-risk occupations, depending on their probability of digitisation. The results are truly eye-opening! According to their estimates, 47% of total US employment is in the high-risk category, ie likely to be automated, and refers to jobs that may not exist within the next 10 years or so.

According to their data, the professions that are most vulnerable in the near future, include employees within the transportation and logistics sectors as well as office and administrative support. Additionally, the production sector is also likely to be disrupted to even a greater degree than it already has been.

The growing divide

Low employment growth and low participation rates in the labour force, especially within the youth, has the makings to broaden the divide between the 'haves' and 'have-nots' thereby creating significant social stress and tension due the distribution of resources within society.

Rapid technological advancements and automation have already, and will continue, to create redundancies in many businesses throughout the world. Together with the overnight disappearance of many long-established fields, this has forced many individuals to fiercely compete in a very narrow employment channel. For those who do secure well-paying employment, the consequence of pushing themselves so hard may be future health instability and compromised well-being.

Aside from the coronavirus pandemic, which stripped South Africa of 2.2 million jobs[36] and Moody's downgrade to 'junk status', South Africa was already grappling with a major unemployment crisis. In the first quarter of 2020, narrow unemployment (those who are unemployed but still looking for work) within the country hit a 16-year high of 30.1% and the broad unemployment rate, which takes into account people who are no longer looking for work (who have basically given up) was as high as 38.5%.

> The greatest protection against unemployment is skills and education. In 2019 the unemployment rate in South Africa, in highly skilled individuals, was only 2.3%.

Looking at the unemployment challenges, it becomes apparent that there is an inverse relationship between skills and unemployment. Towards the end of 2019, the unemployment rate among high-skilled individuals such as managers, professionals, technicians was only 2.3%. By comparison, unemployment in those who were previously employed within low-skilled occupations such as domestic workers and general workers and medium-skilled occupations such as sales assistants and basic machine operators, was a staggering 90.7%.[37]

However, as technology and automation is not only replacing the more routine professions, it is likely to threaten even the most intellectual and creative fields.

Moreover, employment does not ensure material well-being and according to a report entitled 'World Employment and Social Outlook – Trends 2020', income inequality is far greater than previously anticipated or reported.[38] Big data shows that in 2017, a worker falling in the upper 10% of global labour income distribution earned, on average, $7 400 (approximately R122 000) per month. By contrast, a worker in the bottom 10% earned only $22 (R373) per month.

For millions of people across the world, especially in South Africa, who are currently employed, they will still experience a basic lack of material well-being, economic security, future opportunities and scope for personal development. Not only is the reduction in employment opportunities due to economic challenges and technology and automation creating tremendous job and employment insecurity, (associated with a 45% risk of mental and physical health issues) it also perpetuates and amplifies an effort-reward imbalance culminating in ongoing negative emotions and stress.

All of this is taking place against the backdrop of businesses fighting for their survival. The immense pressure of constantly having to be relevant, innovative, streamlined, efficient and agile is taking its toll on organisations, their leadership and employees.

Future-proofing against the radical shifts within the labour market and the effects on employee health and well-being, requires a complex set of solutions. As with productivity, promoting an environment that embraces technology and innovation together with skills development is very much central to the solutions set. But there are many additional factors that need to be considered, including the promotion of a sense of job security and fair reward that encompasses appreciation, opportunities for growth and financial compensation. But arguably the most important future-proofing strategy, with the radical changes occurring within the labour market, is the safeguarding of the health and well-being of the entire workforce. Management, executive teams and primary decision makers ensure the future survival and success of a business and being physically healthy is the foundation of psychological resilience, which is the only assurance of future success in the current conditions.

Promote a culture that centres around people's intrinsic value and the expression of gratitude/ appreciation

→ There must be a strong emphasis on creating growth and potential career advancement opportunities

→ Grow and develop organisational health awareness, knowledge, skills and resources

Leaders and decision makers need to place additional emphasis on their personal health and well-being in order to strengthen their resilience

Challenge #3

Volatility and uncertainty in the labour market

Stress associations

High demands, long working hours, effort-reward imbalance, the risk of unemployment and job insecurity

Negative health associations

Burnout, mental and physical health compromise, increased alcohol abuse as well as other self-destructive behaviours such as smoking, poor diet, lack of exercise

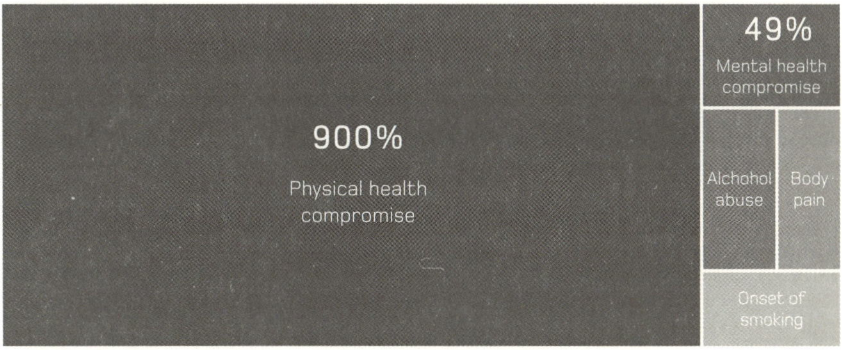

The health impact of a lack of appreciation, career advancement or poor financial compensation

The future of jobs

I have always stuck by the notion that the only time you are truly indispensable is when you are able to do things in a way that achieves successful outcomes that others simply can't. If you are engaged in a 'typical profession' (eg vendors, fast food cooks, agricultural worker, legal secretary) that does not require significant creativity, imagination or decision-making, the likelihood of automation is exceptionally high. For many businesses and millions of individuals around the world, this is already a lived reality and significant source of stress.

I recently had a conversation with Lerato, a travel agent who experienced major upheaval in her industry, and we spoke about the dire consequences of the professional recalibration. Lerato explained that for decades she ran one of the most successful travel agencies in Johannesburg. Her clients included older, high net-worth individuals and from 2004 to 2016, business was good, very good. However, during this time, countless online booking platforms and apps sprung up, resulting in a reduced influx of new clients. This decline in new business wouldn't have been an issue were it not for the fact that many of Lerato's existing clients had retired or immigrated.

Deep down she acknowledged that a 'storm' was brewing in the travel industry, but was in denial and kept herself distracted with positive health practices, physical exercise such as playing tennis, following a proper diet and taking nutritional supplements. People quickly became more web and app-savvy and low-cost flights, low-cost holidays and Airbnb replaced the existing travel model. The stress of future uncertainty became all-consuming as Lerato went from a well-established and trusted expert in the field to almost 'obsolete' within no time. Despite Lerato's health regimen, her well-being began deteriorating. She suffered from constant anxiety, low mood and body aches and after 18 months of chronic stress, she suffered a pulmonary embolism. Thankfully she was treated successfully for it and was fortunate in her circumstances as she had established savings and strong investments that she could rely on.

Lerato now operates from home in a much-reduced capacity. Closing her business affected many lives, livelihoods and the overall economy. Sadly, this scenario is becoming increasingly common and is contributing to tremendous health instability throughout the world.

According to 'The Future of Jobs Report 2018' by the WEF,[39] within the next two years, major companies are expecting a significant shift on the frontier between humans and machines when it comes to existing work tasks.

Based on extensive data, the report assessed 12 different industries and the relative contribution of professional activities performed by humans versus machines in those industries. The findings showed that in 2018 humans performed approximately 71% of all professional activities but by 2022 this is set to drop to 58%. We are almost at a threshold where machines and humans are contributing equally to the world economy.

In 1984 the movie *The Terminator* was released starring Arnold Schwarzenegger. Set against a backdrop of an artificial intelligence defence network that becomes self-aware and takes over the world, it destroys much of humanity, with the exception of a pocket of resistance. A war ensues vetting man against machine. It was a smash hit and received rave reviews and I was a huge fan, probably watching 20 times over. No one could have imagined that by the year 2020, the man versus machine war would become a reality. Only this time, the frontline is jobs and well-paying employment.

> By 2022 more than 42% of professional activities will be performed by machines.

Even jobs in the professional 'safe zone', ie a profession that has a low perceived risk of automation such as a role in communications, coordination, development, management as well as reasoning and decision-making, are not entirely safe. The same report suggests a 7–9% increase in automation in these fields within the same time frame.

> Millions of jobs can be created if companies are willing to embrace the changes brought on by the Fourth Industrial Revolution.

The report also predicts a rapid displacement of 75 million jobs through this shift in the division of labour. However, there are positive outcomes too as this change will bring with it exciting new opportunities. Klaus Schwab from the WEF believes that should businesses embrace the sweeping changes, this recalibration of the job market has the potential to bring with it at least 133 million employment opportunities around the world.

With the unprecedented Terminator-like shift of machines replacing humans in many work-related tasks and activities, skill instability is likely to become a great challenge for many companies and a significant source of stress for their employees. Already many leading businesses across the globe acknowledge that the skills required to perform most jobs are radically shifting. According to the WEF, there will be a 42% shift in required workforce skills by 2022. We have already seen glimpses of this shift following the coronavirus outbreak, where a basic work requirement is an online presence either through Zoom, WebEx, Microsoft Teams or similar platforms.

> More than half of the world's workforce will require retraining and skills development to cope with the rapid changes within their respective fields.

The skills that are required to run a business today are not the same as those that will be required in the coming years. In fact, new research shows that currently more than half of the world's workforce requires significant upskilling. Bear in mind that upskilling is no easy task and the future of work does not entail a one-day workshop or a weekend course once or twice a year, but instead requires training anywhere from six months to well over a year in many professions.

This will be a significant challenge for companies in the current economic climate as it initially presents as a double-edged sword. Should organisations choose to not strongly invest in skills development and training (as many don't), they run the risk of being uncompetitive and may potentially not survive the combined effects of the current crisis of the pandemic and Fourth Industrial Revolution. And if they do, it will be an expensive exercise. Large groups of employees taking time away from current responsibilities to acquire skills and knowledge will temporarily reduce productivity, efficiencies and effectiveness within the organisation. In the short term, this can cause increased stress on those remaining employees having to take on longer working hours and the exposure to competing demands; a strong trigger for burnout.

The cost may also affect businesses, as skills training and education is by no means an inexpensive exercise, especially when up to 50% of your staff are involved at any one time. In some ways it goes against the very fabric of the prevailing business practices over the last decade, which has seen companies migrate to lean and streamlined operating models, aggressively cutting back on costs.

I recently experienced two vastly different approaches to the exponential changes that have taken place in the workplace in recent years. Two managing partners of competing international law firms based in South Africa, have approached the impact of the coronavirus pandemic and the Fourth Industrial Revolution in diametrically opposed ways.

Kevin's firm is a medium-size law practice that is one of the most successful law franchises within South Africa. By industry standards, Kevin is fairly non-conformist. He is progressive, forward-thinking, has a strong commitment to diversity and inclusion and is heavily invested in future-proofing the firm in uncertain times. When Kevin took the position several years ago, he realised that industry changes were imminent and made sure that he was flanked by an exceptional COO and an innovative HR director, giving him a business management and people advantage from the outset.

Although the firm demands a lot of their teams and has exceptionally high targets, even by industry norms, the organisational environment is very people-centric and supportive.

Diversity, inclusion, health, wellness and ongoing education are central to the firm's practice agenda. Their commitment to skills development resulted in a strategic partnership with Harvard Business and Law Schools, affording employees the opportunity to grow and expand their knowledge set through online courses and training. Despite volatile conditions, the firm maintained its spending in those areas, setting the stage for productivity, growth and expansion. When the coronavirus pandemic hit South Africa, the firm maintained and gained dozens of deals – business got better.

By contrast, Joel had a very different approach in his firm. The basis of strategic survival in response to the coronavirus and Fourth Industrial Revolution was consistent with market norms and included immediate restructuring and radical cost-cutting initiatives. The firm focused on augmenting efficiencies, ie reducing the number of people and expenses required to produce the same amount of output. There was no existing skills development or health programmes in place, or a clear urgency to innovate and create organisational niches. Joel relied on a handful of highly competent partners with strong existing relationships to keep the business generating income. Once the country went into lockdown, the number of active deals in the firm trickled down to a handful.

Not surprisingly, Joel's operating model of limited commitment to skills development, health and innovation, was in complete contrast to the WEF's viewpoint that strongly believes that businesses have no choice but to support their existing workforces through upskilling, regardless of circumstances, economic or otherwise.

Skills and training

The decision whether or not to invest strongly in skills and training is a challenge and a major source of stress for corporate leadership around the world, in light of the current economic volatilities and uncertainties. At the same time, having employees with outdated skills is having an equally stressful effect on those within the labour market.

The Fourth Industrial Revolution is a complete paradox. In many ways, it has brought with it challenges and stresses that we are ill-equipped to deal with, but at the same time it also provides the solution set often before the problem even surfaces. Within the context of skills development and limited resources, there are countless training options available that are free and accessible to all. For example, Alison, is an online education platform that focuses primarily on workplace skills. It has millions of registered learners and offers more than 1 500 courses in categories such as technology, business and humanities. The cost? Nothing!

Another large-scale provider of online training and courses is EDX, a non-profit organisation launched by MIT and Harvard University. It offers a wide range of computer science courses and a small number of art-related courses.

Coursera is an online learning platform founded by Stanford professors, Andrew Ng and Daphne Koller. It partners with universities around the world, as well as companies such as Google and IBM, to provide courses for free. In fact, since the outbreak of COVID-19 all 3 800 of the course offerings were free.

However, despite these incredible opportunities that exist in upskilling and education, no matter how current events and future trends are framed, the volatility and scale of change may be construed as unfair and unjust.

Take a moment to reflect on your life journey that has brought you to this point in your career. The long nights of studying, the personal sacrifices and the vast financial toll it has taken. Imagine that everything you have worked so hard for over so many years won't 'cut it' in the future and you will have to commit to hours of additional training for the rest of your life, or face the consequences of redundancy or restrained career growth. That is the reality of the current workplace and the workplace of the future.

> Organisational (or societal) injustice increases the risk of developing mental health issues in those affected by 60% or greater.

While there are those people who enjoy and are passionate about acquiring new knowledge and continued learning, such as myself, for many it can feel disheartening and unjust. Fairness and injustice, both within society and a professional environment, have strong associations with illness, corresponding absenteeism as well as mental health compromise and organisational injustice which is associated with a 60% higher risk of developing mental health issues.[40]

Society is already grappling with numerous sources of injustice such as inequality and a significant lack of reciprocity for efforts. It's fair to say that our threshold for injustice is at its high-water mark and, on its own, perhaps skills instability and the potential for redundancies would be a tolerable injustice, but once added to the collective set it creates a significant health risk.

For almost two decades, global wealth gaps were progressively narrowing. However, since the Great Recession of 2008, the divide has once again increased and following the coronavirus pandemic is set to further widen with no apparent end or limitations in sight. There are two primary reasons for this divide. Firstly, labour markets are becoming increasingly biased towards a restricted range of skills. Secondly, a globally connected economy is yielding supersized rewards to a handful of innovation-driven visionaries with existing access to financial resources. In other words, the highly educated, skilled, innovative and well-funded members of our society will be able to increase their wealth exponentially. By contrast, those with a lower level of skills and education, with no access to funding, will experience fewer and fewer opportunities.

> Inequality is undermining the social balance that exists within the world. Over 50% of the world's assets are owned by the wealthiest 1% of the population.

A 2019 report by Credit Suisse showed that the lower half of the global population collectively owns less than 1% of global wealth, while the richest 10% own 82% of all wealth. Most distressingly, the top 1% account for almost half of all global assets.

> Unfairness in decisions and organisational processes, poor treatment of employees and low respect, result in significant employee stress, impaired health and reduced productivity.

This is part of the reason why striving for organisational justice and fairness is so important. Perceptions of fairness have been shown to positively translate to strong job satisfaction, individual commitment and overall performance, ie higher levels of productivity. Conversely, unfairness in decisions, low respect and poor treatment of subordinates and unfairness, with respect to organisational processes and procedures, doesn't only result in higher stress and impaired health in employees, but can also lead to unethical behaviour that can destroy the foundation of any business.

Rising prevalence of job and employment insecurity

Employment, in all its forms, not only serves as a means of income, but also provides an individual with purpose, status and identity and the opportunity to create social connections and life structure. Owing to the value that employment holds in our lives, any perceived or justified threat to our ability to generate an income has far-reaching consequences within the framework of health and well-being.

Job insecurity is as equally stressful as unemployment and in some respects can be more harmful. Both job and employment insecurity are associated with protracted periods of anticipatory worry about events that may or may not unfold in the future. This can be driven by many factors such as previous life experiences, active restructuring within the workplace, economic uncertainties, speculative behaviours among friends and co-workers, macroeconomic trends, political events and so on. These deep-rooted fears can be triggered in a number of ways and that effect can be felt for weeks, months or even years.

Within the field of psychology it has been well established that worrying about an event is as stressful as the event itself, or in many instances even more stressful.

The days preceding the lockdown in South Africa were marked by fear and uncertainty, driving an entire nation of 59 million people into a state of anxiety, depression, sleeplessness, physical pain and digestive distress. No one knew what the lockdown was going to be like, nor how it was going to impact their business, income and financial futures. Whether there was going to be enough food and basic supplies, how children would cope and what was going to happen to schools and universities. Yet, once lockdown took effect, the mood palpably changed in the country. A sense of acceptance and the creation of new routines soon replaced anxiety and anticipatory worry. Yet, despite the relative drop in perceived stress, none of the material issues fundamentally changed. In fact, in many respects, the challenges were amplifying as most businesses were still unable to operate, personal incomes were further compromised, relationships became increasingly estranged, movement and freedom was severely limited, education was a struggle for parents and students alike and opportunities in all forms became increasingly less accessible. What created the mood shift, despite the existing hardships, was that we were all living and experiencing the new reality as opposed to anticipating it.

This clearly exemplifies the profound impact that job, employment and economic insecurity can have on your psyche and emotional well-being. Yet, we are standing on the edge of a proverbial precipice. By scale and numbers, the combined effects of the coronavirus and the Fourth Industrial Revolution have increased these concerns to levels never before seen in human history. The principal drivers: the steady replacement of human tasks by machines; skills instability; changes in corporate operating models (ie reducing the number of employees, mergers and acquisitions, restructuring, change in work practices and outsourcing) and ongoing recessions.

Economic downturn and recessions are creating heightened uncertainty and insecurity

Having lived through one of the most devastating events in modern history opens up feelings of nostalgia for the time prior to the pandemic. Granted, it was easier in many respects, but the reality was far from idyllic. In 2019 *Forbes* already listed countries or territories that were at risk of going into a recession in 2020. They included Hong Kong (due to months of protests that impacted retail and tourism), the UK (driven by the unbundling from the European Union (EU), Germany (as a result of a decline in manufacturing and lower global demand for luxury cars), Italy (largely through political turmoil and low productivity) and even China who was showing the slowest growth in years. Several smaller economies, including South Africa, were either in a recession already or showing strong markers to go into one. Before the coronavirus pandemic, analysts from institutions like Moody's, J.P. Morgan and several prominent US business schools believed that global recession, or at the very least a period of slow growth in 2020, was inevitable. Following the pandemic, it appears that these assertions were merely the tip of the iceberg. In April 2020, the IMF's Managing Director, Kristalina Georgieva, said that over 170 countries were likely to experience negative per capita income growth for the year.

The global cost of the pandemic is incomprehensible. On 19 May 2020, the Centre for Business Risk Studies at Cambridge University warned that, worst-case scenario, the virus could cost the global economy $82 trillion over five years. Having said that, the consensus among the research team was that the cost would probably land at around $26.8 billion.[41] Bear in mind that the figures related to reduced growth potential (ie opportunity cost) as opposed to global economic shrinkage.

The stress of job and employment insecurity as well and financial uncertainty is impacting millions (potentially billions) of people around the world. The broader human health implications, the organisational repercussions and how recessions impact those who are still employed, are all questions that need answering. Interestingly, several researchers explored these questions during and following the Great Recession in 2008.

Recessions are associated with significant physical and mental health compromise.

In 2018 Michael Frone from the University of Buffalo published a study investigating the impact of this recession on job insecurity, health and organisational commitment.[42] Frone used data from two national surveys of US employees. The first survey was performed on 2 354 workers prior to the recession, and the second analysis on 2 322 employees during the recession. The results showed that the recession was strongly associated with an increase in job and employment insecurity, and overwhelming fear of not being able to find new employment, which certainly doesn't come as a surprise. The study also showed that recessions result in compromised physical, and especially mental, health not to mention reduced organisational commitment. A reduction in commitment to a job in an unstable environment seems absurd and completely counter-intuitive. If you were at risk of losing your job, with limited future opportunities, what would your knee-jerk reaction be? In concept, it would be to push harder, show more commitment and show your value. Yet, in reality, when placed in these circumstances the exact opposite holds true.

These findings were echoed in a 2012 study done in occupational medicine. The paper examined civil servants' work-related stress and absenteeism during a period of economic recession, relative to levels prior to the onset of this period.[43] The analysis compared the findings from two surveys of employees of the Northern Ireland Civil Service. The first survey was conducted in 2005, prior to the onset of the Great Recession, and the second was performed four years later at the height of the recession. In total, 27 037 participants were included in the comparative review. The results clearly showed that not only do recessions increase the prevalence of job insecurity, but they also increase overall stress among employees (ie create environments where there is reduced support, strained relationships and higher demands), resulting in a greater degree of absenteeism because of stress-related health issues.

> Job and employment insecurity cause reduced commitment, a breakdown of organisational support systems, strained relationships and result in higher overall demands on employees.

This study may not be a true reflection of the scale of influence though as within the business space, civil servants are fairly buffered in that they have a greater degree of job security than most professions. But if an economic downturn affects civil servants to this extent, the impact on the rest of the world's workforce is catastrophic.

The psychological contract

What makes job insecurity so destructive is that it can be viewed as a breach, or even a violation, of the 'psychological contract' that exists between businesses and their employees. The psychological contract involves expectations of the employment relationship that extend beyond any formal paperwork. From an employee's perspective, the psychological contract guarantees job security, fair remuneration, certain benefits and a sense of self-worth for professional competencies. From an employer's perspective, they acquire and maintain dedicated employees who perform their roles effectively, are satisfied with their jobs and are entirely committed to the organisation.

A primary function of the psychological contract is a reduction of job insecurity and this agreement provides a tremendous sense of stability and predictability to both parties.

Rapidly changing circumstances are forcing this contract to be rewritten in an impromptu fashion, bringing with it significant stress for both businesses and their employees. Employers simply can't guarantee job security and a stable future, as they themselves are finding themselves having to constantly restructure, re-engineer and recalibrate in light of the ever-changing economic landscape. Although in many instances, organisations are often merely reacting to market forces, the trust between employee and employer progressively disintegrates often resulting in irreparable damage.

The impact of job, employment and economic instability

Research reliably shows that job and employment insecurity corrode our health and well-being. Ongoing fears and nervous tension about your

> At the height of the recession in 2008, almost a third of Americans reported experiencing some kind of physical pain.

financial future can result in a broad range of symptoms including psychiatric disorders, cardiovascular diseases, digestive issues, visual disturbances, hearing compromise as well as a profound rise in physical pain.

The prevalence of physical pain has increased dramatically in recent years and interestingly, this increase parallels the rise in job and economic uncertainty. In 2008, at the height of the financial crisis, more than 100 million Americans were experiencing debilitating physical pain.[44] This may be seen as a coincidence, but researchers Eileen Chou and Bidhan L. Parmar from the University of Virginia, and Adam Galinsky from Columbia University, are certain it isn't and have the evidence to prove it.

In 2016 Chou and her team published a paper entitled 'Economic Insecurity Increases Physical Pain'. The review involved several large studies and found clearly defined associations between job and economic insecurities and the onset of physical pain. Moreover, one study involving 33 720 individuals showed that job and/or economic insecurity could predict the consumption of over-the-counter pain medication.

Incredibly, the review was also able to provide reasons as to why people have a 36% higher risk of developing a pain disorder in response to the experience

> Job and financial insecurity increase anxiety and depression and are associated with low self-esteem.

of job insecurity. The link is generated by several interconnected mediators that include a resultant increase in anxiety and depression, which amplifies feelings of uncertainty and can even manifest in low self-esteem.

The world of neuroscience has shown us that psychological distress and physical pain share similar processes within the brain. For example, physical pain has been associated with the strong activation of the dorsal anterior cingulate cortex, the brain region sensitive to uncertainty and failure in meeting expectations. In other words, the region of the brain that processes fears, uncertainties and failure also drives pain.

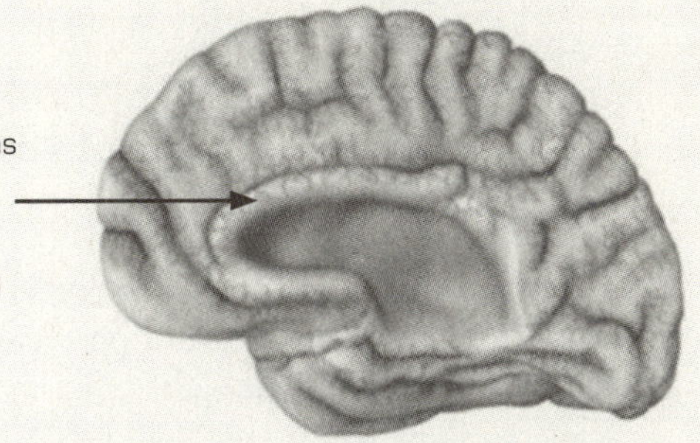

The anterior cingulate cortex is involved in pain perception as well as a number of functions related to emotion. This is why pain can create emotional volatility and vice versa.

The translation of job and employment insecurity into debilitating pain is amplified in people who are already experiencing financial difficulties (which is nearly half of the world's population at this stage), as well as those who have an existing worry or anxiety disorder, which is becoming more and more common.

> 39% of the world's population are experiencing fears and worry on any given day.

According to the 'Gallup 2019 Global Emotions Report' based on 151 000 interviews with adults from 143 countries, more than 1 in 3 people around the world are experiencing significant worry on any given day.[45] This correlates very closely to the global prevalence of physical pain which impacts almost 1 in 3 people. Coincidence? The numbers speak for themselves.

Physical pain hurts your business

Creating links and drawing connections between various stresses, emotional states and health outcomes can be extremely helpful in managing personal stress and negative associations. This is hugely relevant in business and leaders and managers need to pay more attention to these associations.

Job and employment insecurity can increase physical pain and physical pain results in increased stress and mental health compromise. A self-perpetuating

The economic burden of physical pain is greater than many of the world's priority diseases.

cycle quickly unfolds that has substantial financial and productivity repercussions. This can tip the very delicate scales within any business, especially during turbulent times such as those we are living in.

In 2012 a team of health economists at Johns Hopkins University published a study aiming to quantify the costs of physical pain on the US economy.[46] The researchers looked primarily at healthcare costs and lost productivity. Their findings showed that following the recession in 2010, the collective financial cost of pain was estimated to be $635 billion. The economic impact of pain is therefore far greater than the world's priority health conditions such as heart disease, cancer and diabetes.

In 2017 GlaxoSmithKline (GSK), a British multinational pharmaceutical company headquartered in London, published a report on the global pain landscape entitled 'The Global Pain Index'. The index was an in-depth global study looking at attitudes towards physical pain and the impact that physical pain has on people's lives around the world. The research was conducted through online interviews in 32 countries, across six continents, with the participation of 19 000 people. The findings showed that 1 in 3 employees reported having to take time off work due to physical pain at an annual average of 2.6 days every year.

Physical pain affects 1 in 3 employees.

If you run a large business with 1 000 employees, this means that roughly 330 are likely to take 2.6 days off each this year due to physical pain in the neck, back, and joints. This equates to 866 days of lost productivity, which is associated with significant financial and growth implications for the company. The report highlighted that pain-induced absenteeism is costing the economies within the 32 markets surveyed approximately $245 billion per year through lost productivity.

Decision makers and business leaders need to realise that job insecurity not only impacts the well-being of their employees, but also strong growth

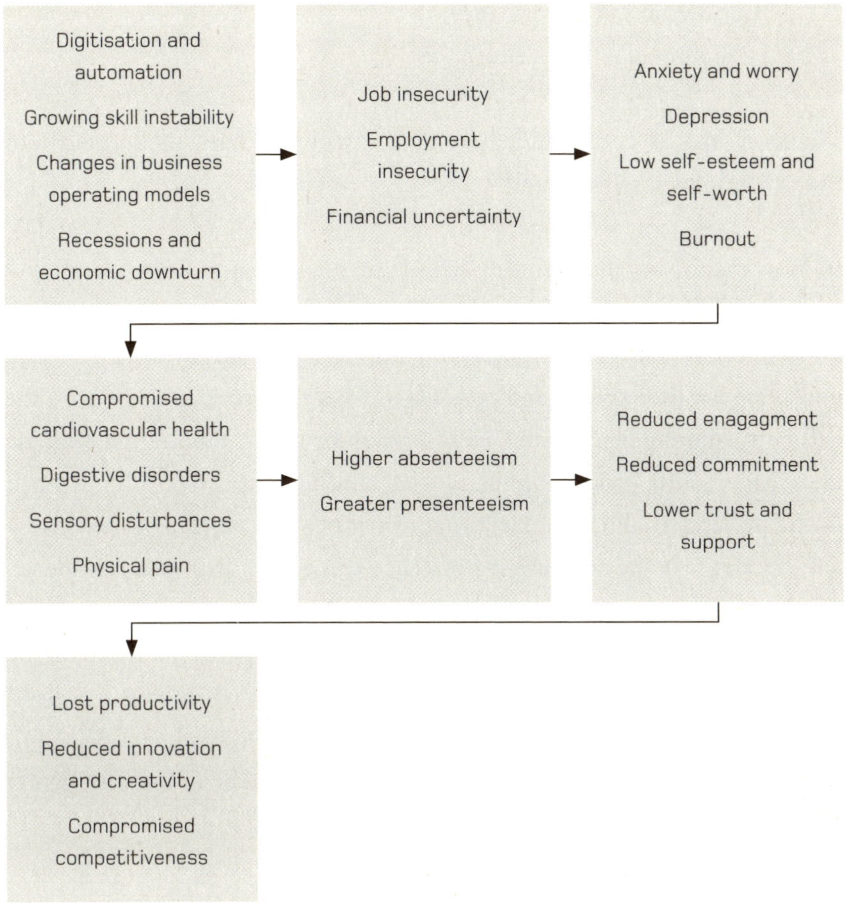

determinants within the business itself. Two large reviews[47] have shown that job and employment insecurity is associated with:

- Reduced job satisfaction
- Less participation in professional responsibilities
- A reduction in commitment
- Higher degree of destructive behaviour
- Lower levels of trust and mutual support

- Poor overall job performance
- High rates of employee turnover

Moreover, this is compounded by higher reported rates of burnout and lowered employee self-esteem.[48]

In May 2020, I began consulting with Lauren, a highly successful entrepreneur. She was struggling with various stress-related health conditions such as low self-esteem, burnout, physical pain, insomnia and anxiety, which were all impacting her professional and personal life. For the previous 10 months, she had been running a successful skills development and training programme for a large South African company. Her and her team were fully invested in the project on all levels. Her commitment to the project was driven by passion and a desire to make a difference to people's lives and, of course, transform the business. She worked nights, weekends and took on several responsibilities that were well beyond the scope of her portfolio. Based on the feedback received from the company's leadership, the tremendous success of the programme and the fiscal success of the company (despite COVID-19), she assumed her contract would be renewed for another 12 months, giving her and her team job security in an uncertain future.

However, towards the end of April she was told that despite all the positive gains, the company had decided on a spend freeze and thus, from 1 July, her team's services would no longer be needed. Lauren was devastated and wondered what more she could have done. More concerning was that she employed a sizeable team who were all on generous salaries.

Fears over the future became overwhelming and all-consuming. The reality was that the market had imploded due to corporate survival strategies such as spend freezes, downsizing, restructuring and remote working taking precedence over growth and innovation. The uncertainties and financial worry and anxiety started to keep Lauren awake at night. She became short-tempered, intolerant and introverted and felt unfulfilled by her work for the first time since the project began.

Lauren had developed tremendous self-awareness in her life journey (as many leaders do) and fully acknowledged that the stress of job insecurity, together with the disappointment in the company's decision, resulted in her behavioural changes and emotional volatility. Yet, the reality was that she still had a live project running for at least two months and was generating significant income from it. Knowing the professional and reputational value, you would assume that she would have intensified her efforts in order to prove the decision makers wrong or, at the very least, get a good endorsement. However, the opposite response unfolded. Her commitment to the project rapidly diminished and her relationships began to disintegrate, along with trust in the company's leadership. While her and her team always maintained high standards and delivered on expectations, they struggled in their personal capacities to actively participate in the programme. Fundamentally, the stress of injustice and employment and economic uncertainty had resulted in an uninspired service provider who had completely disengaged.

Lauren's situation shows how someone who is totally committed, passionate and inspired can disengage based on the fears of future unemployment and lack of fairness or transparency. She was exceptional in her role and made an enormous difference to the company, both materially and in terms of relationships. There were ongoing promises of continuation and expansion of the project into overseas offices which were not delivered upon. As it turns out, Lauren's fears and worries were unfounded as she picked up several lucrative projects shortly after finishing her contract.

A challenge confronting current leaders and managers is that job and employment insecurity triggers low self-esteem, physical and health compromise, a breakdown in relationships and a disconnect from professional responsibilities in their workforce. At the same time, for a business to survive, it requires productive and innovative teams that feel valued and supported, are collaborative, confident in their talents and are fully invested in making the business a success.

The growing consensus among researchers is that the impact of job and employment insecurity on human health and productivity is so profound, that governments and businesses need to rethink policies in order to mitigate some of the risk.[49] The process of future-proofing for skills instability includes:

- Identifying skills and training needed to promote business growth, development and performance
- Aligning the business's best resources possible for skills development
- Allowing teams to take the necessary time to upskill and grow
- Creating a culture that values learning

Future-proofing for perceptions of fairness and injustice

Leaders need to understand that a perceived lack of fairness or injustice (even if it has nothing to do with organisational governance and operations) is a major source of stress for employees and a strong driver in mental health compromise. More concerning for business dynamism and reputation is that injustice perception has strong associations with unethical and destructive employee behaviours.

> To promote fairness and organisational justice, the following actions need to be considered:
> - Always treat subordinates with respect and dignity.
> - Never allow for an abuse of position or power.
> - All major decisions must be accompanied by rationales and good communication.
> - Protocols and procedures must remain fair, reliable and consistent and apply to everyone equally, regardless of seniority.

In order to mitigate the stress of unfairness perception (whatever its source) leadership would be well-served to focus on the promotion of a culture where a strong fairness ethos is central to the organisation. A strong fairness ethos maintains that subordinates are always treated with respect and dignity (ie no abuse of power), all major decisions must be accompanied by rationales and that organisational protocols and procedures consistently remain fair and apply to all, regardless of their role or ranking within the company.

Current recessions, rapidly growing skill instability, ever-shifting business models and broad-scale automation are either independently, or collectively, creating significant job and employment insecurity.

Future-proofing for job and employment insecurity

Evidence shows us that in many respects, job insecurity is as stressful as unemployment, and for many individuals it can be even more emotionally and psychologically damaging. Leaders and managers need to be mindful that job insecurity results in significant mental and physical health compromise that could potentially translate into reduced individual and organisational functionality.

Job insecurity represents a profound violation in trust. There is an unwritten psychological contract that exists between all employees and employers and from an employee's perspective, part of that psychological contract promises job security and compensation stability. When this is not provided, employees tend to not keep up their end of the agreement and this can invariably materialise in reduced commitment and engagement as well as poor job performance and higher staff turnover.

> Measures to combat job and employment insecurity are more important now than any other time in recent history.

Future-proofing businesses will require a strategic approach to reducing the stress of job insecurity. While those charged with steering the corporate ship are most times not in a position to change the external circumstances (ie the economy and markets), especially at this time, there are many actions and initiatives that can be taken which may reduce the effects of this destructive, all-consuming stress. Measures to combat job insecurity and financial uncertainty are more relevant today than ever before and the coronavirus pandemic is unquestionably the catalyst for this urgency.

The following is an extract of a communication on 9 April 2020, in the midst of the pandemic, by the UN secretary general to member states:

> We are all struggling to absorb the unfolding shock: the jobs that have disappeared and businesses that have suffered; the fundamental and drastic shift to our daily lives, and the fear that the worst is still yet to come, especially in the developing world and countries already battered by armed conflict. While the COVID-19 pandemic is first and foremost a health crisis, its implications are much more far-reaching. We are already seeing its ruinous social and economic impacts, as governments around the world struggle to find the most effective responses to rising unemployment and the economic downturn.

These views surrounding the fact that this pandemic was so much more than a health crisis became evident to me during the initial stages of the South African lockdown. In April 2020 I was asked to take part in a webinar panel discussion focusing on the stress of the shutdown and the events leading up to this national emergency. The panel was well attended by approximately 1 000 people and my co-panellists were some of the foremost experts in the areas of anxiety, psychology and crisis management. The session lasted two hours but it passed in what felt like minutes. The audience was engaging and there was cohesion between all the panellists and we were able to build on and develop each other's narratives. As one would expect from a stress panel discussion, typical areas of questioning included how to parent under these extenuating circumstances, how to manage personal anxiety, how to manage the feeling of being overwhelmed, but there was one question that felt as if it were on repeat. Phrased in a number of different ways was, 'How can I overcome this sense of financial and economic uncertainty?'

There is no simple answer to this question as everyone's circumstances are vastly different. Financial counselling and advisory services, debt relief and a complete recalibration of life are critical steps, but they don't offer psychological respite (or enough of it). What does help in alleviating some of the stress burden is the knowledge that when this is all over, you are re-employable or that your business will offer a service and/or product that is sought after.

Extensive research shows that re-employability has been shown to dramatically reduce the stress of job insecurity, no matter the macroeconomic circumstances. While the prospect of a new, equally good job might not be quite as desirable as the one a person already has, it can prevent the loss of income and go a long way in ameliorating the potential psychological loss and anticipatory stress. This assertion has been strongly supported by recent studies in Australia and Germany.[50]

Re-employability strongly offsets the stress of job insecurity and is underpinned by skills development.

Maximising chances of re-employability, or ensuring you have a successful business within a period of unprecedented uncertainty and exponential change, can be done by receiving relevant education, ongoing training and skills development or refinement.

Under the restraint of lockdown or during periods of profound economic instability, this action step can be extremely comforting on a psychological level. Knowing that your expertise is unique, at the highest level and relevant, doesn't only offer respite from the fears of job insecurity and economic uncertainty, but also rebuilds confidence and self-belief.

As a business leader know that the more training and skills your employees receive during their time of employment, the greater their opportunities in the future (either within your organisation or outside). This will translate into reduced job and employment insecurity and a greater sense of health, well-being and productivity in the company.

Contrary to the common perception that exists within many businesses, where the belief is that training and skills development may create an exodus of employees, the reality is that with greater employment security comes more commitment, better engagement, higher levels of trust and better overall work performance.

The encouragement and investment of the development of others within your business, or even within your personal sphere, is not only 'people-centric' but also fundamentally moral. In his book, *Morality: Restoring the Common Good in Divided Times*,[51] Rabbi Lord Jonathan Sacks defines morality as follows:

> Morality, at its core, is about strengthening the bonds between us, helping others, engaging in reciprocal altruism, and understanding the demands of group loyalty, which are the price of group belonging. A sense of morality safeguards something deeply engraved within us, a legacy from a distant life's past, when we lived together in small groups. Then, as now, the ability to rely on the help of others when facing life's challenges is a powerful source of resilience.

Time and time again, selfless investment in the growth and development of people is showing exceptional outcomes, not just in mitigating stress, but also in promoting organisational productivity and ultimately success.

> Contrary to the common perception that exists within many businesses that training and skills development will create an exodus of employees, the reality is that with greater employment security comes more commitment, better engagement, higher levels of trust, not to mention better overall work performance.

One of the world's top-rated CEOs, Bob Chapman, strongly lives by this 'people-centric' principle. He believes that corporate leaders and managers have a responsibility to steer and improve the lives of their employees. His view is that first and foremost, the people that come to work are husbands, wives, daughters and sons who have family members who love and care for them. Leaders should ensure that at the end of each day, their workforce return to their families in good shape, capable of living fulfilled lives outside of their professional responsibilities. Chapman has been exceptionally successful in growing a manufacturing business that is currently worth $2.5 billion. Harvard Business School recently released a case study featuring Bob's successful leadership approach.

Over and above training and skills development, leaders can successfully reduce the stress of job insecurity by structuring income protection plans, increasing communication and creating support platforms. There is tremendous value associated with each of these strategic levers and the 'to-do list' includes:

- Establish welfare policies or create income protection plans
- Increase workforce participation in unfolding events and maintain transparent communication with those affected
- Give teams a sense of influence over decision-making
- Always champion fairness and procedural justice
- Encourage and develop social support networks as much as possible

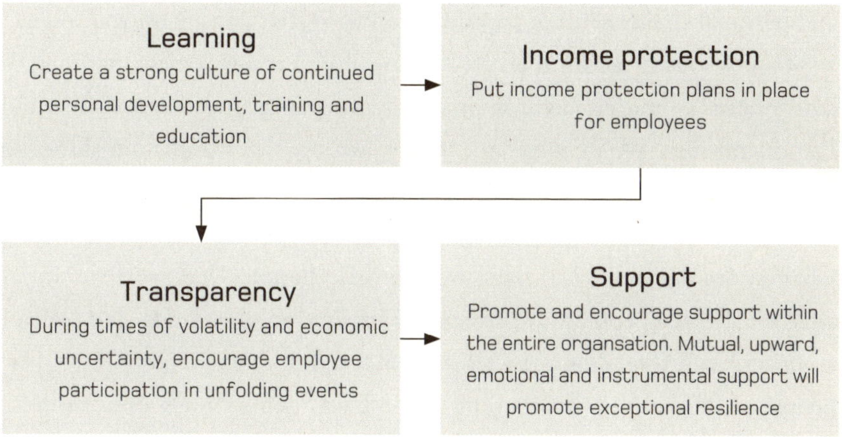

Connection and unity create a significant source of strength

In 2016 Sebastian Junger published his book *Tribe: On Homecoming and Belonging*,[52] which delves into our evolutionary past as a communal species and explains some of the reasons why we are stronger when we come together. In the book, Junger describes how early humans were distinguished by two things they did effectively: the organised sharing of food and selfless defence of the group.

Looking back through time, the challenges and threats we have all faced have been insurmountable. We were able to overcome infectious disease epidemics, two world wars, severe famines and prolonged food shortages, not to mention radically changing natural environments. This was all achieved by supporting one another and through strong mutual cooperation on a family, community, regional and even national level. History has shown us that we are always strong as a collective and vulnerable when we are isolated.

Yet, the practice of this historic fail-safe for overcoming challenges and difficulties has become a rarity. Outright disconnection has replaced support and connectivity during periods of crisis and hardships. Whether social media or a new order of societal norms have perpetuated this phenomenon is hard to say, but unfortunately in today's society when you experience stress and personal challenges, the prevailing feeling is that you are on your own.

Modern society seems to perceive vulnerability as a weakness that may be construed as a limiting factor in professional advancement, relationships and even friendships. We are forced to create a pretence that we are flourishing, no matter the circumstances, when in truth we are barely coping. Take a moment to revisit some of your communications with people during lockdown. Chances are that not all of them were entirely honest. Under the surface of what we showed people was perhaps the frustration of isolation and fears of an uncertain future, that impacted your mood, health and relationships. Few people admit that they are battling in some way and so much of our time is committed to keeping up the façade and inauthentic connection.

For many, stress and crisis management amounts to periods of withdrawal from society on an emotional and/or physical level and possibly even taking medication. Only when we start to feel stronger or the circumstances that created the stress begin to shift, can we rediscover our former selves and take our place in society again. This is extremely difficult when the stress is so extreme and extends over such a lengthy period of time as is the case with COVID-19.

The best thing we can do for others and for ourselves is connect and share our experiences and encourage them to do the same. Reaching out for support and care can often strengthen and fortify relationships, not undermine or derail them. Although it is comforting on a deep psychological level as it transports us back in time to when our tightly knit community protected us, the greatest benefits attributed to reaching out for support is that by doing so, the body releases the powerful neurochemical and hormone, oxytocin.

Oxytocin has incredible effects on both our psychological and physical well-being and can counterbalance many of the adverse effects of stress, no matter the source. Due to its inhibitory effect on the brain's fear and stress centre – the amygdala – oxytocin can reduce perceptions of stress and reactivity to unsettling situations. Secondly, it has positive effects on health and studies show that oxytocin lowers blood pressure and heart rate, has strong anti-inflammatory and antioxidant qualities and also causes robust increases in neurochemicals and proteins such as serotonin and dopamine that promote emotional stability and cognition, physical strength and vitality through the release of insulin growth factor-1.[53]

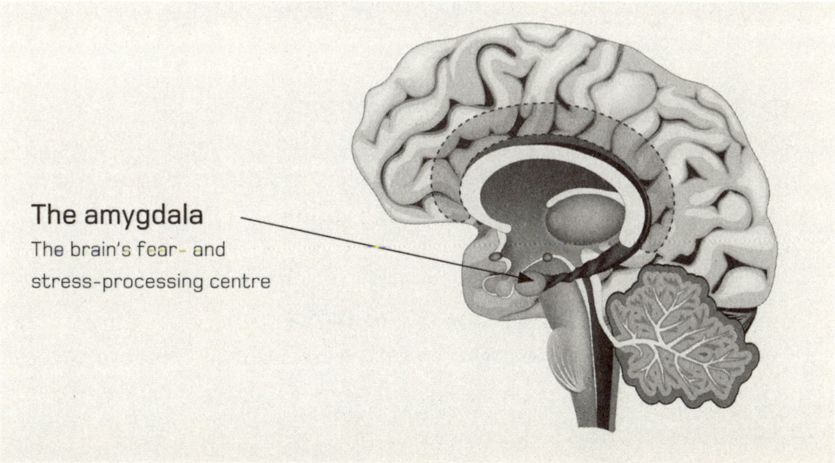

But the greatest advantage is that oxytocin strongly influences behaviour and perception of self. A 2005 study by Swedish researchers[54] showed that oxytocin promotes feelings of self-worth, confidence, fearlessness, optimism, trust, a sense of calm, generosity, connectedness, and empathy towards others. Any leading CEO would list those as qualities they would look for in a high-performing team and remarkably this profile has a strong hormonal basis – ie oxytocin.

With the knowledge that oxytocin can transform ill health to well-being, insecurity to surety, and disengagement to potential, leaders should take every opportunity to create environments that increase this biological state.

> By connecting and supporting others when you experience stress will enhance your own mental health and physical well-being.

A weekend away or afternoon team-building session may offer some value, and decision makers need to understand that an infrequent release of this 'superhero' molecule will not suffice in mitigating the stress of skills instability, injustice and job insecurity.

Challenges #4 and #5

Skills instability and job insecurity

Stress associations

Perceptions of injustice, job and employment insecurity, unemployment

Negative health associations

Increased anxiety and depression as well as other psychiatric diseases, burnout, higher prevalence of pain disorders and cardiovascular disease, sensory compromise (visual and auditory), digestive system dysfunction

Business performance

Reduced engagement and organisational trust, lowered commitment, poor work performance, increased staff turnover and destructive behaviour

A shift in culture, policy and corporate ethos from one that is cut-throat, competitive and self-orientated, to one of mutual and upward support, collaboration, care, empathy and generosity will take employees back to a safe space. Leaders can then be assured of achieving greater engagement, proficiencies, trust and loyalty.

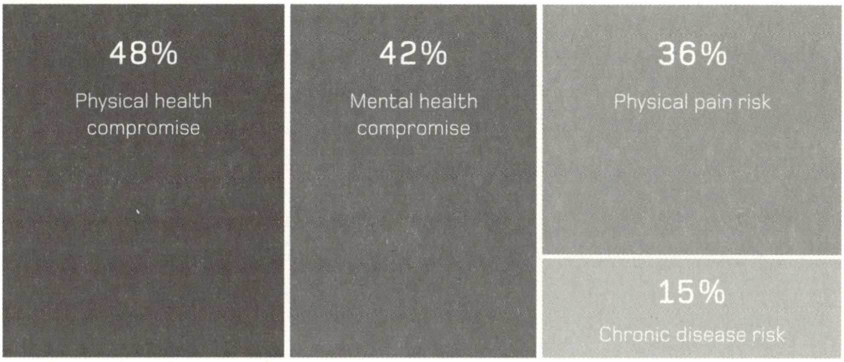

Health risks associated with job and fiscal insecurity

A RECALIBRATION OF WORK

The Fourth Industrial Revolution and coronavirus pandemic have brought about change, in some cases forced, in the way companies and employees engage. The world has surged into a phase where an on-demand economy prevails, and it is altering our relationship with work and the social fabric in which it is embedded. In response to the global economic uncertainty, more employers are pushed into using the human cloud as a means of operation, as full-time staffing is becoming increasingly difficult due to the volatility and uncertainty.

> In 2018 the gig economy, which encompasses online work platforms, independent contractors, temporary agency workers and consultants, was valued at over $4.5 trillion.

The human cloud is an emerging set of online/digital labour marketplaces where talent, and those looking to hire talent or services, can find and engage one another in a work arrangement.

According to a report done by the WEF, during 2018, digital work or services platforms such as Uber and Upwork, processed approximately $126 billion in spending globally.[55] This figure excludes independent contractors, temporary agency workers and temporary workers sourced directly by companies, which all form part of the broader $4.5 trillion gig economy. The gig economy also includes other forms of contingent work outside of online platforms such as freelance contracting and consulting and temporary workers provided by staffing agencies.

Businesses are moving towards hiring experts for short and defined projects, which is facilitated by the increased accessibility to online talent anywhere in the world. Law firms and banks looking to understand a market better will hire business development specialists, from different regions of the world, at specific intervals throughout the year, as opposed to creating a full-time position.

Regardless of sector, country or the size of a business, this trend has become increasingly more common, even at the highest level of sport. In July 2005 I was introduced to a young, charismatic Serbian tennis player who had just broken into the Top 100. He was confident and energetic and it was inspiring to be around him at the courts and in social settings. For the next few years, I spent a lot of time at tournaments with him and his team. As he continued to improve his ranking, he made some surprising decisions to change a few core members of his team, including his coach and physio, which seemed strange as they had been part of his initial success journey.

In hindsight, it was the right decision and his new coach was a perfect fit and is still with him today. Within a few months of the partnership, he exploded into the Top 10 and by 2009 held a steady ranking of number 2 in the world. In 2011 Novak Djoković became world number 1, a position he still holds today in what is the greatest era in history of men's tennis, with iconic rivals such as Roger Federer and Raphael Nadal. While his coach and other members of his team have been instrumental in his success, Novak acknowledged that additional specialists need to be brought in periodically to create injections of passion and vision and to overcome performance barriers. Coaches like Boris Becker and Goran Ivanišević are some of the iconic figures brought in to assist him in his highly successful career.

Many businesses are using similar models, where core teams are supplemented by top specialists from around the world for short periods of time (approximately 1 year) to propel the business forward and into uncharted territory.

The benefits

What drives many individuals to participate in the human cloud and gig economy is the opportunity to generate additional income. In addition, there is a significant degree of professional autonomy and flexibility. This makes for a great fit for Millennials and Generation Zs whose relationship to traditional employment differs from those of previous generations.

The gig economy provides opportunities to those with an entrepreneurial drive, and is a platform that enables individuals to transcend local labour markets and step onto the global stage. All 'pull' reasons why professionals are drawn to platform work.

However, there is also a set of 'push' factors that drive people into the platform space that include financial difficulties, unemployment, economic insecurity and even existing disabilities. With the current climate of change and uncertainty, the push factors are the greatest driver in an individual's participation in this emerging independent economy.

The gig economy can create opportunities, irrespective of a person's age or stage in life and Ben, a long-time family friend, was a perfect example of this. Ben ran a highly profitable and successful furniture import and distribution business in the US. From 2010 to 2018, the business flourished, and new markets continuously opened up. At 70 years of age, Ben welcomed this success as he had been involved in several ventures over the years that had

had limited success. With three kids to support to some degree or another, financial security was always a concern. During these flourishing years, Ben bought a beautiful house in the suburbs of Boston, travelled regularly, owned several luxury cars and had all the freedoms anyone could want. At the same time, he was still modest and conservative in his lifestyle.

In 2018 the market quickly started to change. More competition in the industry, an overall change in clients' interior design preferences and some poor financial decisions saw Ben's business begin to contract. Within 18 months he had to fund the business in his personal capacity and his whole world changed. He wasn't sleeping or eating, due to anxiety, and soon became depressed. But unlike many people who found themselves in similar circumstances, Ben still owned certain assets and his luxury vehicles proved to be an opportunity to get back on his feet. Within a few months, he started an airport shuttle service which grew into a thriving business. It may not be what Ben had envisaged for his life or his career, but the gig economy offers opportunities in circumstances where there appears to be none and enabled Ben to establish a brand-new business venture.

Like individuals, businesses of all sizes can benefit immensely from the growing gig economy. One key advantage of this platform is adaptability. The human cloud allows organisations to expand their workforce in periods of peak demand and then revert to a leaner core team when the workload normalises. Companies can hire people quickly and gain specialised skills required for a specific project that then allows growth in a multitude of new and innovative directions. 'The Platform' also enables companies to change their operations model accordingly and unbundle jobs into a series of tasks that can be performed by any number of gig workers. Over and above the advantage of gaining a greater degree of specialist skills, it also creates shorter tenures, a lower risk of employee errors and less liability in the form of reliance or dependency on specific individuals or broader teams.

The greatest value for organisations is unquestionably the cost benefits.

These benefits are realised through the full utilisation of the independent contractor where they work only when there is a need for their service, charge lower rates for services due to increased competitiveness and platform incentives and reduced benefits costs (ie no healthcare, skills development, wellness programmes or retirement plans). Companies can become even leaner as they require smaller offices and less operational equipment such as PCs, cellphones, office furniture, canteens, etc.

The downside

The gig economy has generated opportunities for flexible work and business innovation, but it has also created significant economic and social stress for many individuals. Some of the biggest issues confronting professionals operating in this space are ratings systems, information asymmetry, social isolation, limited (or non-existent) benefits and protections and reduced learning opportunities and skill development.

Ratings systems are used in virtually all platform businesses to establish trust between service providers and clients. Airbnb, TripAdvisor, Amazon and Uber were some of the first platforms to use ratings scales. Ratings scales are extremely useful as good services and expertise can be openly recognised, valued and promoted. However, great concepts and reality only seldom converge.

One of the primary issues with a ratings scale is that it can often reflect bias and customer prejudice. Moreover, these biases can be influenced by countless factors often beyond the control of the dedicated service provider. For example, an unexpected price surge, bad traffic or a passenger having a bad day, can all have a direct impact on an Uber driver's ratings. For the service provider participating in the platform, low ratings means fewer working opportunities due to algorithmic and client preferences.

TripAdvisor, while a useful platform and one I frequently use, is unfortunately one that shows the extent of the ineffectiveness of a ratings model. For more than a decade, I travelled up to 10 months a year while working on the ATP and WTA tours. I was often asked how I managed based on the fact that there are so many basic hurdles and frustrations to overcome as a stranger in a new city or country. Language barriers, cultural differences and inaccessibility to the things that we take for granted such as laundry facilities or doctors, are some of the basic challenges I was confronted with on an ongoing basis.

To expedite my settling-in process, it was important to create basic day-to-day structure as soon as I possibly could. This entailed finding a local supermarket, health store, gym or pool, laundromat and a few core restaurants. TripAdvisor was a lifeline in this process as it assisted in helping me get the lay of the land, so to speak. I could instantaneously access all the information I needed from business descriptions, web pages, travel distances and operating hours. But one of the annoyances I had was the platform's rating system. Initially, I would base my decision to use a service provider such as a hotel, or restaurant on their ratings, but the more I used it, the more inaccurate the ratings were. Restaurants and hotels that received high ratings could turn out to be downright disappointing, whereas there were times when hotels or restaurants that had received low ratings on the platform turned out to be of the highest standard. This model is based on subjectivity and good quality service providers can often be rated poorly for circumstances beyond their control, which in turn impacts their business's ability to grow and thrive.

> Ratings systems are highly subjective and often result in significant stress to gig workers. Lack of appreciation, feeling undervalued, together with a lack of fairness and job insecurity can undermine mental and physical health as well as lower productivity.

Ratings are creating significant stress and anxiety for many platform workers, but without good ratings there is the constant threat of deactivation with little to no recourse. This invariably leads to grossly unfair working conditions where service providers feel they need to lower their rates, offer free services or even perform emotional labour by being exceptionally affable or tolerating inappropriate behaviour from companies, in order to earn a basic living. This leads to feeling unappreciated and undervalued and the broader experiences of injustice and job insecurity. In time this will impact productivity and professional competencies and corrode mental and physical health.

Another challenge that gig workers face is information asymmetry. As an independent contractor you often need to price a project before you know the full extent of the assignment. Correct pricing can be a major source of stress for gig workers, as many don't have financial training. Going in too high means you risk losing the job due to fierce global competition, but if you go in too low you may end up working countless hours without compensation. Finding this balance and mitigating potential risk develops through experience and gaining a strong professional reputation, but due to the rapidly changing professional landscape, may potentially never actualise.

Being an independent contractor comes with additional liabilities that include social isolation, a potential loss of social identity, a reduced sense of belonging and limited benefits. Despite the fact that gig workers are exposed to the same array of health risks as permanent employees, they do not receive health insurance, sick pay or any form of disability benefits. Ironically, the stress of not having health insurance is one of the major risk factors in the onset of many chronic diseases. Health benefits aside, contract workers have no traditional employee protections such as minimum wage, workplace safety or anti-discrimination laws.

While many gig workers may see greater flexibility and autonomy as a fair trade-off for traditional employee benefits and securities, there is no reconciling for the loss of reskilling, upskilling and training opportunities within a company. Both the WEF and the ILO are of the opinion that professional relevance, following COVID-19 and into the Fourth Industrial Revolution, is largely dependent on developing, expanding and the acquisition of skills. Without a well-funded and structured educational drive, individuals (whether platform workers or not) will be confronted with a high risk of being left out of the economy through redundancy or even automation. Though this may not be a reality in the short term, with time, workers will develop feelings of financial and employment insecurity.

Organisations are also feeling the effects of the paradigm shift in labour practices. Concerns are being raised about converting functions traditionally performed in-house to independent contractors, potentially creating a greater churn. In countries or regions where business practices are very transactional (like many EU states) this may not be that impactful, but in other regions where relationships form the basic fabric of business practice such as South Africa and Israel, churn can be an organisational liability.

Another realisation being made about platform workers is that not every role is well suited to being bundled and handed over to external operators. In some instances, smooth coordination of the independent parts is more important than the strength of an individual component. In these situations, long-standing employees who are part of a cohesive team may be better equipped to provide growth opportunities for companies. Of course, churn and the bundling of projects is very dependent on the company, industry and market expectations and therefore what may be a risk for some could be an advantage for others.

The primary issues leaders and decision makers need to be aware of when making use of platform workers, is that outside contractors don't share a single identity with the business and so the expected level of customer service and organisational stability may not be realised. Another significant threat posed by a platform workforce is internal knowledge leaks either intentionally or unintentionally. A gig worker has an area of expertise in a specific sector and it is not uncommon for gig workers to run several projects concurrently or have them overlapping from time to time. An outside workforce with knowledge of your business's strengths and weaknesses can make the most trusting leaders hold their breath. Naturally all stakeholders assume a degree of confidentiality, but there is a certain degree of conflict. Finally, the relationship between employees and contract workers can often be fraught with animosity and distrust, something no business can afford.

Trust and success

Trust within a business is an interesting dynamic and in modern society we delegate our financial well-being to our place of work. This means our entire livelihood and future well-being is placed in the hands of an institution. This is why each and every employee needs to trust that their employer will act with integrity and with their best interests at heart. Should trust diminish, regardless of the reason, employees begin to fear that they are no longer in safe and reliable hands, causing them to experience significant stress and anxiety.

> Trust is unique in that it is a forward-looking metric that not only predicts credibility but also enables support in future endeavours.

Trust is unique in that it is a forward-looking metric. As a leader, it is central to success as it is a predictor of whether all stakeholders (employees, the board, as well as investors) will find you credible in the future, will embrace new innovations you introduce and will enthusiastically support or defend you when things become challenging. Leaders and managers have a vested interest in promoting and maintaining a high level of organisational trust.

In the last few years, there have been some interesting insights pertaining to trust, both in a societal and business context. The Edelman Trust Barometer done in 2015[56] showed a strong link between trust and innovation. It is a fairly logical relationship as the more trust you have in a process, organisation, team or person, the greater the likelihood of creative outcomes. We have all been in situations where mentors, leaders and colleagues have had complete faith and trust in us and its highly likely you were inspired to come up with the exceptional, often to the extent where your own expectations were exceeded.

By contrast, when your every move, motivation, and the entire process is questioned, it lends itself to self-doubt, fear and anxieties that ultimately materialise in poor outcomes, regardless of the endeavour.

One of the great challenges that society faces is the rapid corrosion of trust on almost every level. The Edelman report points out that between 2016 and 2018 trust was at a global low, to the extent that 2017 was dubbed the year 'trust in crisis' and 2018 'the battle for the truth'.

2015	2016	2017	2018	2019	2020
Trust seen as essential to innovation	Growing inequality of trust	Global trust in crisis	Battle for the truth	Trust is questioned in the workplace	Trust in competence and ethics

As South Africans, we can identify with experiencing a complete lack of trust with years fraught with ongoing scandals, overt corruption, increasing fraud and societal injustice as Jacob Zuma and his crew of henchmen were well entrenched in their state capture mission.

76% of employees have trust that their employer has their best interests at heart.

Governments around the world have breached the important institution of trust, ie national security and public policy, but the media has also done a fine job of breaking down the public's confidence in credible information and knowledge. Based on the Edelman report, corporate trust is the only institution of trust that remains intact largely due to a strong belief in competence. In fact, 76% of people still have trust in their employer. This is a gift to leadership, but at the same time a huge responsibility. Trust must be built, nurtured and vehemently protected at all times. This is why decision makers need to measure the benefits of bringing in gig workers against the potential destabilisation of organisational trust.

All on its head

Since the early 1900s, the global workplace has been steadily moving in a direction that offers employment security, and away from the uncertainty of self-employment. By the beginning of the 1970s, 94% of the labour force in the US was formally employed and 9 out of 10 workers in Europe had traditional work engagements.[57] This steady trend brought with it labour unions and movements to combat the gross exploitation that low- and medium-skilled workers faced. Decades of fierce struggles between activists and employers culminated in vastly improved working conditions. This included 80-hour weeks eventually reduced to the 40 hours that we have come to expect today. Moreover, the enforcement of a minimum wage, workers safety rights and compensation, strict restrictions in underage labour and overtime pay, enhanced and improved the lives of all employees in developed countries. Since then, additional protection regulations have been steadily increasing for the legislation on governing procedures for firing workers. Some may even argue that these laws have become so rigid that they have stifled the labour market and have resulted in an increase in unemployment.

Traditional employment has historically been associated with benefits to all stakeholders, as well as greater global prosperity. According to the ILO, only 30% to 40% of adults are traditional employees in low-income countries. This increases to 60% to 70% in middle-income countries and is as high as 80% to 90% in high-income countries. The gig economy is unravelling this societal progression at a remarkably rapid pace. But what does this mean for the labour force? In a McKinsey global report on independent work, it comments that the future of independent work is looking remarkably similar to the past, specifically the early 1900s, where self-employment constituted almost 50% of the workforce. Many sociologists are concerned about this trajectory, arguing that the gig economy undermines the decades of hard-fought labour battles to the extent that it is as if they were never fought, let alone won. They also point out that in the labour world, gig workers are treated as second-class citizens who are denied the basic rights of workers in traditional positions. In the years to come, government policy and corporate awareness of social responsibilities will change this landscape, but for now it is a significant stress for all gig workers.

Following the coronavirus pandemic, businesses need to carefully weigh up all the pros and cons, as well as the legalities, of staffing through the gig economy. But the advantages offered through this professional vehicle might offer businesses the perfect opportunity to adapt, innovate and grow, even under these highly uncertain conditions. According to the IMF, 170 of their 189 members have been plunged into negative growth.[58] The negative effects on the global economy and business landscape are likely to be long-lasting and with the urgency to downsize and restructure, many businesses won't have the ability to retain the same numbers of employees. Another consideration is that many organisations may need to restructure and repackage their services and core offerings. This makes the gig economy highly advantageous as it

Challenge #6
The recalibration of work

Stress associations

Perceptions of injustice, job insecurity, an effort-reward imbalance, low social support, limited health insurance/health protections

Negative health associations

Increased risk of psychiatric diseases, burnout, physical health issues, chronic disease diagnosis and premature mortality

Business performance

Potential information leaks, distrust, greater churn, reduced organisational commitment and loyalty, class actions, brand risk

Personal advantages of the gig economy

- Additional income
- Autonomy and flexibility
- New opportunities
- Access to global markets

Disadvantages

- Job and employment insecurity
- Ratings systems
- Information asymmetry
- Limited benefits
- NO benefits
- Limited learning opportunties
- Skills development
- Social isolation and loss of identity
- Reduced sense of belonging

Organisational advantages of the gig economy

- Adaptability
- Rapid scaling of workforce
- Specialised skills
- Lower rates for services
- Reduced benefits costs
- Reduced hard expenses

Disadvantages or limitations

- Greater staff turnover
- Lack of shared identity
- Reduced business stability
- Knowledge leaks
- Distrust
- Brand risk/reputation
- Class actions

±100%
Chronic disease diagnosis

±50%
Physical health compromise

±25%
Premature death from all causes

The collective health risk of not having medical aid (health insurance) or access to proper health care offers additional skills and diverse talents that can be acquired at a moment's notice.

South Africa's gig economy currently touches 1% of the country's workforce, with the strongest contributions stemming from cleaning services such as SweepSouth and Domestly, food delivery services such as Uber Eats and transport services such as Uber and Bolt, as well as the digitally mediated freelancing space. The local gig economy is growing rapidly at an annual rate of 10%.[59]

The overwhelming stress of uncertainty and a lack of control

Whether driven by job and employment insecurity, overwhelming financial pressures, professional skills recalibration, the consistent move to digitisation and automation or the overnight change in the framework of professional relationships, the overwhelming uncertainty within the workplace is unquestionably fuelling global stress and the mental health epidemic.

Never before has all of humanity been confronted with two simultaneous health epidemics – COVID-19 and stress. What's most concerning is that there may be an additional health epidemic looming that is a direct consequence of chronic stress – chronic disease.

COVID-19 has amplified existing stresses and brought with it a wave of unimaginable fear and anxiety. Chronic stress has been shown to lower immunity and resistance to infectious diseases as well as further increase worry, anxieties and fear. Simply put, stress increases the risk of infection and the risk of infection amplifies stress, creating a self-perpetuating cycle.

Coronavirus – we've got your number

To date, there have been six previous coronaviruses, dating back as far as 3300 years BCE (Before the Common Era) and COVID-19 is not the first, but rather the third major coronavirus outbreak in the last 20 years. In 2002 Severe Acute Respiratory Syndrome (SARS) broke out in Asia and in 2012, Middle East Respiratory Syndrome (MERS) first appeared on the Arabian Peninsula. Although both these coronaviruses were more deadly, their ability to spread was limited by comparison, allowing for containment measures to measurably reduce the public health risk. These outbreaks gave scientists and policy makers the opportunity to gain deep insights into COVID-19 in a very short space of time. This culminated in radical and swift responses at governmental level and vaccine trials within a matter of weeks.

The first case of COVID-19 was reported on 17 November 2019 in Wuhan, China and by 11 January 2020, the genetic sequence of COVID-19 was published. By 16 March, the first COVID-19 vaccine candidate entered human clinical testing at Moderna in the US.

By 8 April 2020, the global COVID-19 vaccine research and development landscape included no less than 115 vaccine candidates, some confirmed and some unconfirmed.[60]

By October 2020, the WHO published a report showing that the number of vaccine candidates had increased to 193. Remarkably, 42 of these candidates had already progressed to human trials, many already on phase III.[61]

What is so remarkable about this drive to bring the pandemic to an end is the range of different vaccine approaches being explored. These include DNA and RNA preparations (made from the virus' own genetic information), virus-like particles (multi-protein structures that mimic the organisation and conformation of authentic viruses), peptides,[62] viral vectors,[63] recombinant proteins[64] and live-attenuated virus and inactivated virus.

The global effort to curb the spread of the virus and save lives is unprecedented and saw almost 3 billion people around the world on some form of lockdown by April 2020. The drive to develop a vaccine in response to the virus has also been extraordinary in terms of worldwide collaboration, available funding, scale and speed. Given the urgency, there is an indication that a vaccine could be available, under emergency use or similar protocols, by as early as 2021. Considering that a vaccine normally takes over 10 years to be developed, tested and made available, this timeframe is remarkable.

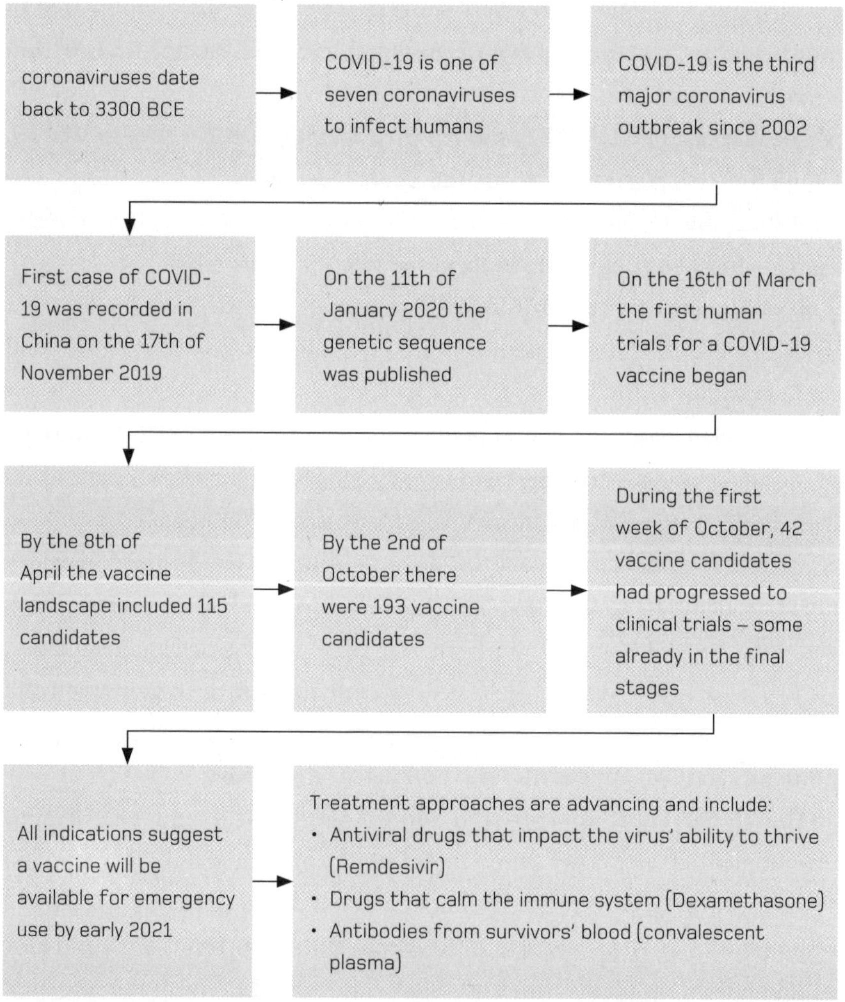

Stress triggers, responses and resolutions

Unlike the coronavirus pandemic which will come to an end, the stress crisis has no known parameters or containment measures (at least on a macro level). For almost seven decades, scientists and researchers have been trying to establish the primary triggers in the human stress condition as well as the short, medium and long-term health implications. The motivation for such a deep dive into chronic stress is to derive answers and solutions to a growing epidemic for which there is no vaccine.

My previously published book, *The Stress Code*, describes two acclaimed studies performed by Sir Michael Marmot,[65] Professor of Epidemiology and Public Health at University College London, that were able to illuminate some understanding pertaining to the burden of chronic stress.

The studies were remarkable due to the sheer scale of the research project. Marmot's team carefully monitored almost 28 000 British civil servants over a 40-year period. Incidentally, these studies were the first to show strong negative associations between chronic stress, mental and physical health.

What set the studies apart from all previous research was that they identified that the grade of employment, or the employee's rank or position within an organisation, is a reliable predictor of perceived stress and increased risk of premature mortality from a wide range of diseases.

> The lower-ranking members within a business experience greater stress than leadership and have a significantly higher risk of developing stress-related health issues.

You would assume that senior, high-ranking employees such as managers and people in positions of leadership would be more prone to stress-induced health issues, due to a greater degree of responsibilities, more accountability for their actions and decisions and often, the age factor. Seniority within an organisation is typically associated with work experience and happens later in life, in most careers. In other words, management and organisational heads are older and more prone to health issues. Of course, this is a generalisation as there are many young leaders and managers.

In a surprising twist, the studies revealed the exact opposite. It was the younger, lower-ranking employees within the organisation that had the greatest degree of perceived stress, worst health and even the highest risk of premature death. In fact, in a 10-year period, those in the lower ranks of the company, compared to those in leadership roles, had a 300% higher risk of premature mortality.

Anyone who has worked their way up from the bottom in a big corporate, doesn't need this research, or any hard science, to validate their experience and what they already know.

One of the talks I give to companies centres on the triggers in organisational stress and what proactive measures need to be taken to reduce them. Within the session, I present more details on these findings and their implications and I can usually predict, with a fairly high degree of certainty, what the audience responses are going to be. A small group of people, usually the executive teams and managers, will appear shocked and a bit confused and may even shake their heads subconsciously. While the rest of the workforce will nod and smile as their experiences and circumstances are finally validated.

While this trend was identified in the first study and strongly reaffirmed in the second, it was key data from the second study that cracked the entire stress code. The findings showed that lower-ranking employees had less social support and less variety at work (which means higher levels of boredom) which are both strong stress triggers. But the fundamental issue within the bottom end of the employee hierarchy was a clearly defined lack of control. When you have limited say in the decisions that directly affect you, no control over the direction of your career, no jurisdiction over your daily routine or limited authority in your life, it creates stress on a scale that is almost unimaginable.

> Stress is typically caused by a sense of a 'lack of control' over the events and circumstances that influence our lives.

That is precisely that reason why the coronavirus pandemic has created the greatest global stress event in recorded history. Billions of people around the world have lost their ability to make decisions that relate to their lives. The order, structure and routine we once knew have all but disappeared. What has been the most emotionally destabilising is that we have a limited ability to influence the direction of our lives for the foreseeable future.

> A feeling that our lives are 'out of control' is rocket fuel for fear.

We've all experienced numerous stressful times in our lives and while the specifics of the events, people and circumstances vary, the common denominator is the emotion involved. Feeling like your life, or the circumstances you were confronted with felt completely out of control and chaotic, is the rocket fuel for fear.

This is what makes the times we are living in so destructive within the context of human health and well-being. The collective effect of the overnight reorganisation and decline of the global economy (encompassing the financial markets, trade and investment, travel and even government policy), the rapid, and wide-scale disruption, across so many fields, the contraction in employment growth and the rapid disappearance of established professions, are independently and collectively creating and driving worry and uncertainly. These fears of the unknown are impacting each and every one of us whether consciously or unconsciously.

> The unforeseen collapse of the global economy, wide-scale disruption across every profession, the contraction of employment growth and the disappearance of established professions due to technology and automation has created worry and uncertainty throughout the world.

It is hardwired in our DNA to search, understand, predict and control. This is how we learn and keep ourselves safe. Uncertainty makes us feel insecure as we are unable to predict what will happen in our lives, both in the short and long term. As our mind races and we catastrophise, it triggers our stress axis into overdrive, which causes our heart to pound, respiration to become shallow and, in some instances, our palms may begin to sweat.

For those who are intrinsically resilient (either through previous life experiences, good genetic wiring or have had some form of training) this experience is merely uncomfortable and can be intellectualised and worked through with relative ease. But for many it is nothing short of unbearable.

Psychologists have identified a prevalent human condition known as 'intolerance of uncertainty'. For the countless individuals suffering from this syndrome, uncertainty has been shown to occur alongside depression, GAD, OCD, eating disorders and, in extreme cases, psychosis.[66] While strong associations exist between the intolerance to uncertainty and mental health compromise, it has been speculated that the experience of uncertainty may actually be the protagonist in depression and many anxiety states, as opposed to the other way around. There is a common belief that being anxious or depressed results in an inability to cope with uncertainties and this notion is now being questioned.

In 2019 psychology professor Benjamin Rosser performed a comprehensive meta-analysis aiming to clarify whether intolerance to uncertainty could be the primary trigger in numerous psychological difficulties.[67] Understanding in this area will be invaluable in attempting to predict the impact COVID-19 and the Fourth Industrial Revolution have had on stress and mental health, and in the creation of action steps to prevent this scenario from unfolding.

The experience of uncertainty can be upsetting and threatening. Intolerance of uncertainty refers to difficulty enduring the experience of *not knowing* and can give rise to a range of cognitive, emotional and behavioural responses. These responses are aimed at avoiding and/or resolving the experience, yet often become an issue themselves.

Although Rosser cautioned that more research is needed due to some inconsistencies in the literature, he did find strong associations for anxiety and mood compromise. Simply put, the feeling of uncertainty can trigger an anxiety disorder or result in significant emotional compromise.

All of this isn't that surprising considering that when we struggle to cope with the experience of uncertainty, we come up with an increasing number of frightening possibilities that play over and over in our minds.

Within our professional lives, a lack of control and authority over the decisions that impact us today and in the future, has been shown to be extremely detrimental to health. Research shows that a lack of control increases the risk of dying prematurely (from all causes) by more than 40%.[68] This risk is greater than exposure to second-hand cigarette smoke or the stress of unemployment.

The challenge that we are now all confronted with, no matter where you live in the world, your socio-economic circumstances, age, gender or race, is that we have no control over the exponential shifts and unprecedented changes that are taking place. We can however learn how to deal with them more successfully, mitigating most of the mental and physical health risks. My book, *The Stress Code*, provides a systematic approach to personal resilience and how to thrive in the most difficult of circumstances. Managers, leaders and decision makers have added responsibilities as they will actively need to shield and protect their teams.

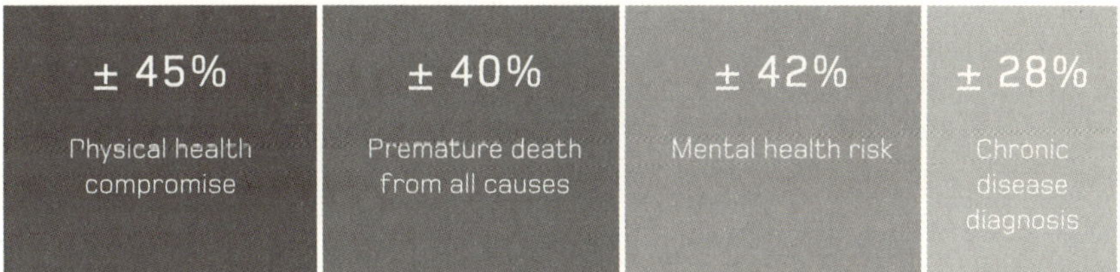

The health risks associated with a lack of control and uncertainty

A LACK OF CONTROL PLUS ONE

While it is fair to say that uncertainty, a lack of control, and fear of the unknown are firmly in the stress and mental health compromise driving seat, another growing societal phenomenon cannot be discounted. This social feature is impacting more people now than at any other time in history and during lockdown, when its true and most concrete impact was felt. That phenomenon is loneliness and social isolation.

According to a 2019 study done by Cigna,[69] a large US health insurer, involving more than 10 000 adults, 61% of American adults are experiencing loneliness (feeling excluded, poorly understood or materially lacking in companionship). The measure used in the study was the 20-item UCLA loneliness scale, a standard in psychology research. You would assume that this trend is largely a consequence of an ageing population, yet this appears not to be the case. The Cigna report showed that 79% of Generation Z and 71% of Millennials feel socially isolated compared with only 50% of those people born between 1946 and 1964.

Europe and the UK is also grappling with social isolation among its citizens. According to a 2018 European Commission report, 75 million adults only meet with family or friends, at most, once a month. The study also shows that 30 million Europeans frequently feel isolated and lonely, especially those with unfavourable economic circumstances, who are unemployed or suffer from health issues – a percentage that has radically increased since the outbreak of COVID-19.

Loneliness has significant health repercussion and a large meta-analysis involving 40 studies for more than 65 years, showed that social isolation and loneliness is associated with a higher risk of cardiovascular disease and stroke and mental health compromise.[70]

Loneliness and isolation is also strongly associated with physical pain, fatigue, cognitive decline, depression, personality disorders, psychosis and even Alzheimer's disease. Moreover, according to researchers from the University College London, the degree of loneliness is a predictor for symptom severity in those with existing mental health issues.[71] Yet there has been a steady trend in developed countries towards living alone and experiencing social isolation. Even a family-orientated country like South Africa, where only a little over 8% of the population is over 60,[72] is profoundly affected. In fact, since 1996 there has been over a 10% increase in one-person households within the country. Current estimates show that more than 1 in 4 South Africans live alone.[73]

While the Fourth Industrial Revolution and the exponential changes in values, education, work and personal interactions is a large contributor to the feelings of growing isolation, nothing could have prepared any of us for the rolling lockdowns driven by the coronavirus pandemic.

The stress on those already experiencing loneliness and even those who had never before experienced social isolation, is incalculable. While many of the contributing factors relate to broader social shifts, there are several steps that can be taken within the workplace that can alleviate this societal burden.

- Encourage social connections and mutual support. Team-building exercises, shared learning experiences, group projects and collective accountability can mitigate the stress of loneliness.
- Create an environment where your workforce is able to share a collective identity. Pride in the company's values, ethos and moral code can bring teams together.
- Check in personally with those directly under your care and encourage all leaders and managers to do the same.

By implementing these steps not only will you enhance the well-being and health of those around you, but it will also reduce absenteeism and staff turnover as well as increase productivity and the standard of work.

3

THE IMPACT OF THE GIANT STORM

Humanity is in the midst of a storm – chronic stress. However, unlike typical hurricanes which eventually pass, this one appears to be building and growing with every passing year and none more so than 2020. The destructive potential of chronic stress has been recognised by governments, research institutions and health agencies throughout the world. Well before the coronavirus pandemic, the WHO cites stress as the 'health epidemic of the 21st century'. On the surface, this statement appears alarmist and disproportionate, considering the devastating impact of COVID-19, together with the growing prevalence of complex chronic diseases. But when we dive deeper into the biological mechanisms that result in health compromise (on both a mental and physical level) chronic stress invariably plays a central role in the unfolding story.

According to the American Psychological Association, 77% of people who experience chronic stress will develop physical symptoms (ie digestive, immune compromise, pain, etc) and 73% will experience mental and emotional symptoms (ie poor concentration, emotional instability, low mood).[1]

Within the last decade, the spotlight has been placed on stress in the workplace due to the immense human cost and financial burden on the world economy. For corporates, higher rates of absenteeism, presenteeism, lost output, disability benefits and treatment costs are reducing productivity, innovation and competitiveness. For employees, chronic diseases, mental health challenges and physical pain and have sadly become an accepted norm and in a sense, a 'causality of war'.

BADGE OF HONOUR

At the beginning of 2020 (pre-COVID-19), I was contacted by David, a highly respected CEO of a successful multinational business with offices in South Africa. He asked me for a referral to a healthcare practitioner, with no further information given. We had an existing relationship as I had consulted to his local offices on health and organisational performance fairly regularly. David was a classic high-achiever and had risen to the top at a young age. He projected mental toughness, lived off adrenaline and coffee, hardly slept, and no challenge seemed too great, or at least that was the impression he gave.

It was difficult for me to provide him with a referral, without knowing the issues at hand, so we set up an appointment for the following day. I hadn't seen David for a few weeks and was taken aback when he walked through the door. He had gained a significant amount of weight, was more visibly grey and his posture was stooped and withdrawn.

We chatted about the business landscape and its exponential rate of change and how it was impacting David and his team and the organisation as a whole. David was innovative and a visionary and had already put plans in place to future-proof the business through strong stress-management programmes, skills development and more engagement with contract workers. The current challenge he was facing was a compounding stress that no one could have foreseen – COVID-19. The demands were enormous, relentless and taking their toll and the conversation progressed to the issue at hand – David's health. David complained about weight gain despite a fairly stringent diet and other physical symptoms included increased body pain, recurring sinus infections, a persistent cough and no energy.

Getting out of bed in the morning was almost impossible and it took several hours for his head to be 'semi-clear' and for him to feel awake, despite the consumption of litres of coffee. His digestive system was compromised with constant diarrhoea, bloating or constipation and kidney pain was ongoing. But David's symptoms weren't limited to a purely physical set and he also mentioned that he didn't feel like himself. He complained of an unusual emotional instability and vulnerability and was experiencing a degree of distance in personal and professional interactions. What he was describing is known as depersonalisation disorder, marked by periods of disconnection or detachment from your body and thoughts. However, David's biggest concern was that he wasn't living up to his own standards in his personal and professional life and it was affecting his sense of self-worth and self-esteem.

On the surface it appeared that none of David's symptoms were connected or even remotely related, but in reality they were. He was experiencing extreme burnout, brought on by a prolonged state of hyper-vigilance in a world where uncertainty, unpredictability and insecurity had become the established norm.

The solution was clear – we needed to develop David's resilience and ability to maintain sustained functioning through adversity. Resilience is strongly influenced by neurochemicals such as brain-derived neurotrophic factor (BDNF), neuropeptide Y, oxytocin, serotonin, dopamine and noradrenaline and so the action steps required were genetic and metabolic assessments.

For the genetic evaluation, I used a resilience and mind panel that I had developed in conjunction with a biotechnology lab based in South Africa. It assesses an array of genes that can impact mood, cognition and coping mechanisms. The metabolic testing involved a test that identifies 75 health markers, especially in the areas of energy production, nutrient balance and neurological health. From David's results, I was able to tailor-make a personalised health plan including nutritional supplements, diet, exercise and mind-body interventions that would not only address David's burnout, but also promote molecular balance, thereby helping him cope with and overcome the relentless challenges all leaders are being confronted with all time.

For many years, burnout was considered a badge of honour – a measure of success and ascendancy within an accomplished career journey. Until 2020, burnout was principally a subjective experience that, at best, could be corroborated by a family physician. This is no longer the case. In 2019 the WHO officially added burnout to the 11th International Classification of Diseases List (ICD-11)[2] and according to the ICD-11: 'Burnout is a syndrome conceptualised as resulting from chronic workplace stress that has not been successfully managed. It is characterised by three dimensions:

- feelings of energy depletion or exhaustion
- increased mental distance from one's job, or feelings of negativism or cynicism related to one's job
- reduced professional efficacy

Burnout is typically a result of a chronic combination of two principal stresses: long working hours and high demands, both of which were central to David's breakdown. The challenge most organisations and employees face is that both of these stressors are key drivers in competitiveness in the workplace, not to mention individual career advancement. Outside of the direct short-term impact of COVID-19 such as lockdown and economic slowdown, the likelihood of demands decreasing and working weeks becoming shorter is fairly low in the coming future.

In 2018 a large team of researchers from Harvard University published a review on the prevalence of burnout in physicians around the world.[3] Physicians are a perfect sample group for a large study focusing on burnout as they

> More than two-thirds of practicing physicians are currently experiencing burnout and emotional exhaustion.

experience both long working hours and high demands, to the extreme. The research team evaluated 182 studies, from 45 countries, involving 109 628 practitioners.

The findings showed the prevalence of overall burnout and were able to disentangle the composites that make up the burnout experience. These factors include emotional exhaustion, depersonalisation and a sense of low personal accomplishment. Alarmingly, 67% of the physicians were completely burnt out, 72% were experiencing emotional exhaustion and as many as 68% were feeling completely detached from their physical and mental state.

Although this meta-analysis was performed on a very specific group, the results can be superimposed onto any sector that combines long working hours and high demands, on a protracted basis. Professional services such as law, finance and consultancy are all subject to the same cause-and-effect relationship.

Solving the burnout puzzle

From mid-2019 to mid-2020, I worked with one of the world's premier law firms. The firm is a showcase for high performance and has more globally ranked lawyers than almost any other law brand. They also lead and close approximately three transactions a day, which translates to an extraordinary level of achievement and pressure on a daily basis.

The firm lives and breathes a performance culture and I was appointed to create a health and wellness programme at their Johannesburg office. From the outset, it was obvious that the key productivity drivers were already in place and included good infrastructure, a high level of skills, business dynamism and innovation capabilities. There was, however, a prevailing sense that chronic stress and its negative health associations was taking its toll on the entire workforce. Sustained growth and the human cost of pushing for higher levels of excellence were pressing concerns for the company's leadership.

The first step in any health and performance intervention programme is to establish a material understanding of the present landscape. As mentioned, the legal profession is one of the most stressful occupations in the world and is associated with significant mental and physical health compromise.

In the build-up to the launch of the new wellness vision at the firm, the managing partner and operations team briefed me on the current organisational health challenges and the level of urgency they wanted to implement. I accepted the challenge and knew I needed to deliver. The more industry standard wellness approaches, that include a handful of motivational seminars, some coaching sessions and some reactive measures would unlikely be effective in this situation and create the desired outcomes.

I needed to create a far more comprehensive and nuanced model. Following the preliminary briefings, I compiled a survey that would determine the type and levels of stress, the degree of psychological resilience within the firm as well as the existing mental health landscape. I made use of the Patient Health Questionnaire-9 (PHQ-9), a 9-question instrument given to patients in a primary care setting to screen for the presence and severity of depression. This data provided the basis for the strategic intervention model going forward.

> We experience stress through a variety of pathways. These include psychological, physical and environmental. Often it is the collective influence that is more impactful than an individual part.

From the 12 primary life and workplace stresses listed in the questionnaire, the results showed that, not surprisingly, high demands and long working hours were the principal challenges confronting the entire organisation. In truth, this was not unexpected due to the success of the firm.

What I didn't anticipate was the scale and magnitude of the impact of overall stress within the firm's workforce. 80% of the organisation was experiencing stress at levels that had adverse effects on health. As I slowly unpacked the data, several prominent reasons for this emerged. When you combine a high-stress profession and extreme performance expectations from international offices, operating in a country that is rated as one of the most stressed in the world and based in one of the most polluted cities in the world, the combination creates an overwhelming set. It was fairly evident that the sum of all these combined factors were driving the stress crisis in the firm, as opposed to the weighting of an individual part.

What I also discovered, was that 88% of the firm was experiencing a considerable degree of burnout. Through my work over the years, I have seen that the combination of high self-rated scores due to long working hours and high demands and where the average exceeds a given percentage, is a reliable predictor of burnout. The issue with burnout is that it profoundly impacts your emotional state, perceived reality and ultimately the ability to actualise your intrinsic potential and consequently the company's.

Burnout is usually understood to be a purely physical condition causing extreme exhaustion and fatigue and while this is certainly one of its manifestations, and is included in the WHO's definition, the reality is that it is by far the most complex and destructive, impacting almost every system within the body.

Shortly after completing the evaluation and data capturing, I reported my findings to the firm's partners, COO and HR director, who all signed off the project.

While the merits of the new vision were sound enough to get sign-off, what was more important was to get buy-in from each and every member of the firm. But there was a roadblock. One of the biggest challenges within any high-performing environment is that the primary burnout drivers – long working hours and high demands – are part of a complex set that determines business growth and earnings. Logic suggests that if you want to address an issue then identify the cause and the outcomes will be favourable. In this instance, the very thing that was causing the burnout, ie long working hours and high demands, were not possible to remove in this context.

Because of this, I was stretched to find solutions. Instead of suggesting reduced working hours and a lower set of demands on individuals (which could be construed as insanity in a professional services firm) I decided on a multi-layered approach that could be applied to almost every business or team. The layered approach was made up of four interconnecting parts and covered the following areas:

- To equip the firm with the knowledge, skills and resources to support and promote health and manage stress
- Reduce the burden of additional stressors
- Encourage self-empowerment and personal accountability
- The building and development of trust

1. Knowledge, skills and resources

The first step was the training in, and practice of, reframing. Reframing simply refers to an adjustment in the way we perceive the challenges that we are confronted with and our biological responses to them (ie elevated heart rate, change in respiration, etc). Numerous Harvard studies[4] have shown that simply seeing stress as an opportunity, as opposed to a burden or liability, provides cardiovascular protection, increases focus and attention, reduces stress-induced anxiety and even enhances cognition.

The second part of the model strongly promoted the power of connectivity and the strength of the collective. Greater support, care, empathy and protection formed the working framework.

The third part of the health programme involved awareness and the skills to tame the stress response. From a biological standpoint, stress has an off button. It's not a molecule, protein or hormone, but rather a nerve system known as the vagus nerve. By frequently activating and strengthening this stress fail-safe, the entire team was able to turn their stress off at times when it was not necessary to be hyper-aroused or adrenalised (ie in the evenings, outside of working hours and during downtime). My book, *The Stress Code*, details these activities, which include yoga, deep breathing exercises, meditation, music and many physical therapies.

The final part of the programme included lifestyle choices. The food we eat determines our well-being and performance, especially during demanding periods. Additionally, nutritional supplements can offer significant advantages in emotional, mental and physical well-being. Exercise can help lower anxiety, improve focus and concentration and protect against stress-related diseases. And lastly, spending lunch breaks outside, or time in the garden at the end of the day, can promote emotional stability, lower stress hormones and drive performance. Fundamentally, all these lifestyle activities are able to enhance key hormones and molecules (such as growth hormone, serotonin, dopamine, brain-derived neurotrophic factor) that neutralise the adverse effects of stress and help protect the body from the wear and tear (often referred to as allostatic load) that ultimately contribute to burnout.

When the programme was first launched at the firm, a senior member approached me to assist her on a personal level. She, like many others, was struggling with the symptoms of burnout, especially emotional outbursts. She couldn't sleep and conflicts had become a daily occurrence. In our initial conversations, she was fairly intense and irritable, which was understandable considering that the organisation had been driving projects at all costs. One of the big frustrations she had was that she was working 65 to 70 hours a week, but only billing a small percentage of that. The pressure destroyed many of her personal relationships and corroded her self-worth. She, and many others, were at a loss as they needed to continue at the intensity they were, but knew they didn't have the physical and emotional reserves to do so.

By teaching her to manage her stress responses better, changing her diet to promote more consistent energy levels and providing techniques to help with focus and concentration, she was able to increase productivity by 30%, reducing the number of hours spent at her desk. As the weeks passed, a smile reappeared on her face, her social connectivity grew and she was able to develop interests outside of work.

2. Long working hours and high demands

Common to most work environments, these stresses are fairly fixed within high-performing teams and therefore other stresses need to be lowered in order to reduce the overall stress load and lower the risk of burnout. In this instance, my approach was to create an environment where people felt more valued and respected, were more supported, where conflict was resolved quickly and where everyone felt that they had a voice and were treated fairly.

3. Self-empowerment and personal accountability

These two facets of personality are a central characteristic of Olympic champions and the cornerstone of psychological resilience. It is the ability to positively reframe challenging events and circumstances as opportunities as opposed to adversities. Awareness of the immense power of our mind in shaping our reality, the strength of our actions in moulding the world around us, creates a powerful set that allows for intrinsic potential to be fully actualised.

Many years ago, I worked for an Olympic silver medallist who had suffered a series of injury setbacks. He underwent more than one surgery to try and save his sporting career and one evening at dinner I asked him how he kept going. Whether he ever felt like the challenges were too great and not worth the pain and effort. He smiled, took a sip of his drink, looked up and said, 'I don't recall ever feeling like it's too much. What I do is remove myself from the challenges and circumstances and rather evaluate my own thoughts.'

Simply put, he focused on controlling his thoughts and responses as opposed to dwelling on the circumstances, which are often beyond our control. I asked him how that was possible and with an intense stare, he said, 'I self-talk, set small achievable goals, remain positive and try to be as proactive as possible.' He ended by saying, 'I have always benefited in some way from the challenges. Look, you are here now helping me with this challenge.' These wise words have always stuck with me.

By applying these fundamental principles of separating themselves from the daily stresses (which were often not within their control) and evaluating their own set of thoughts, emotional responses and actions (which were firmly within our control), members of the firm were able to significantly reduce their experience of stress and subsequent degree of emotional, mental and physical strain.

The practical application follows a process of understanding that our stress and challenges don't define us. We will not resent them, lay blame, become enraged, pessimistic, rigid or unforgiving. Instead, we are able to reflect on how we are thinking and feeling and what the right action responses should be, thereby regaining a sense of control. This facilitated response will lead to challenges, demand courage and require strength of will and self-control. But as Jonathan Sacks puts its so perfectly, it represents the ultimate 'triumph of choice over fate' and as such leads to success and positive realities.

4. Building and development of trust

Trust is central to both individual and organisational success. Organisational trust increases support, reduces conflict, eliminates perceptions of injustice, and increases the feeling of appreciation.

In 2019 I had the opportunity to sit in on a trust-building session for a very high-performing executive team. Some people often perceive these kinds of sessions to be something held at a remote resort where group members dive backwards off a stage and are caught by their overexcited colleagues. This session was nothing like that. The trust 'expert' spent 20 minutes expounding on the importance of organisational trust using a white board and a crude drawing and then opened the floor as a moderator. The mandate was to share honest views and feelings, which each of the 20 attendees did. Needless to say, it was a very heated and tense two hours and I was relieved when it was over, but it did bring the entire team together and helped to rebuild relationships.

While this is one approach to building trust, my goal at the firm was to earn trust gradually. Whether it be a process, vision, group or person, the approach I decided on was done through competency, consistency in messaging and deliverables, transparency and honesty, helping those in need and living the vision.

The overall resilience programme I set up involved monthly talks, weekly podcasts, use of The Stress Code app, short videos on topical issues (such as immunity or sleep), the installation of fitness facilities, a cognitive performance menu, on-site yoga classes, daily massages, personal coaching

> Trust is developed through competency, consistency, transparency, honesty and ethics.

This may sound like an Olympic village not a law firm, but there is actually very little that separates elite athletes from high-performing professionals. While athletes rely principally on their physical capabilities to earn a living and prestige, professionals use their minds. This said, an athlete who does not focus on the mental side of their development is unlikely to be successful, while a professional who doesn't nurture their physical well-being is also unlikely to achieve their fullest potential.

> There is very little that separates elite athletes from high-performing professionals.

Six months into the implementation of the programme, the number of lawyers experiencing stress at levels that would negatively impact their health and productivity, dropped by 50%. Burnout rates reduced to only 13%, while at the same time fee earnings hit a seven-year high. What made this particular outcome so remarkable was that working hours and individual demands increased during this period in order to accommodate the greater flow of work.

The multi-layered approach I adopted at the law firm to tackle burnout could be implemented in any business and based on the success of the programme, this narrative shows that burnout can impact you, your team *and* your business:

- Any company, group, team or person who performs at a high level is at risk of burnout. It's not a case of if, but rather when, and to what degree.
- Burnout will jeopardise any business or individual. It creates emotional instability, negative feelings towards the work and the environment, and creates lowered self-esteem and self-doubt.
- Due to the competitive nature of the modern workplace, it is very difficult to reduce the primary burnout triggers, ie long working hours, high demands and role uncertainty. If the primary burnout drivers cannot be managed, the most practical way to address burnout in the modern workplace and prevent future occurrences, is to buffer unnecessary stresses (ie lack of support, lack of respect, lack of appreciation, role uncertainty, abuse of power). The workforce must be equipped with the knowledge, skills and resources to better cope with the stress and promote personal health and well-being. A special emphasis needs to be placed on restorative therapies and activities. Meditation, breathing, yoga and physical therapies can help immeasurably. All this needs to be brought together by creating an environment of support, understanding and strong values.

WHY WE NEED TO TAKE STRESS MORE SERIOUSLY

While burnout has only recently been recognised as a 'real' health disorder, mental wellness and the negative relationship to stress has been known and studied for some time. Chronic stress has been associated with a significant disruption in the production, transportation and uptake of several brain chemicals involved in emotional and cognitive functionality. For example, chronic stress reduces levels of brain-derived neurotrophic, BDNF, by over 40% within a six-week period.[5] BDNF is a protein produced inside nerve cells that promotes the structural integrity and functionality of the brain through new brain cell formation, maturation and retention, as well as by building connections between the cells. Research has consistently shown that BDNF is a reliable biomarker for depression and anxiety.[6] In other words, stress-induced reductions in BDNF increases the likelihood of experiencing depression or anxiety.

Another molecule profoundly impacted by stress is serotonin. Serotonin is a powerful neurochemical that strongly influences mood and social behaviour, appetite and digestion, sleep, memory and sexual desire and function. Four to six weeks of stress has shown to have a profound effect of serotonin function, which can also have an effect on the structure of the brain (principally through the reduced formation of new cells). Disruptions to this finely tuned system can result in depression, anger and poor coping skills, as well as a host of other mental health challenges.[7]

These are only two examples of the negative impact of overstimulating the stress axis through the repeated experiences of fear, uncertainty and other challenges. There are many other neurochemicals, including dopamine and norepinephrine that are profoundly impacted by stress, that could have an equally, if not more damaging effect, on mental health and well-being.

It should come as no surprise that the prevalence of mental health issues around the world has been steadily increasing in recent years and pre-COVID-19 has amplified this crisis. According to the Institute for Health Metrics and Evaluation, a research institute working in the area of global health statistics and impact evaluation at the University of Washington in Seattle, in 2017, 971 million people had a mental or substance abuse disorder.[8] Not even two years on, experts were of the opinion that this estimate of 1 in 7 may actually have been on the conservative end. This figure is likely to rise significantly following the events of 2020.

This mental health crisis has created a boom for the pharmaceutical sector. The use of prescription medications used in the treatment of mental health disorders, including antipsychotics, antidepressants, anxiolytics and anti-seizure medications tell the real story. In 2015 BCC Research, a leading information resource that produces high-quality market research reports and newsletters and hosts conferences, estimated that the value of the mental health drug market was worth $88.3 billion showing an annual compound growth rate of 1.9%.

According to a 2019 report by Reports and Data, a boutique market intelligence and strategic consulting firm, the depression and anxiety medication sector alone is growing at a rate of 2.4% (1.5 times that of the current global population growth).

Consider that any natural disaster or global crisis that causes a significant amount of stress to those affected, will create a huge surge in mental health compromise. This is precisely what has happened with the coronavirus; it pushed the world into a state of fear, worry and uncertainty within a matter of weeks. The fear of exposure to the virus, prolonged social distancing, financial insecurity and uncertainty, with no end in sight, has raised stress and anxiety to such a degree that mental health agencies like SADAG are barely able to cope with societal demands.

Another growing concern in the mental health space is the impact of social distancing as a direct result of the uncontrolled spread of the virus. By the end of May 2020, more than three billion people in 70 countries were asked to not leave their houses.

Human beings thrive on social connection and strong relationships and even the most antisocial people still require some degree of interaction and human engagement. The stress of social distancing has had a profound impact on mental health and well-being, the effects of which will be seen for many years following the event.

On 26 February 2020, only weeks before the global lockdown, *The Lancet* published a review article on the psychological effects of historic quarantines and the steps and measures that need to be taken to reduce the negative impact (which include acquiring relevant knowledge, ensuring adequate supplies, maintaining strong connections and limiting boredom).[9] The researchers from Kings College in London showed that social distancing measures such as quarantines, are strongly associated with PTSD, depression, emotional exhaustion, irritability, insomnia, nervousness, fear and anxiety.

Prior to COVID-19, the world was already overwhelmed by chronic stress and mental health compromise. The combined and superimposed effects of economic, health and educational fallout, together with fragmented connections and reduced support networks, places a tremendous moral responsibility on all leaders and decision makers to do everything in their power to reduce, buffer or even combat the current challenges.

In his book, *Morality: Restoring the Common Good in Divided Times,*[10] Rabbi Lord Jonathan Sacks eloquently defines this obligation as: 'Any position of leadership, however, makes you responsible to the people who have entrusted some part of their destiny to you.'

While the relationship between chronic stress and human health is still being explored, what we already know and understand is that different stresses have unique effects on health and well-being. For example, some stresses have stronger associations with chronic disease (ie injustice, racial and gender bias) or physical health compromise (ie job and employment insecurity) while others can trigger a rise in the prevalence of physical pain (ie financial challenges, job insecurity and lack of sleep).

As the chart shows, the primary stresses that increase the risk of developing mental health issues include financial pressure, conflict between work and personal responsibilities, relationship challenges, injustice, high demands and, most notably, a lack of control or authority in your own life.

It is probably safe to say that most of us, due to a variety of reasons, are

Type of stress	Physical health	Mental health	Pain	Chronic disease
High demands	x	x		x
Lack of support	x	x		
Conflict	x	x		
Lack of control	x	x		x
Financial pressure		x	x	x
Injustice/prejudice	x			x
Sleep issues			x	x
Job insecurity	x		x	

feeling out of control, experiencing financial pressures, are overwhelmed by high demands, are facing conflicts between work and personal life and many are being subjected to prejudices and injustices that exist within society. The rise in chronic stress, and these very specific stresses, parallel the rise in the prevalence of mental health compromise.

STRESS AROUND THE WORLD

Chronic stress and mental health compromise in the workplace are inextricably linked to over-commitment, long working hours and high demands, and while these are strong contributing factors, they often coincide with additional strains that include low levels of support, financial challenges, lack of control and a lack of appreciation. This is why simply applying the logic of shorter working weeks or longer annual leave may not necessarily have a mitigating effect. Looking at stress and mental health in different regions of the world, this understanding is strongly supported. In the EU, the average annual working hours are lower than many parts of the world, but the prevalence of stress and mental health compromise is still exceptionally high.

The European stress landscape

In 2011 a large team of researchers from Europe and Canada performed a systematic review on the prevalence of mental disorders in Europe.[11] The aim of the meta-analysis was to provide a 12-month view into the prevalence and liability estimates of a broad range of mental and neurological disorders. The results were jaw-dropping and according to the researchers, 'It is estimated that each year 38.2% of the EU population suffers from a mental disorder'.

> More than a third of the EU population suffers from a common mental health disorder such as depression.

This corresponds to 165 million people that were experiencing either anxiety disorders, major depression or insomnia. Interestingly, the study found no substantial cultural or country variations. This certainly comes as a surprise, considering the aspirational lifestyle seen in many of the Mediterranean nations.

With data drawn from a broad range of sources, including national health programmes, the analysis also revealed that there have been significant increases in sick leave, early retirement and treatment rates due to mental disorders.

In 2013 Matrix, a research group commissioned by the Executive Agency for Health and Consumers, published an extensive report that analysed workplace stress and mental-health promotion programmes within the EU. The aim of the analysis was to assess the potential contribution that mental health promotion and mental disorder prevention programmes can make in increasing employment and productivity within the EU.

The report contained many valuable insights that have helped health professionals better understand the stress, mental health and work performance relationship. For example, much of the research into stress and common mental health disorders ascribes a 100% overlap between stress and depression. In other words, a person who experiences depression also suffers from chronic stress with a high degree of certainty.[12]

> 60% of all lost working days within the EU is related to work stress.

The report also showed that the total cost of work-related depression in the EU was €620 billion annually (in a post COVID-19 world this estimate is likely to be considerably higher in most of the EU states). This estimate encompasses presenteeism, absenteeism, lost output as well as treatment costs and disability benefits.

EU-OSHA (European Agency for Safety and Health at Work, a decentralised agency of the EU with the task of collecting, analysing and disseminating relevant information that can serve the needs of people involved in safety and health at work) also identified that 60% of all lost working days are related to work-related stress, amounting to an annual cost of almost 4% of the EU's GDP. It is plausible that the low growth figures within the EU over the last 20 years, may have some association to stress and the mental health landscape.

> The primary causes of lost productivity within the workplace include:
> - Depression (primary)
> - Allergies
> - High blood pressure
> - Anxiety
> - Physical pain
> - Respiratory disorders
> - Diabetes
> - Headaches
> - Migraines
> - Asthma
>
> It is a fair assumption that stress is central to many of these health disorders.

According to a 2017 report by EU-OSHA, the current cost of stress and mental health in Europe exceeds €240 billion annually.[13] However, the report has some limitations as it only looks at the economic burden within the context of lost productivity and direct medical costs. The study points out that absenteeism costs within the EU account for losses of €136 billion per year and direct medical treatment amounts to €104 billion annually. The €380 billion difference between the Matrix study of 2013 and the 2017 EU-OSHA study, centres around presenteeism.

Presenteeism-related losses in productivity are primarily driven by several chronic medical conditions that include depression and other mental health disorders, allergies, physical pain, headaches and migraines, high blood pressure, asthma and other respiratory disorders as well as diabetes, etc.[14] Presenteeism is far more costly on any business or economy than absenteeism. To put this into context, consider that low levels of depression are associated with a 30% reduction in productivity. This means that instead of being productive for eight hours in a workday, an employee is effectively only productive for 5.5 hours. This may sound insignificant but over a week it amounts to a loss of 12 hours of work. Taken over an extended period, such as a month, this translates to 48 hours and over a year that's a staggering 576 hours of lost productivity, or the equivalent of two months.

Because the burden of presenteeism on individuals and businesses is 4 to 10

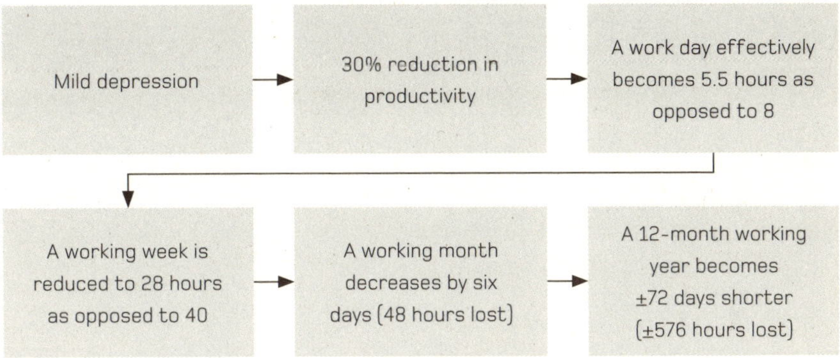

times greater than absenteeism, it is easy to appreciate why researchers have become so invested in understanding, quantifying and managing this phenomenon.

European companies acknowledge the need for action

It has become clear that leaders and decision makers across the EU recognise the enormity of the stress and mental health crisis, both from a human cost and financial perspective.

According to the EU-OSHA's European Survey of Enterprises on New and Emerging Risks (ESENER), an extensive survey that draws on the responses from almost 50 000 establishments across all size classes and activity sectors in 36 countries, work-related stress is a major concern in nearly 80% of EU businesses.[15] Yet, surprisingly less than 30% of organisations in Europe have procedures for dealing with workplace stress.

I have experienced this level of stress first-hand, having spoken at European HR conventions and to executives on the promotion of resilience and health in the workplace. The topic draws a large crowd and consistently runs overtime with an emotional Q&A. Much of the audience conversation is spent discussing personal struggles, growing family and organisational challenges as well as appeals for direction in management and prevention.

The general understanding of stress and mental health compromise has grown significantly, as has the urgency to deal with the growing challenge. However, setting in motion an effective health and resilience programme is

According to Johns Hopkins University, the symptoms of depression include:

- Lasting sad, anxious or 'empty' mood
- Loss of interest in almost all activities
- Appetite and weight changes
- Changes in sleep patterns
- Slowing of physical activity, speech and thinking, or the opposite
- Fatigue
- Ongoing feelings of worthlessness or guilt
- Trouble concentrating or making decisions
- Thoughts of self-injurious behaviour

complex, with many moving parts, which may be a deterrent for a number of organisations and could possibly explain the slow uptake. What every leader, manager and business should bear in mind is the cost (human and economic) and burden of not managing organisational health and stress.

Low mood or depression is associated with significant productivity losses and the journal, *Annals of Family Medicine*, published a study showing moderate depression associated with a 51% increase in absenteeism and presenteeism.[16] It is this point in history, with the global economy ravaged by the coronavirus pandemic, that no business or team can afford not to invest in the well-being of their individual members.

Of the EU's workforce of 299 million people (taken from 2019),[17] 113 million economically active individuals may have experienced some degree of presenteeism or increased absenteeism due to illness, as a consequence of stress and associated mental health challenges. This suggests that the stress and mental health cost estimate of €620 billion annually might be too conservative.

There are two additional considerations that leaders and decision makers need to be mindful of that haven't been factored into the cost-modelling of the studies mentioned above.

Firstly, any form of absence by employees is likely to result in an increased workload, and consequently higher levels of stress on the remaining workforce. High demands, longer working hours and overcommitment are major triggers in mental health compromise and burnout thereby perpetuating the vicious cycle.

Secondly, consider that when skilled and more senior employees suffer from mental or physical health challenges (whether stress-induced or not) and are unwilling or unable to continue in their designated role, there will be additional recruitment and training costs ranging from 75% to over 200% of annual compensation.[18] Yet, according to a report by Oxford Economics, the biggest blow stems from the fact that new employees only reach the maximum productivity level after a 5- to 8-month period.[19]

Should this occur in the professional services sectors such as law, management consultancies, accounting and medicine (which take more than 32 weeks to reach optimal productivity), these additional costs have the potential to impact the success of the entire business.[20]

Is the other side of the Channel any better?

The UK has been subject to tremendous volatility over the last few years, driven largely by a referendum that was held on 23 June 2016. The referendum saw 51.9% of voters supporting the UK leaving the EU. Following this, the government invoked Article 50 in the EU's Lisbon Treaty, initiating a two-year process which was due to conclude with the UK's planned exit on 29 March 2019 – a deadline that had to be extended to 31 January 2020.

The negative impact of Brexit was not only felt across the UK and in Europe, but throughout the world. The world's sixth largest economy has seen considerable negative shifts in its GDP, the job market, retail and inflation and by mid-January 2020, half of UK firms were of the opinion that the country would slide into a recession. Sterling hit a 15-year low against the US dollar and 2019 saw British retail drop to a 25-year low[21] (although incomparable to the collapse in April 2020). Job postings reflected a 10-year low and the UK inflation target of below 2% has been a huge struggle to meet. The years of uncertainty and indecision within the country has profoundly impacted the UK economy and British society as a whole.

Yet nothing could have prepared the UK for the socio-economic impact of the coronavirus. According to a BBC news article entitled 'Coronavirus: A visual guide to the economic impact'[22] there have been several profound shifts within the economy that will take decades for the country to fully recover from. For example, from the beginning of January 2020 to the middle of March 2020, the FTSE 100 Index dropped by 34.1%.

The travel industry came to a standstill and restaurants saw an 82% drop in customers. In April 2020, GDP dropped by a record 20.4% as the country came to a standstill. Despite a colossal £30-billion effort by the government to reduce the societal and economic impact of the pandemic, it could not curb the growing stress and mental health situation.

Prior to the coronavirus pandemic and political and economic turmoil that was triggered in 2016, Britain was already struggling with a high prevalence of chronic stress and mental health issues. This is not dissimilar to many other leading industrialised nations, but the combination of the coronavirus pandemic and Brexit is likely to push the British stress and mental health crisis into uncharted territory.

Towards the end of 2018, the UK's Health and Safety Executive (HSE) published the annual statistics related to work-related stress, depression and anxiety.[23] From 2017 to 2018, stress and associated mental health issues accounted for 44% of all work-related ill health cases and 57% of absenteeism.

The biggest trigger in work-related mental health compromise within the UK is excessive workload. This involves deadlines, excess work volume and perceived pressure. All are factors contributing to corroding mental health, according to doctors.

According to the Centre for Mental Health,[24] mental health issues result in 72 million lost working days every year, costing businesses at least £33–£42 billion annually.[25]

In recent years, the General Practitioners Network (GPN)[26] has carefully analysed work-related mental health cases by the precipitating events, thereby creating a cause and effect model. What the data showed was that the biggest trigger in stress-induced mental health compromise was excess workload. This involved tight deadlines, an excess of work volume or just too much perceived pressure.

From March through to August 2020, I was involved in different community panels and web-based talks on stress and resilience. The audience involved many leading companies with offices throughout the world, YPO groups (the global leadership community of more than 29 000 chief executives in 130 countries who are driven by the belief that the world needs better leaders) as well as the business media such as Business Day TV. For many of the sessions, I created a real-time online stress and resilience survey to get a sense of what stresses were impacting the groups, and essentially the nation, the most. I used the data to talk to the groups' challenges and to create a more authentic connection. The survey was very specific to the current socio-economic landscape and looked at the 10 most common stresses that included: long working hours, high demands, financial difficulties, job and employment insecurity, reduced support, social isolation, conflicts, sleep, and family health concerns.

Drawing from the data of approximately 3 000 individuals, the prevailing stress was a combination of high demands and long working hours. In follow-up conversations, many attendees reported working at least two to four hours longer every day following the events of COVID-19. This increase in working hours and demands was a consequence of trying to find potential opportunities in a changing market and save existing jobs and businesses.

The collective hyper-vigilance and urgency was creating a stage for burnout and mental health compromise that is likely to be felt for months, if not years, to come. But there were other stresses that hadn't been properly recognised and that will further contribute to health instability. Compromised mental health also occurs in response to a lack of managerial support, significant organisational changes and professional role uncertainty.

When such a large percentage of the world's labour force are not in their traditional work environments and support (whether emotional or instrumental) has significantly diminished, these factors further add to the mental health crisis. Also, sweeping organisational changes as a consequence of downsizing, restructuring and changing markets has also created tremendous role uncertainty further fuelling an existing crisis.

> Within the last year, 74% of adults in the UK felt that they could not cope with their stress.

Pre-COVID, the Mental Health Foundation performed one of the largest studies on stress and mental health in the UK. The research showed that within the previous 12 months, 74% of adults felt so stressed that they were unable to effectively cope and felt completely overwhelmed.

It is plausible that this inability to cope strongly correlates with the high prevalence of mental health compromise seen in the UK. Common mental disorders such as depression and anxiety are strongly associated with reduced stress coping mechanisms. A 2014 paper entitled 'Mental Health and Wellbeing in England' captured data over two decades that involved four independent surveys involving 7 500 individuals.[27] The study revealed that, at the time, one in six adults in the UK had a common mental disorder such as depression, GAD, panic disorder, phobias, social anxiety disorder, OCD and

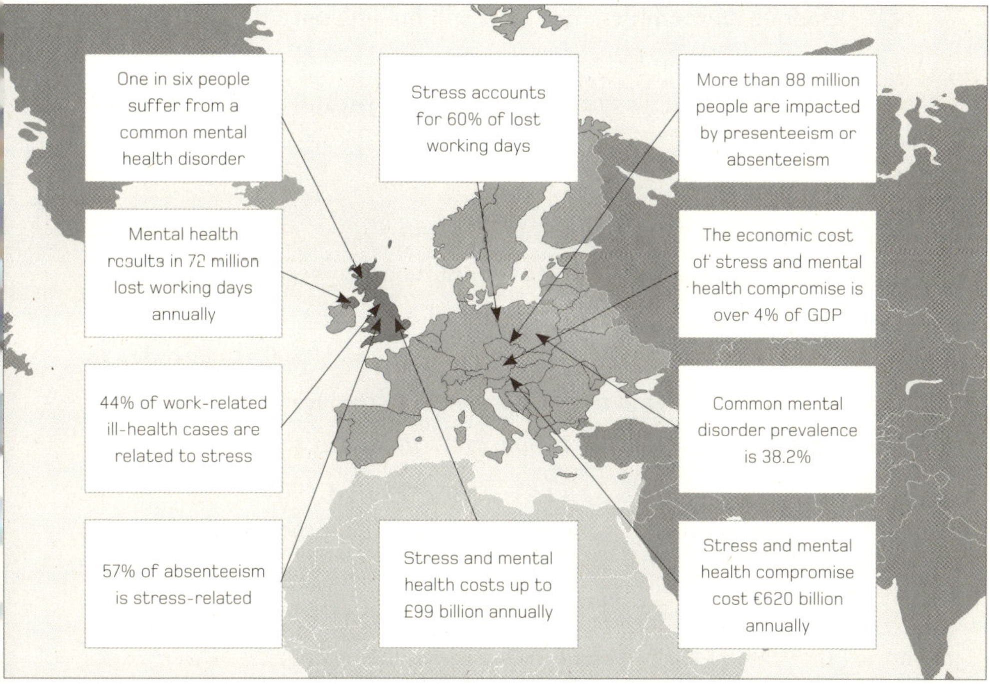

Health and economic burden of stress in Europe and the United Kingdom

PTSD. What was equally alarming about the report was that only a third of those who were experiencing a common mental disorder were receiving any form of treatment.

Despite the high prevalence of stress and the enormity of mental health challenges within UK as well as the rest of Europe, by global standards, they are considered to be relatively low stress regions. This assertion is strongly supported by the 'World Happiness Report 2020', an annual publication of the United Nations Sustainable Development Solutions Network. The WHR ranks 153 countries[28] on several key metrics that include GDP per capita, social support, health and life expectancy, freedom, generosity and absence of corruption. Of the 10 'happiest nations', Europe occupies nine spots and with all the above-mentioned stresses of Brexit, COVID-19 and the prevailing socio-economic uncertainties, the UK is still holding onto the 13th position on the happiest nation list.

Sadly, South Africa has a negative rating on the list and we are ranked 109.

Across the pond

Like the UK, the US has experienced a tumultuous few years, which is reflecting strongly in their stress and mental health statistics. During the Great Recession, Gallup established a National Health and Well-Being Index to track and better understand the key factors that drive health and well-being. Gallup surveys roughly 10 000 people every month in 50 US states and in 2018, despite a surging economy, it was found that Americans are some of the most stressed people in the world.

> 60% of Americans are experiencing significant stress and 58% worry on any given day.

The paper entitled 'Americans' Stress, Worry and Anger Intensified in 2018', showed that 22% of the population were experiencing anger, 45% were experiencing worry and 55% were experiencing significant stress on a daily basis. The report rated the US as the seventh most stressed nation on the planet.[29]

Not surprisingly, these figures have risen substantially in 2020 and a large survey carried out in April showed that 60% of Americans were experiencing a significant amount of stress and 58% were worried or anxious on any given day.[30]

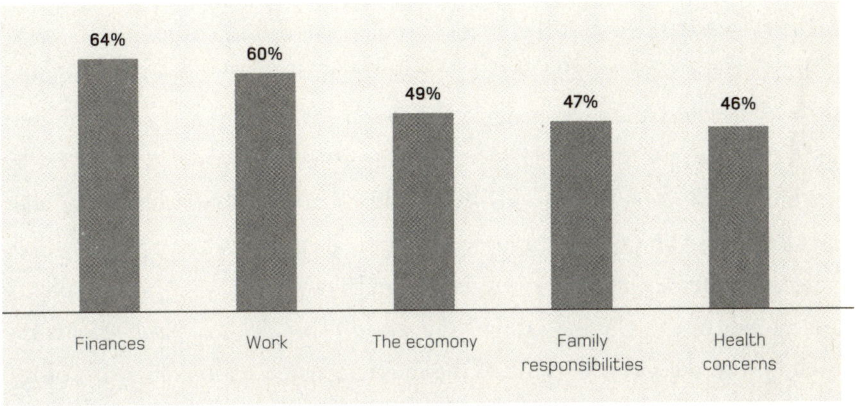

Stress in America in 2014

Americans are so stressed because of a collection of many factors that fluctuate according to the socio-economic conditions of the time. For example, in 2014 the primary stresses included finances, work, the economy, family responsibilities and health concerns.

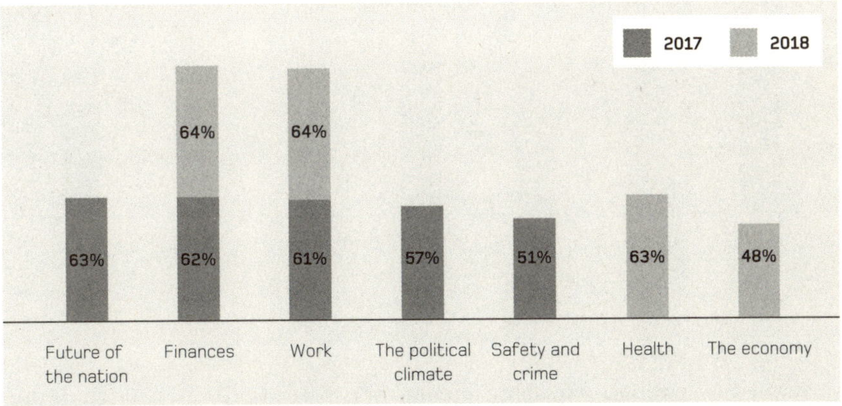

Stress in America in 2017 and 2018

A few years on and the stress landscape has changed considerably and according to the annual Stress in America survey conducted by the Harris Poll on behalf of the American Psychological Association, in 2017 and 2018, Americans were experiencing significant stress about the future of the nation, finances, work, the political climate as well as safety and crime.[31]

In 2020 the same annual report by the American Psychological Association showed that the nation was being destabilised by two additional and significant sources of stress – the coronavirus and racism/discrimination[32] spurred on by the killing of George Floyd, a 46-year-old black man, who was killed by police on 25 May in Minneapolis during an arrest for allegedly using a counterfeit $20 note at a supermarket. The event set off weeks of protests over police violence and racism in the US and around the world. This all took place against the backdrop of the US being one of the most impacted nations in terms of the coronavirus pandemic, its spread, death rate and equipment crisis.

The overwhelming set of stresses experienced by the broader population shifted to the uncertainty of the future of the nation, the coronavirus, the economy and work.

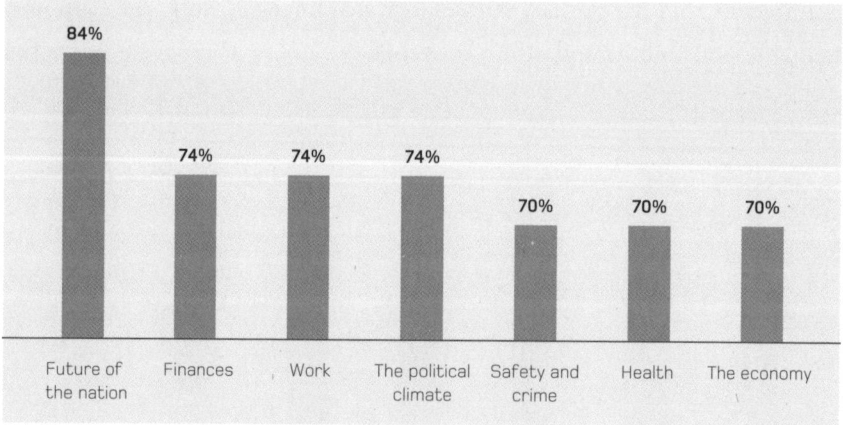

Stress in America in 2020

While any nation's stress and mental health landscape is strongly influenced by the existing socio-economic climate, culture, broader health and environmental conditions, together with government policies, we have to be mindful of the profound and rising influence of stress in the workplace.

In 2016 researchers from Harvard and Stanford Universities published a paper aiming to quantify the human toll of workplace stress.[33] These stresses included job insecurity, work-family conflict, long working hours, lack of medical aid, exposure to shift work, low job control, high job demands, low social support at work and low organisational justice – a very familiar set to all professionals.

According to the researchers: 'We find that more than 120,000 deaths per year and approximately 5% to 8% of annual healthcare costs are associated with and may be attributable to how US companies manage their work force'.

At the time, 8% of annual healthcare costs amounted to $190 billion. According to the American Institute of Stress, a non-profit organisation that aims to educate the public on the topic of stress, stress costs the US economy more than $300 billion annually in absenteeism, staff turnover, diminished productivity and medical, legal and insurance costs.[34]

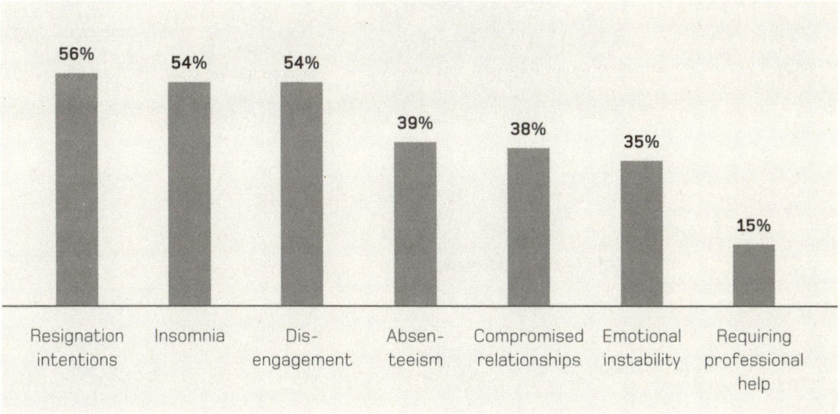

Typical employee responses to ongoing work stress

In a 2018 survey done by Wrike, a project management company with over two million clients around the world, it was shown that 94% of US employees report feeling stress at work[35] with a third experiencing high or extreme stress. According to the report, work stress has several negative outcomes that include resignation intentions, insomnia, absenteeism, fractured relationships, emotional volatility and disengagement.

Disengagement, whether triggered by stress or other factors is having a significant impact on the US fiscal landscape. According to a report entitled 'The State of the American Workplace', 70% of the American workforce is disengaged, costing the economy up to $550 billion every year. Stress and poor management practices are at the centre of this storm, but so too is the growing mental health burden.

According to the National Alliance of Mental Illness, 1 in 5 adults in the US experience mental illness. The most prevalent mental condition is anxiety

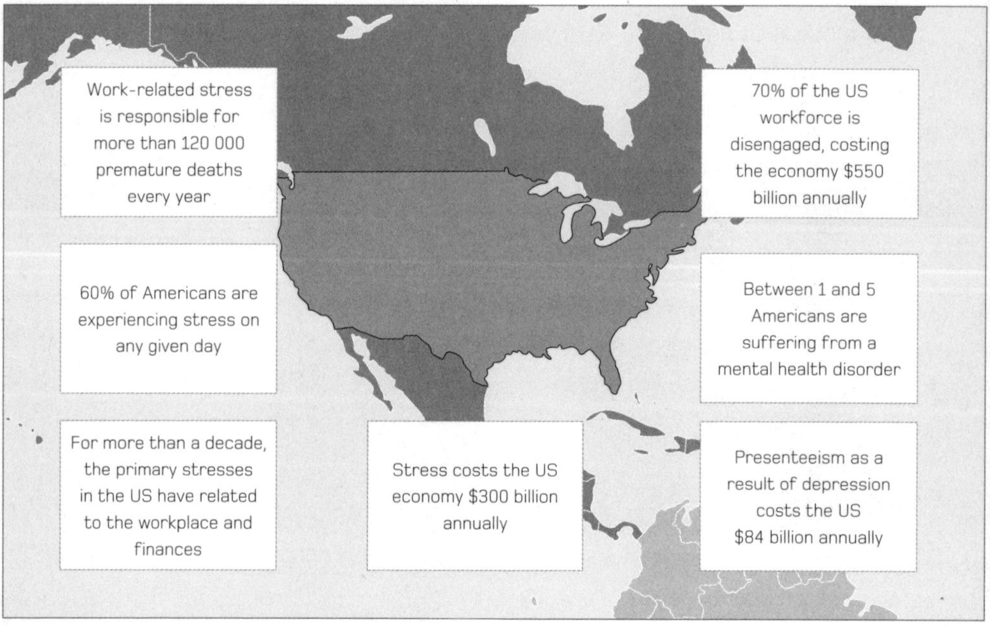

Health and economic burden of stress in the US

followed by depression and in a landmark study that examined the impact of depression on workplace productivity in eight diverse regions, found that presenteeism costs in the US exceed $84 billion annually, which equates to 0.5% of GDP.[36] These statistics are pre-COVID-19 and are likely to be significantly higher following the events of 2020.

SOUTH AFRICA – A NATION ON ITS KNEES

As the second most stressed nation on the planet, South Africans are all too familiar with chronic and relentless stress. For nearly two decades I have consulted to athletes, teams, high-performing groups, executives and businesses around the world on overcoming health and performance obstacles and the advancement of potential. The role has required a fair amount of travel; sometimes for days, sometimes months and even sometimes years on end, when on long-term contracts.

Landing at OR Tambo always filled me with a range of positive emotions and walking from the plane to customs always made me feel that I was returning to the place I belong and made me excited, knowing I was going to see my family and friends. Plus, there is nothing more welcoming than the South African accent!

As I went through customs there was always the personal race to the luggage carousel, even though I always ended up waiting for my bag. Nevertheless, it was part of the routine. Once my luggage was safely on a trolley, a different set of emotions started to emerge, largely driven by the general feeling of stress that saturated the building. Fortunately, my prevailing mood was still one of anticipation and excitement but by the time I walked into the arrivals hall, my excitement was merged with growing concerns over personal safety.

The walk from the arrivals hall to the car was predominantly a positive one and once in the car, and out of the airport building, the sense of belonging and elation to be home became overshadowed by the heartbreak at the scale of poverty and desperation on the faces of people on the street. I always found it really hard to reconcile the inequality and municipal neglect, especially when compared to places like Australia, New Zealand, Canada and some of the European states.

Walking through the front door resulted in the most conflicting emotions. There was a peace and safety that accompanied being in my own space, but it wouldn't last long. Within a few hours, I would hear about a scandal, a corruption fiasco, the high levels of crime, but mostly, the struggling socio-economic conditions. The streets were quiet, the restaurants only half full and the general mood was low. Within a few days, I would slot into the collective psyche of the country and get on with it, but in that time of adjustment I clearly saw the strain on the faces of the people, the economy and the nation that I love.

Stress in South Africa takes many shapes and forms, but its negative effects are clearly defined by the immense mental and physical health challenges that the nation faces. Witnessing extreme poverty on the daily drive to and from work, ongoing corruption scandals, repeated blows to the economy, rising unemployment, poor, sometimes non-existent, service delivery and an overriding feeling of anger among citizens are a few of the larger stress triggers.

Bloomberg rates South Africa as the second most stressed nation on the planet. Nigeria is rated as number 1.

These stresses are very real for all of us on some level and it appears that the world recognises the scale of stress that exists within our nation. Most especially after Bloomberg released a report in 2013[37] on the 'Most Stressed-Out: Countries'. The report was done in the middle of Jacob Zuma's controversial presidency and the ranking system was not simply a survey that set out to establish general public perceptions, but included a data set that was highly objective, taking into consideration seven equally weighted variables. This information included homicide rates, GDP per capita on a purchasing-power-parity basis, income inequality, corruption perception, unemployment, urban air pollution and life expectancy.

The information was drawn from organisations such as the UN, the IMF, Transparency International, the WHO and other highly respected agencies. South Africa was unfortunately ranked number 2 on the index out of a total of 74 countries. Not a list a country wants to be near the top of.

The unemployment calamity

According to Stats SA, the unemployment rate in the first quarter of 2020 was a staggering 30.1%. The 'Quarterly Labour Force Survey'[38] showed that there are more than 7 million unemployed people out of a potential workforce of 38 million. However, this doesn't factor in the 3 million discouraged work seekers, those who have given up trying to find a job, or the 13 million people who are not economically active. In simple terms, only a small percentage of people are able to put food on the table and pay taxes.

Moreover, annual GDP hasn't increased by more than 1.8% since 2013. In fact, annual GDP growth in 2018 was a mere 0.7% and in 2019 it was as low as 0.15%.[39] The first half of 2020 saw a 0.1% decline in GDP and by the middle of the year it plummeted to –17,1%.[40] Unemployment will likely further increase as economists say annual GDP must rise by 3% to 5% for a fairly protracted period of time in order for the unemployment rate to recede.

> Unemployment has devastating effects on mental and physical health. Businesses need to consider the heavy human and societal cost before embarking on this path.

South African businesses have been in a fight for survival and frantically engaged in large-scale restructuring, downsizing and retrenchments for a number of years, ie pre-COVID. Not only has this added to the current unemployment crisis and rising poverty, but it has also had catastrophic health consequences for those who have been retrenched and for those employees left behind manning the fort, who now work longer hours and have vastly expanded portfolios.

During 2009, in the throes of the previous global economic crisis, Kate Strully from the University of Albany published a research paper[41] on the health implications of job loss. In the study, she showed that job loss increases the odds of reporting poor physical health by 80% and developing new health conditions by 43%. Moreover, according to researchers from the School of Social Ecology at the University of California, retrenchment and unemployment increase the risk of developing depression by a staggering 200%.[42]

> Retrenchment can increase the risk of premature mortality by 100% in the year following the event.

Many South African employees are faced with the double-edged sword and are either facing burnout or retrenchment, ill health or depression. What's even more concerning in the South African professional landscape is that studies show that retrenchment has also been linked to an increased risk of dying prematurely, from all causes.

Swedish researchers discovered that unemployment can reduce life expectancy by approximately 44% following retrenchment.[43] In 2009 the *Quarterly Journal of Economics* published a study on job displacement and mortality[44] and discovered that for high seniority male workers, mortality rates in the year after retrenchment are as much as 100% higher than would otherwise have been expected. Simply put, if you hold a senior position in an organisation and suddenly lose your job, your risk of dying prematurely increases dramatically.

Retrenchment doesn't only impact those affected, but also those who have managed to hold onto their treasured positions. Job and employment insecurity is a major source of stress throughout the world and has significant health, psychological and proficiency implications.

Profit over people

Having been on the frontline with many employers and employees during the COVID-19 pandemic, I have witnessed the emergence of two very distinctive leadership styles. The first has been shareholder-centric and the other people-centric.

Shareholder-centric is about the preservation of company assets with finances being the central focus, to the exclusion of almost everything else. In order to achieve this, those businesses have rapidly implemented sweeping retrenchments, spending freezes, aggressive wage decreases as well as negotiated rental payment 'holidays' and new customer pricing. While this approach does ensure survival in the short term, the human price tag is immense. For those left behind, their connection between their daily work and the company's identity disintegrates. Moreover, the culture becomes slowly corroded as the workforce's purpose, values and beliefs are re-evaluated.

A year before the COVID-19 crisis, Jodi was recruited as head of HR for the 'trendiest' advertising firm in Johannesburg. The firm had had a hugely successful run for nearly a decade and had won numerous prestigious awards, both locally and abroad, and developed a very robust balance sheet along the way. It was Jodi's dream job and for the first year she loved the culture and identified with the 'cool' company vision. She became an all-star employee in a high-performing organisation. However, in April 2020 everything changed. The coronavirus and rolling lockdowns corroded an already fragile economy and the agency was no longer in the driver's seat and business was tough. Despite being in a financial position to weather a lengthy storm, management's decision was to protect their balance sheet and lay off a large portion of their staff. As head of HR, it was Jodi's role to oversee the lay-offs. It was the most difficult experience, witnessing husbands cry, single mothers break down and the fears and desperation in the faces of those affected. While Jodi retained her position, she could not reconcile the events and no longer identified with the company's purpose and mission. Although a consummate professional, Jodi disengaged and within days started looking for another job as her respect and admiration for the company had been replaced with contempt and distrust. Jodi's situation is one of millions played out in countless organisations throughout the world.

The people-centric approach is socially biased and leadership can begin the journey by showing their personal and the business's vulnerabilities. This gains tremendous support and trust among the workforce and an authentic connection among the staff. The second step is to secure funding, or tap into existing reserves, to ensure that as many staff as possible hold onto their positions, albeit at slightly lower salaries. The next action piece entails strong customer price negotiations and rental payment holidays. This is overlaid by dynamic operational planning and improved communication to ensure that remote working environments are as productive as possible. The last step involves a commitment to the growth of digitalisation in the key areas that could benefit.

This people-centric approach has a positive overflow to organisational culture as it shows that the leadership and decision makers have the courage to take informed risks, an openness to embrace stretch missions as well as a high degree of integrity. Moreover, it demonstrates a strong personal accountability (ie looking at the best interests of those who form part of the greater whole) and shows the value of teamwork and the ability to be agile.

Shayne and his two brothers run a successful media and large events business that had been growing exponentially prior to the South African lockdown. Because business was booming, they had taken on a large team of specialists to service their local and international projects. However, unbeknown to them, and like many businesses around the world, their business model, plans and aspirations were going to come to an abrupt end.

The South African lockdown and fears of infection resulted in an immediate termination of all their existing contracts, with no exception. They were left without a business and a large team to support, not to mention hefty overheads. Within days, they communicated their current vulnerabilities and challenges to the entire team as a collective as well as on an individual basis.

The consensus was to press on, with the understanding that they would all have to take a 50% salary cut for two months and then 30% for a further two months, with no exceptions. Although there was no end in sight, the brothers decided to access all their existing financial reserves and continue for as long as possible, hoping for new opportunities to appear sooner rather than later. Amazingly, they had the full support of every team member in the struggle and were completely united.

Because they had an existing bond on their premises, the next action step was to negotiate with the bank for payment leniencies for as long as possible. Looking forward, the dynamic leaders reinvented their offerings and used their historic personal relationships with big corporates to open doors to new ideas and offerings, albeit at a reduced cost. They managed to get on their feet again and their team was full of support and overflowing encouragement.

As tech aficionados, they kept their eyes open to new opportunities and ideas that could help them overcome the limitations of the time. This passion culminated in their discovery of an online communication platform that, from a functionality and user interface perspective, superseded anything that was currently available in the space. Essentially, they had found a way of simulating a live event experience through a digital platform. They were officially back in business but this time was different. Unlike before, there were no limitations based on geographical region – it was truly a global operation.

They had achieved the impossible, while at the same time living up to the moral responsibility to the people in their care. Remarkably, only one person left the business.

Increasing demands on South African professionals

The recent urgency to downsize and need for restructuring within organisations has resulted in fewer employees manning the organisational ship. But the rules of business practice have changed as the market simply doesn't tolerate outdated or complacent operating models. The relentless drive to be more competitive, more innovative and offer better goods and services is on the shoulders of an exhausted few. This translates into greater demands and extended working hours, essentially creating the perfect conditions for burn-out and mental health compromise.

> Long working hours impact our health and well-being on many levels. Not only is it physically and emotionally exhausting but it also limits our ability to properly manage our lives in a way that promotes our intrinsic potential.

Longer working hours not only detract from living and developing in your personal life and interests, but as has been shown, also causes tremendous stress and jeopardises health.

In 2015 a large team of researchers from various European states performed an extensive meta-analysis on the effects of long working hours on cardiovascular health and stroke risk.[45] The analysis included 25 studies involving 603 838 men and women from around the world who were healthy at the outset of the analysis. What the researchers found was that when compared to working the average 35 to 40 hours a week, those individuals who worked 55 hours a week or more, had a 13% higher risk of developing cardiovascular disease and a staggering 33% higher risk of a stroke event. Another overall analysis of 18 studies of 189 729 people from 35 countries[46] also showed an elevated risk of developing depression when working more than 55 hours.

It is important to consider that long working hours does more than merely impact cardiovascular health. The large disruption in work-life balance, utter exhaustion, no time to exercise, the higher demand for convenience foods, the strong attraction to stimulants like caffeine and sugar, added to the emotional distress will collectively place the stress axis into a state of overdrive. This opens the door to a wide variety of physical and mental ailments, which will further amplify existing stresses.

The challenge we all face, no matter where you live and work in the world, is that 35- to 40-hour working weeks have all but disappeared. While you may not necessarily be spending more than 40 hours a week in the office per se, there is a professional expectation of 24-hour availability, seven days a week. In fact, it is considered absurd to create personal boundaries in many industries in the professional world. Innovation and technology have connected global markets, removed all borders and provided opportunities that were previously unavailable and while we all have 24-hour access to global markets, service providers, clients and colleagues, being 'always-on' comes at a price – exhaustion and physical health compromise.

What is being felt on the ground in South Africa?

In recent years, Profmed, a restricted medical aid scheme for professionals who have obtained a tertiary qualification and relevant professional experience, has produced an annual stress index report evaluating the health landscape among graduate professionals within a range of respected fields.[47] The report involves a survey of over 2 000 members that looks at stress, mental health, coping skills, medication habits, together with other perceived wellness data.

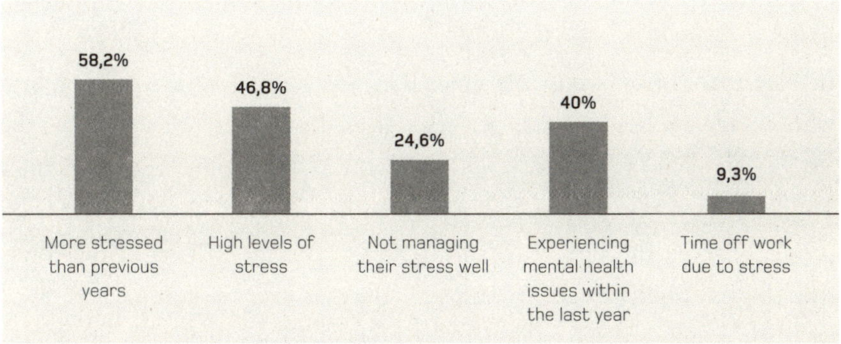

2018 stress landscape among South African professionals

According to its 2018 survey, almost half of the respondents reported high or very high levels of stress and among this highly educated group, 1 in 4 were not handling their stress. The report showed that almost 10% of the group needed to take time off work due to significant stress-related health issues. Mental health also featured prominently with about 40% of those surveyed stating that they had experienced either depression or anxiety within the survey year.

This snapshot of the level of stress among South Africa's brightest professionals is very much a reflection of the steady rise of negative sentiment within the country, regardless of education, economic or social circumstances.

The last 18 months have shown a profound shift in the well-being of many of the country's foremost leaders and decision makers in business. Some of the sessions I have had with leaders feel scripted at times, with the conversation typically starting off with a few pleasantries and then launching into a commentary on how bad things are from a socio-economic standpoint and the accelerating downward trajectory. Once this narrative has concluded, attention then turns to a discussion about the participants' growing set of physical and mental health ailments. This discussion is an important part of the resilience and performance journey, but in previous years the negative commentary was less frequent and interspersed with positivity and optimism.

In May 2020, Ipsos Group SA, a global market research and consulting firm with worldwide headquarters in Paris, released a report, 'What Worries the World'.[48] The report was based on a monthly survey of almost 20 000 people between the ages of 16 and 64 in 27 countries. Many of the countries showed similar trends in terms of concerns over the coronavirus, fiscal well-being, political uncertainties, growing social inequality, rising unemployment, crime and questions around healthcare. The researchers performed an inter-country comparison as to whether or not people thought that their country was going in the right direction as a nation and an economy.

60% of South Africans are currently concerned about unemployment.

According to the survey, South Africans were some of the most negative in the world with 59% of the population experiencing pessimism about their future and believe that we are headed in the wrong direction as a nation. Also, when measured against the other countries in the report, South Africa shows some of the highest levels of distress over unemployment and what the financial future holds, with almost two out of three people feeling apprehensive in this space.

When evaluating this sentiment through less subjective measures such as surveys, the Misery Index, an economic indicator created by economist Arthur Okun, is probably the most representative analysis currently available. The index helps determine how the average citizen is coping economically (which is a strong predictor of their emotional well-being) and it is calculated by adding the seasonally adjusted unemployment rate to the annual rate of inflation. It is assumed that both a higher rate of unemployment and worsening inflation create economic and social costs for any country.

In July 2020, the index evaluated 60 countries around the world, including those countries with only robust economic data such as countries in the eurozone, China, Japan, Singapore, Turkey, Thailand, the US and UK. Based on the narrative around the high rate of unemployment and chronic stress that currently exists within South Africa, it should come as no surprise that we are

Health and economic burden in South Africa

ranked number 3 in the world. I would far rather our soccer and cricket teams ranked as high as 2 and 3 than our stress and misery indicators. We need only look at the mental health statistics in our country to acknowledge the impact of stress and the correlation between stress and the misery indicators.

MENTAL HEALTH IN SOUTH AFRICA

According to the South African Depression and Anxiety Group (SADAG) as many as 1 in 6 South Africans suffer from anxiety, depression or some sort of addiction issue. What is most concerning is that this statistic excludes some of the more severe mental health issues such as bipolar disorder and schizophrenia.

1 in 6 South Africans suffers from anxiety, depression or addiction.

It is widely believed that the limited access to specialist practitioners, properly equipped medical facilities and a stigma surrounding mental health, especially within the rural communities, are dramatically affecting these statistics, which are believed to be far higher; possibly reflecting the numbers seen within the corporate mental health landscape. With such a high prevalence of common mental disorders and limited access to treatment, many local health agencies are calling the situation a 'national crisis'.

In 2016 the *International Journal of Depression and Anxiety* published a study on the prevalence of depression in the South African workplace.[49] Depression is profoundly impactful on a personal, relationship and professional level and not only has a significant impact on those affected, but also on family members, friends and colleagues. Studies like this, provide businesses with invaluable information that can be used not only to improve the

Depression is a condition characterised by low mood, feelings of hopelessness, loss of interest (in practically everything), feelings of low self-worth, irritability, fatigue, little to no motivation and impaired focus and concentration.

lives and well-being of their employees and their families, but also enhance productivity and organisational growth.

In recent years there has been a huge investment into understanding depression within corporate environments due to the fact that when compared to many other health conditions, depression may have the greatest impact on productivity, overall time management and organisational success.[50]

The *International Journal of Depression and Anxiety* study, entitled 'Depression and the Impact on Productivity in the Workplace: Findings from a South African Survey on Depression in the Workplace', focused on addressing the gap in the research in terms of basic data for assessing the burden and impact that depression has in the South African workplace. Another objective of the paper was to better quantify some of the established connections between depression, cognitive dysfunction, absenteeism and presenteeism. Of the 1061 respondents, 26.2% had been previously diagnosed, by a trained medical professional, with depression.

As high as this figure is, in some organisations 1 in 4 may still lean towards the conservative end. Over the last few years, I've gathered vast amounts of data on employee health and stress in order to create and enable strategic direction for businesses' wellness visions. Using standardised depression assessments and other mental health metrics, my findings show that depression levels within many of South Africa's leading companies ranges from 20% to 37% and mental health compromise indicators from 40% to as high as 53%. These indicators reflect a specific set of stresses at high levels that are known to trigger worry, anxiety, low mood and other mental health challenges.

The study also pointed out that in small (up to 49 employees) and medium-size organisations (50–249 employees), depression rates appear to be significantly higher than larger institutions (>250 employees). Additionally, depression rates are higher in females as well as in individuals over 45 and employees experiencing depression are likely to be absent from work for between 13.2 to 21.5 days every year.

Depression is associated with a 50% self-related decline in performance and competency.

Presenteeism is arguably the most destructive consequence of depression within an organisational and professional context. Among respondents who continued to work during their last experience of depression, the average rating of job performance was significantly lower when compared to a depression-free period. Depressed employees typically rated their professional competency, on average, as a 5 out of 10 when measured against their own personal and the organisational expectations.

Common symptoms of presenteeism include a higher frequency of errors, trouble concentrating, crying or aggressive outbursts with little provocation, indecisiveness, forgetfulness and difficulty in planning.

When presenteeism happens to a handful of individuals, the impact on a business's dynamism and productivity will be fairly low, but if 1 in 4 employees are feeling this way, it is impossible for any company to thrive during this time of market hyper-competitiveness and volatility. A team of indecisive lawyers, a tearful sales force, a careless surgeon or forgetful lecturers will struggle to move our embattled economy forward, let alone the nation, and as a result, presenteeism is costing the South African economy and businesses $14.8 billion annually.

In 2020 I worked closely with a team of highly intelligent and capable lawyers. One of the stars of the group was an outgoing and social woman in her early 30s. She loved what she did and was brilliant at it. She would often get called upon to address incompetencies, create solutions where none seemed possible and she always knew where to find opportunity amid the chaos. She was a huge asset to the firm and to everyone around her.

While she was relatively unaffected by the initial stages of the South African lockdown, as time went by there was a noticeable decline in her mood and appreciable changes in her behaviour. The personal disconnect from friends and family members was taking its toll and, eight weeks into the lockdown, the early signs of depression began to emerge. At first she experienced low mood and little motivation and then complained of constant fatigue and irritability, together with complete disinterest in work. She spent more time avoiding professional responsibilities than actively engaging in them.

Poor concentration, overlaid with forgetfulness, severely hampered her work and basic errors became all too common. She would reply more than once to the same email and frequently forgot about scheduled meetings and conference calls. From being one of the most organised and efficient people, she became increasingly underprepared as she struggled to plan ahead. Although her level of depression was considered mild and had not overtly affected her personal relationships, the impact on her work had become significant. Her assumption was that it was simply a vitamin deficiency, hormonal imbalance or rare health issue which required extensive blood tests.

However, once we took an objective view of her current cluster of physical symptoms and her uncharacteristic behavioural changes, it exposed her existing emotional struggles and the fact that she needed professional help. Through reflection, greater awareness, support and guidance by a trained professional, within a matter of weeks, she was back to her old dynamic self.

Prior to the coronavirus pandemic many, if not most, South African businesses did not fully comprehend the current mental health burden, nor were they equipped to handle the enormity of the situation. Following the events of 2020, the mental health landscape has become even more volatile and unless urgent and deliberate action is taken by the private sector and government, the situation is likely to impact lives and the economy for many years to come.

4

THE ACTION PLAN

A few years ago, I worked with the iconic tennis player, Maria Sharapova. One of the most ambitious and driven people I have ever met, her drive transcended the sport of tennis and she had become a highly respected entrepreneur and business mentor.

When we first started working together, she asked me a string of questions pertaining to her personal health and future performance. I responded by saying that if she had asked me those questions 20 years ago, I could have answered quickly and definitively. But through the acquisition of knowledge, and an additional two decades of experience, comes the realisation of the infinite possibilities and complexity in every situation. I no longer had a short answer for her, but instead could paint several scenarios related to each of her concerns and with that provide modifiable success strategies.

We live in a time of unprecedented complexity. How do we as leaders, decision makers, managers, parents, spouses and community members positively impact the lives of those within our sphere of influence, not to mention those in our care?

As was the case with Maria, the answer is not simple and in many ways far more complex, and the road is not easy, but the rewards from a business, personal and societal level will far exceed the efforts.

The famous Chinese proverb, 'A journey of a thousand miles begins with a single step', holds true as much now as it did before. The only difference is that amid the uncertainty, volatility, fears, stresses, worries, vulnerabilities and ambiguity it is not enough to merely begin a process, you have to have a vision and a plan.

The goals and objectives are simple, ie to improve lives, bring human potential to life and secure a professional advantage. The process and way this is achieved, resembles the multiple adaptable scenarios that I communicated to Maria on that warm summer's day in Los Angeles.

Yet within each of these possibilities for success and positive change, lies fundamental truths and governing principles. Many of these are based on ownership of our personal responsibilities to reduce the burden of stress on the people whose lives and destinies are inextricably linked to our own. This chapter provides the framework for personal, organisational and ultimately, societal change.

ACKNOWLEDGE YOUR ROLE

We typically delegate important aspects of our well-being to four institutions: business for our fiscal well-being; government for our security (in all domains); the media for information and knowledge; and NGOs to address social causes and complex societal issues.

Edelman, a global communications firm that partners with businesses and organisations to evolve, promote and protect their brands and reputations has studied dynamic shifts in trust for more than 20 years. The group asserts that trust defines an organisation's licence to operate, lead and succeed, and that it is the ultimate currency in all relationships.

Edelman has been involved in extensive research in this space and publishes a comprehensive annual report on the topic. Their research has involved more than 2 million respondents from over 400 companies. Moreover, it encompasses more than 80 000 employee reviews and detailed interviews with well over 50 leading CEOs.

Their 2020 report, released at the World Economic Forum in Davos,[1] showed that society's trust in governments, the media and NGOs is at one of the lowest points in recorded history, causing widespread fear and tremendous insecurity in an already frenzied world. It also revealed that the last remaining trust sanctuary is in the workplace, where 76% of employees still feel that they have an institution looking out for their best interests.

> Employees have handed their trust to managers, leaders and decision makers and it is important for them to safeguard that trust, and those employees, to the best of their ability.

As a leader, decision maker or manager this level of trust might not be what you signed up for, but it is an incredible gift. CEOs and management teams are no longer solely assigned the role of steering the company in a direction of survival, competitiveness and profitability, but also in safeguarding the lives and well-being of those members that form part of it.

Today's leaders have been designated a more expansive role that requires not only responsiveness to industry issues, but also leadership pertaining to political events, national challenges and employee wellness. More than three-quarters of an organisation expects this of its leadership team and not just sporadically, but all the time.

> Modern leadership requires responsiveness to:
> - Business and industry issues
> - Political events
> - National challenges
> - Employee health and wellness

Over and above the traditional day-to-day business challenges (ie market changes, restructuring, increased demands for competitiveness, increased automation, rapid skills recalibration) your team is grappling with an overwhelming sense of uncertainty about their future.

> Your thoughts become your words, your words become your actions and your actions shape your future'.

Research done in 2019 showed that 31% of South Africans believe that they will not be better off in five years. It should come as no surprise that, according to Sable International, 25 000 highly skilled people are leaving our shores every year.[2]

Considering the events of 2020, this percentage will be dramatically higher. Uncertainty, insecurity and a lack of control result in significant stress, and if not effectively managed, will lead to an increased prevalence of mental and physical health issues as well as a decline in productivity, innovation and creativity. Research has repeatedly shown that negative perceptions materialise in negative realities in almost every sphere of life.

Knowing this, leaders and management teams need to constantly set their own challenges aside and work tirelessly to try and provide an environment that radiates optimism, enthusiasm and, most importantly, trust.

Trust in others, trust in self and belief in the company ethos and value set is central to future success. More than ever it is a responsibility that has a direct bearing on organisational success.

> Trust in others, trust in self and belief in the company ethos is central to success in the future.

Modern leadership demands that we assume new responsibilities and a widely expanded role. Due to the complexity and the substantial increase in demands, there are several checklists that will simplify and solidify your journey.

My 'role and responsibilities' checklist

Project optimism	Be enthusiastic	Put trust in your team	Promote trust within the workforce	Project self-belief and confidence	Show firm belief and alignment in the company's values

LOOKING FOR LEADERSHIP

In 2016 *Forbes* magazine published an article comparing leaders to mangers within the context of their roles and value to the company.[3] While both are critical to organisational and team success, their functions differ and are complementary.

Leaders are fundamentally change agents. They are able to create a new vision, are prepared to take calculated risks, are always looking at long-term outcomes (sometimes at the expense of short term ones), are constantly striving towards building and expanding professional relationships and have a strong commitment to developing new skills and expanding their own thinking, as well as the organisation's.

In essence, leadership builds new systems or radically transforms old ones, often taking the business, and themselves, into new and unknown territory and are comfortable in doing so.

Managers, by contrast, will happily trade the notion of change or innovation for concrete goals and concrete outcomes. They work tirelessly to achieve both their own objectives and those of the organisation's. Managers are hugely successful at augmenting existing operational models

GREAT LEADERS:

- Are change agents
- Are visionaries
- Do not fear failure
- Are non-conformists
- Have their own unique brand
- Have big and distant goals
- Are focused on new learnings
- Have expanded thinking

GREAT MANAGERS:

- Enhance and grow existing systems
- Are strong goal setters
- Are risk averse
- Do not like to fail
- Are more conformist
- Can fit into existing cultures
- Focus on short and medium-term goals
- Prefer to refine and enhance existing skills

through ongoing improvements and by promoting refinements. Managers are intrinsically cautious and risk-averse. They tend to focus more on short and medium-term goals by setting milestones and monitoring core metrics. Managers are able to strongly focus on the people around them and assist them in achieving their goals and objectives. Lastly, managers will place tremendous emphasis on refinement and perfection of their existing skills as opposed to the acquisition of new ones.

In essence, managers makes a system work and help it to do what it does well.

The expanded portfolio

With exponential change being the only certainty in life, the need for leadership is becoming increasingly more apparent within every business or institution. Leaders must consider that the people in their care expect more from them today than in previous years.

Research shows that more than three-quarters of employees want leaders to act decisively and proactively on key issues that have a direct bearing on their lives and well-being. These issues include core diversity and inclusion precepts such as ensuring equal pay, rooting out discrimination and prejudice, rooting out sexual harassment and strong initiatives to future-proof skills. This is a set that falls comfortably within any modern corporate leadership mandate.

> Modern leaders are expected to act decisively and proactively to issues such as:
> - Diversity and inclusion
> - Health
> - Environmental issues
> - Personal data security
> - Screening of fake news

But this is only part of a leader's role. Business and industry leaders of the future will also be responsible for tackling key health and environmental issues, providing a safe space for employees' personal data and screening fake news.

Changing the script

With all the economic uncertainties that currently exist, companies are no longer able to provide the same degree of job security or much-needed stability to their employees. The knee-jerk reaction of employees (whether consciously or unconsciously) is to be less engaged within their roles and to show less overall commitment to the organisation. In many respects, this does make sense as we can all appreciate how challenging it is to be committed and invested in something that may not exist tomorrow.

> Today's leaders will need to rewrite the long-standing psychological contract between employees and employers.

The impact of this breakdown in the employer-employee psychological contract will invariably impact survival, growth, innovation potential and productivity, not to mention employee health and well-being. Knowing this, it is imperative that today's leaders rewrite the fragile psychological contract that has existed for the last 80 years.

I have always been drawn to achievers, leaders and innovators across all walks of life, as to what makes them so successful, how they achieved what others couldn't and saw what others didn't. This was brought home after being privy to a conversation a few years ago between two successful tennis coaches who were discussing their approaches to developing talent. One of the coaches believed that to create successful athletes or teams, you must look at the best player or team within the current era, and work to emulate their unique set of skills and abilities. His rationale was that those players are at the top because of their differences.

The other coach held a very different opinion and wasn't holding back in expressing it. He believed that to create champions you must not look at what separates the team or individual at the top, but rather at the collective set of skills and traits that all the top players and teams possess. So instead of looking at the world number 1 tennis player and trying to recreate their unique skills in aspiring players, rather take an overview of the top 10 tennis players in the world at the time, look at what they all have in common and create a working model that focuses on developing those core skills.

I completely subscribe to the second coach's viewpoint on the collective approach and it is the reason why I endeavour to listen to the ideas and opinions of industry leaders and form my working model on the basis of the collective sentiment. Many times, engaging with industry giants, forces you to relook at the way you are approaching your business and your offering. It helps you to be more objective and, when called for, more critical. Experience has taught me that the growth point comes from listening and not speaking. Fortunately, my nature is to listen and to limit speaking to selected moments.

A few years ago, I was fortunate enough to spend some one-on-one time with a highly respected leadership coach. She was consulting to every major company at the time, was highly intelligent, communicated well and commanded respect. During one of our conversations, I asked her what it takes to be a great leader and without any hesitation, she replied, 'You have to know yourself.'

This really resonated and has always stuck with me. At the same time, having worked with some of the world's foremost CEOs and most iconic athletes, I have picked up on an extra gear that they possess. An unseen commonality or superpower that I try to apply to my own life, and one that has been incredibly successful for me.

Great leaders know people and truly value them. Our success is almost always linked to the role others play in our lives (despite what we sometimes think). A business's success is not partially attributed, but rather solely attributed, to their employees' wellness and happiness.

> Great leaders know people and truly value them. A business's success is directly attributed to the wellness and happiness of their employees.

A leader and their team share a common vision (with a few exceptions) and as a leader and decision maker, you require greater productivity to move the business forward and at the same time your employees want to be more productive. You need greater engagement in the business while at the same time your team wants to be more engaged and motivated at work. Every business wishes to reduce presenteeism and absenteeism and, again, there is a synergy as employees and contract workers want to be healthier and more functional. They don't choose to be stressed and unwell and will avoid being in this state. This shared vision can be built on and reignited by rewriting the fragmented psychological contract between employers and employees.

Several months into the 2020 lockdown, I received a call from a good friend of mine, Rob, who needed some advice. He was struggling with his role at work and it was impacting him both emotionally and physically. This took me by surprise as Rob is usually very positive, can make any situation work and always saw the best in people.

He took on his new role a year after a long wooing process. He holds a senior position and runs a division central to the business's growth and innovation agenda. When he started in his position, he felt that he had a seat at the table, so to speak, and that his views and inputs were respected, valued and considered by the organisation's leadership. He felt empowered and inspired to put in countless extra hours, even at the expense of his personal and family life. His motivation was to create a name for himself by unlocking the business's intrinsic potential. Rob took on countless additional responsibilities with the intention of building and securing a long-term relationship with this multinational company.

Like so many professional relationships it started well, which strongly motivated him to make a difference. As the months passed, the facades disappeared and the egos appeared and he found the environment became more challenging to work in. Rob described the mood in the office as constantly sombre and oozed negativity. Moreover, he discovered that the workforce was divided into factions who did not engage, speak or tolerate each other. Rob, the consummate peacemaker, assumed that it was typical office politics amplified by the challenges at the time and made every effort to rebuild relationships and bring the different factions together. But as hard as he tried, the divide was too great and leadership had no desire to intervene. Eventually, he gave up on the idea and focused on his work.

Rob is forward-thinking and innovative and he proposed new strategies for growth in the company, which were vital for the business's survival in the challenging times. Without fail, every idea he had or suggestion he made fell on deaf ears and was shot down and rejected by management without justification or explanation. Rob soon realised that he had a designated space with narrow parameters and the expectation was that he not step out of these confines. No matter how Rob approached the leadership, his ideas, views and change vision were always a non-starter.

The frustration for Rob, and the entire workforce, was that problems needed to be solved for the company to remain competitive and stay in business – their jobs depended on it. Yet, the MD and his management coalition clung tightly to historic policy and personal agendas and the environment became overtly authoritarian and egocentric.

After a few more months, Rob found it increasingly difficult to be productive in his job. From being able to comfortably handle many projects simultaneously, he struggled to manage the bare minimum. His motivation trickled down to a stream and there were days where he didn't do anything on the work front. Unfortunately, it was not only his work that was affected, but his mental well-being and self-esteem too. He was experiencing mild depression, something he had never experienced before.

The more he unpacked office events and described the circumstances he was working under, the more apparent it became how it was a case of appalling leadership. And the reason this was not apparent at the outset was because the global economy was yet to be affected by the coronavirus pandemic and so the company's leadership were not under the same pressure.

The truest measure of a leader, a person or an institution is not how they treat people when things are running smoothly, but rather how they treat people when circumstances are difficult and the challenges are great. Rob found himself in a position where passion, productivity, engagement and health can be eroded and dreams destroyed. He started going for therapy and took on many positive lifestyle practices that have helped him deal with his stress on an emotional and physical level. Shortly after our conversation, he started the process of looking for a new job.

This authoritarian version of leadership will not be tolerated going forward by society or a business's stakeholders. Leaders have to stand tall in way that they haven't had to before. Role models such as Nelson Mandela, Mahatma Gandhi and Martin Luther King Jr have shown us the path to greatness and that exceptional leadership is not centred on ego, authority and personal agendas, but rather a selfless commitment to others and the values you represent. The role requires that you create the change everyone so desperately needs.

In order to create this change, leaders have to address four key areas so as to rewrite this critical psychological contract that has been corroded by the recent monumental shifts in our society. They need to lead the change, empower their people, solve problems and regardless of their title, be a CEO.

Rewrite the script

- Lead
- Solve
- Empower
- Assume responsibility

Lead

Leading change begins with a journey into yourself. The leadership coach I spoke to, knew the value of this and built her entire career based on this critical ethos. A central part of being an agent of positive change requires you to be aspirational to the people you lead. This demands that you embody and represent your vision that encompasses positive behaviours and lifestyle practices, both solidified by a strong commitment to growth, ongoing improvement and the actualisation of your own potential. This has a powerful spillover effect that will spread to the organisation and to your teams.

But like all things that contain inherent value, this spillover of ideals, values and vision won't happen overnight. Inspiration has a life of its own and will filter through the organisation organically and at its own pace. We are strongly influenced by the people around us, both positively and negatively, which is why leaders have to set not only the precedent, but also the bar in creating a culture that nurtures potential and aspires to achieve greatness.

Leadership through crisis:

- **Decide with speed and conviction**
  (even at the expense of precision). Embrace action and don't punish mistakes. As the saying goes: 'Failure to act is worse than failure itself'.
- **Adapt quickly**
  What worked yesterday is unlikely to be relevant going forward, especially today. Capture inputs from diverse sources and incorporate technology where possible.
- **Take ownership**
  This includes self-care, the establishment of organisational performance metrics and a focus on only core priorities.
- **Amplify positivity**
  All accomplishments (no matter how big or small), acts of kindness, care and empathy and hurdles that have been overcome should be recognised. This promotes connection within your team and keeps everyone engaged and inspired.

Communication through regular meetings, talks, emails, podcasts and video feeds is powerful, but there is an inherent limitation to this and that is the question of authenticity. The most credible form of communication, whether it is promoting a new agenda, outlining a future strategy or illumination of an unfolding vision, is leading by example and the promotion of consistency.

When you and your team live and embody the change you are pursuing for the business, it overshadows every email, any number of conferences, team-building off site or webinars. It dispels any questions of authenticity, integrity and potential lip service. Actions have always spoken louder than words, and because humanity is being confronted with some of the greatest challenges it has ever had to face in recorded history, it is the only thing that counts.

Several years ago, I ran a wellness initiative for a multinational company. The CEO and his immediate team were very progressive and future-orientated and took every possible step to gain market share and grow the business by fully utilising technology, embracing innovation and making full use of the gig economy by hiring specialists for short tenures.

Their vision was clear, deliberate and had urgency. Realising the value of employee health in productivity as well as the value of wellness programmes in attracting talent, they put together one of the best employee health programmes in the industry.

However, as perfect as everything was on paper, there was one fundamental oversight; the CEO did not embody his vision. He didn't eat healthily, exercise or manage his stress well. While he encouraged his teams to engage and participate in the programme, they did so reluctantly and with suspicion. Interestingly enough, only one member within his coalition came on board with the programme and lost 16 kilograms of excess weight in the process.

> Words inspire actions, but only actions can create change. Don't underestimate your power as a role model.

After suffering from ongoing health issues, the CEO finally began to participate in the programme (about eight months in) and the company finally began to embrace the vision, and within a matter of months there was a steep upturn in productivity and overall positivity. With this momentum, the wellness initiative became so successful that it received accolades within the broader international group and local business community.

The moral of the story is that words do inspire actions, but only actions can create change.

The connection factor

Leading a business, team, group or even a family requires more than being aspirational, the personification of the change vision and the ability to inspire the people around you. It also demands genuine connection. Regular pulse checks and compassionate personal engagements create resilience, unity and trust. But reaching out can, and should not be, robotic or formulaic, but rather something that is personal, sincere, compassionate and empathetic. When leaders are in the trenches with their employees and attempt to understand them, it gives people tremendous comfort and hope.

Finally, as part of the mandate to support, guide and enhance the lives of those within your sphere of influence there has to be an additional focus – mitigating the stress and demands of the challenges that lie ahead. In other words, future-proofing. By continually investing in growing support networks, coaching (group or individual), skills development, self-care, as well as overall health education, you will be able to create significant change that transcends your organisation and that has the potential to shape the lives of future generations.

My 'deliverables' checklist

- Lead by example
- Be aspirational
- Be authentic
- Create a forum for personal interactions
- Be compassionate and empathetic
- Invest in growth and the future
- Sincerely commit to the well-being of others

Empower your people

Monumental changes and shifts in the world have changed the way we live, learn, relate to one another and work. In many respects, these changes have eroded communities and even some family units, replacing these support structures with virtual or disconnected worlds bombarded by social media and fake news. Millions of people feel sidelined, underappreciated, and even inadequate, in both their professional and personal lives. If you are not portraying success, (notwithstanding a once-in-a-century crisis), hyper-intelligence, above-average attractiveness, wealth or another socially impressive characteristic, no one seems to take notice. Or so it appears.

The pressure on the younger generations is unremitting and not sustainable in the long term. Central to everyone's well-being is a sense of purpose and being valued by those around us. A leader's role is to reignite an individual's sense of purpose, self-worth and value, not only within their immediate circle (professional, family and friends) but within their entire sphere of influence.

> A modern leader's role is to ignite purpose, self-worth and a sense of personal value within every member of their team.

To achieve this will require that opportunities be created for shared action to take place. Your team needs a voice, they need a forum to impart their views and experiences and most importantly, they need to feel that their contribution to the organisation they trust and respect matters.

My 'empowerment' checklist

Create opportunities for shared action	Give your team a voice and say in the decisions that influence their lives	Create a platform for your team to contribute beyond their immediate role

Solve problems

While business leaders and decision makers have broader societal responsibilities that include environmental and social issues, it is important to consider that problem-solving has to begin within your immediate environment.

I recently heard a powerful anecdote told by a community leader that perfectly encapsulates this level of responsibility. The leader described that for years he had been trying to change the world but with little success. Eventually, he decided to focus his passion and efforts on the social and societal issues that existed within his own country. Again, over time, his efforts showed limited success. He then decided to invest his time and energy into his own city and local community. Again, despite his best effort, success was not forthcoming. He then decided to invest in creating positive influence and change within his wide circle of friends, but again, no measurable change followed. Still passionate and believing in his dreams for a better world he decided to try and positively influence and change his close family. Again, this yielded no results.

Upon reflection, he finally came to the realisation that the only person he could change was himself, so that's what he did. He transformed himself and became the expression of everything he believed in and shortly after, his family followed suit, as did his friends, the local community, the country and eventually the world!

To be championing outside causes and values while your own organisation or team is in crisis, is inappropriate and misplaced and can even cause resentment and animosity. A strong commitment to problem-solving within your business not only facilitates a better working environment, but also builds significant trust. Challenges and obstacles will always exist in life and in every business, regardless of size, location or sector. Whether these ongoing challenges have a negative or positive impact on the organisation and its workforce depends on the commitment, speed and effectiveness of its leadership in dealing with difficulties.

> Many times the obstacles and challenges we face in life have a positive outcome and act as a vehicle for growth and positive transformation. Whether or not these difficulties have a positive or negative impact on the workforce depends largely on the commitment, speed and effectiveness of leadership in resolving difficulties.

A business culture where management is rapidly mobilised when challenges arise, can provide a secure and motivating business environment. The difficulties we are confronted with are often the catalyst to our greatest successes, on the condition that we confront them and are prepared to learn from the experience.

One of the greatest leaders and problem solvers I have met is a restaurateur by the name of Paulo. For decades Paulo has run one of the most successful Italian restaurants in Johannesburg with regular patrons including South Africa's business elite, government officials, sports stars and local celebrities.

One evening, pre-COVID-19, while eating at his restaurant, Paulo sat down with my wife and I and chatted about the nature of the hospitality industry and its challenges. One of Paulo's admirable qualities and the way he leads is that if a customer complains about any aspect of their meal, it will be replaced, regardless of the circumstances.

Every night, Paulo and his highly capable team rapidly address the night's challenges. This made me wonder whether there are customers who abuse Paulo's model (ie order incorrectly or change their mind once their meal arrives) so I put my question to Paulo. He smiled and his response is now ingrained in my own professional model. He said that the cost of replacing a meal versus the cost associated with a broken relationship cannot be compared. He saw these issues as an opportunity to build trust and solidify a connection with his clients.

Paulo also runs and operates some of the best corporate canteens in the country, servicing thousands of customers every day. His business was so successful it was recently bought by one of South Africa's largest listed companies. The opportunities Paulo created for himself have been through his work ethos where building relationships and dealing with challenges is central to his business philosophy.

With the unprecedented changes taking place in the world and rise in uncertainty, fears and insecurities of every kind, a great leader's problem-solving mandate will need to extend beyond only their people and to the families and the local community in which the business operates. The new psychological employer-employee contract rewards leaders that extend themselves and their management teams to uplift the socio-economic conditions of their operational region. This is especially important for developing nations like South

Africa where so many communities are heavily disadvantaged.

Not only is betterment of the broader community a moral and social responsibility amid the growing poverty and financial uncertainty, it also gains valuable community support and promotes connection. In a world that has become increasingly detached, fragmented and insular, it is these actions that promote unity, create a shared identity and build trust and mutual protection.

My 'problem-solving' checklist

Commit all leadership to problem-solving within the business	Be available to help your teams overcome the challenges and issues they face	Tackle challenges with urgency and speed	Strive to uplift the people in your care, their families and the local communities

Regardless of your title, be a CEO

Leadership is often confused with a title, yet it transcends a label, designation or a weighty benefits package. Leadership is about positive actions and strong values and to gain trust and a dedicated following as a leader, and requires you to live this set all the time. Going to a pulmonologist who smokes twenty cigarettes a day wouldn't engender your trust in that doctor. Credibility and trust must be earned and the starting point is authenticity to the principles you and your business represent.

> A leader needs to live and embody their value set.

My experience of exceptional leaders is that they engage directly and not by proxy or via intermediaries. They are on the ground and building connections with the people that hold the reins of success – their employees. Visibility and a personal commitment to them beyond the traditional scope of their role, creates the best environment for growth, success and the realisation of potential.

My 'CEO' checklist

Acknowledge the importance of values and actions	Be authentic	Engage directly	Be visible – especially when things are tough

Boosting productivity

In 2017 Harvard Business School published a leadership article entitled 'Great Companies Obsess over Productivity, Not Efficiency'.[4] The paper compared efficiency to productivity within the context of future business success amid the prevailing global uncertainties.

For nearly three decades, leaders and decision makers have operated on an efficiency model that has shown exceptional returns. This model focuses on eliminating operational waste and identifying labour hours and materials that are not necessary in order to deliver the same amount of output. In other words, leaner and more streamlined operational platforms generate saving and increase profits, but unfortunately they also increase organisational stress and corrode employee health.

> Efficiency is about producing the same amount of output with less resources.

Essentially, efficiency is about doing the same with less and many senior executives can testify to the fact that an efficiency emphasis has historically increased overall profitability, which is why this strategy has been so widely adopted for such a long period of time.

Michael Mankins, a partner from American consultancy firm (one of the top three in the world), Bain & Company, describes a measurable shift that occurred in late 2015 where the efficiency paradigm appeared to no longer yield the same profitable results, using the S&P500 as the benchmark. This performance shift has prompted many leading companies to focus on improving productivity as a means of generating better returns and many did with great success and less of a human cost.

Although productivity and efficiency appear to be the same, there are core differences between the two. Mankins was able to sum it up perfectly: 'Productivity is about doing more with the same, while efficiency is about doing the same with less'.

> Productivity is about producing more with the same resources.

COVID-19 and in some respects the Fourth Industrial Revolution, have forced many companies to scramble to secure finance, radically cut costs, renegotiate contracts (supplier, employee and client), restructure, lay off staff and work towards preserving revenue in any way, shape or form they can – ie efficiency.

The stress on leadership, management and employees has been incalculable and the effects will be seen in the months and years to come. While this is a necessary survival strategy, leaders will need to keep their eye on the future, not just the present, and this will require a very different way of thinking.

Experts are of the opinion that when markets and economies begin to recover, which history has shown us they invariably do, it will be a period where productivity will greatly supersede efficiency in impacting the performance and success of any business. While preservation is necessary amid the current global challenges, once the clouds begin to lift, the businesses who adapt quickly by pushing for growth as opposed to survival, expansion as opposed to fixed models and innovation as opposed to stagnation, will be best positioned to capitalise on future opportunities.

> Leaders who push for growth, expansion and innovation will be well positioned to capitalise on future opportunities.

But the challenge that businesses have been confronted with for some time is that productivity, the vehicle and measure of success, has been decreasing steadily in developed countries. This trend followed the 2008 global recession and, in light of recent events, is likely to decrease further.

We can clearly see this decrease in its magnified state during the global lockdown. While everyone remained globally connected via MS Teams, Zoom, Skype, WhatsApp and working 12-hour days (and in some cases even longer), relative productivity was low. For many, lengthy meetings

> Unnecessarily lengthy meetings, endless calls, countless emails, organisational bureaucracy and slow decision-making are a strong counterweight for productivity and can result in longer working hours, higher demands, burnout and health compromise.

would flow from one to the next, leaving not much time to do any meaningful work. Emails flooded our inboxes as we were copied in on all correspondence and phone calls competed for the precious (and very limited) hours in the day. The biggest challenge was that all major decisions and corresponding actions were put on hold. With no clear picture of the future, no one within any business was prepared to make a decision.

The reality that exists in businesses and organisations everywhere is that the time and effort required to complete any significant professional task has grown exponentially. This brings with it increased stress due to ongoing frustrations, work-family conflicts, longer working days and higher overall demands.

> On average, senior management devotes more than two days every week to meetings.

Advancements in technology and innovation have exponentially increased the speed and pace of life, but many businesses are operating slower than ever due to the endless stream of unnecessary communication, bureaucracy and indecisive leadership and management. Not only does this decrease output and increase stress but also saps people of their motivation and destroys inspiration.

Productivity is different to efficiency, not only in its definition, but also in its effect on the workforce. Creating organisational efficiencies such as cost-cutting, contract renegotiation and restructuring, often increases the demands on the workforce, creates job and employment insecurity, drives for longer working hours, creates work-family conflict and increases perceptions of injustice.

Conversely, the promotion of productivity within the business not only reduces stress, but also inspires tremendous positivity. Basic productivity drivers include simplifying working models, reducing wasted time, improving employee health and well-being, inspiring the workforce, the promotion of skills development, talent recognition and the adoption of technology and innovation.

> '40% of time can be liberated by reducing meeting frequency, reducing invitees, and/or reducing email' – Bain & Company

These productivity enhancers ultimately unlock human potential, and greater potential, on both a team and individual level, translates into improved productivity.

A firm awareness and detailed understanding of the core productivity drivers and drains within a business can be highly advantageous, especially during these uncertain and complex times. With this knowledge, you are able to pull on the productivity levers in a way that will allow the business and its teams to capitalise on opportunities that exist within the marketplace both today and in the future.

THE PRODUCTIVITY SILOS

The WEF describes 12 pillars that contribute to a nation's overall productivity, which predict future competitiveness.[5] These include:

- Institutions
  Encompasses security, public sector performance, property rights, corporate governance, transparency

- Basic infrastructure
  Includes transport and utilities

- Information and communication technology (ICT) adoption
  Pertains to internet (fibre, broadband) and mobile-cellular subscriptions and utilisation

- Macroeconomic stability
  Centres around inflation and debt dynamics

- Skills
  Refers to the current and future workforce that considers the mean number of years of schooling, ongoing training, critical thinking in teaching and many other factors

- Product market
  Includes domestic competition and trade openness

- Labour market
  Centres around flexibility, meritocracy and incentivisation

- Financial system
  Encompasses depth and stability

- Market size
  Includes GDP and imports of goods and services

- Business dynamism
  Refers to administrative requirements and entrepreneurial culture

- Innovation capability
  Encompasses interaction, diversity, research and development and commercialisation

- Health
  Measures by healthy life expectancy in years

These pillars can be viewed as a compass for policy makers and stakeholders as they provide guidance on what matters to ensure long-term growth. Fundamentally, the framework consists of four primary categories that include: enabling the environment (institutions, infrastructure, IT adoption, macroeconomic stability), human capital (health and skills), markets (product, labour, size, financial system) and innovation ecosystem (innovation capability, business dynamism).

Although not everything within the 12-pillar framework is necessarily relevant to productivity on an individual, team or organisational level, there is immense value in spotlighting and strengthening the ones that do carry over.

Providing an enabling environment that is stable, has good organisational infrastructure, together with strong technology adoption, would allow for more streamlined day-to-day operations, would eliminate time and resource wastage, improve productivity and efficiencies as well as lower employee stress, strengthen trust and improve employee engagement.

> Any business ultimately consists of a collection of individuals with unique skills and talents and the time these individuals dedicate to the organisation. Healthier employees can access their skills and talents far more effectively and dedicate more time to their professional responsibilities

Enhancing the innovation ecosystem through greater dynamism and creativity will position the business better for growth and agility and will future-proof it against unanticipated changes within the volatile economic landscape. Better understanding of the markets will ensure better positioning and strategic decisions.

Finally, spotlighting human capital through skills development and training will improve professional competency, build self-esteem and nurture talent as well as remove the stress of job and employment insecurity. At the same time, the greatest productivity and growth lever is undeniably organisational health as health is the foundation upon which *all* human potential exists.

Over the last decade, I have been in a very privileged position that has allowed me to speak and engage with YPO groups from around the

Productivity drivers

- Health
- Health promotion programmes
- Good organisational infrastructure
- Technology adoption
- Organisational stability
- Ongoing skills development
- Business dynamism and innovation
- An inspired workforce
- Inspiring leadership
- Setting priorities
- Reducing unnecessary attendance at meetings

Productivity drains

- Chronic stress
- Mental health compromise
- Physical health issues
- An unhappy workforce
- Unnecessary bureaucracy
- Long email chains
- Needless conference calls
- Unnecessary meetings
- Dysfunctional meeting behaviour (ie sending emails, scanning social media)
- Meetings that don't have a clear agenda

world. YPO is the global leadership community of more than 29 000 chief executives in 142 countries. The combined annual revenue of YPO member-led companies is in excess of USD $9 trillion.

Since many YPO members run large hugely successful organisations, you would assume that they would suggest sessions that specifically relate to organisational stress, resilience and related topics. Yet, from my initial briefing in 2015, my content mandate has always been to focus on personal well-being and health promotion. This speaks volumes for two reasons: Firstly, the world's top CEOs and business leaders have a full understanding of the value of health in promoting success and secondly, they also acknowledge their responsibility to create an example to the teams and people in their care.

The phrase, 'Without your health, you have nothing', has never been more apt, both on a personal level and an organisational one.

I have had several recent experiences where companies strongly shifted their focus to employee health and wellness and within a matter of months there were measurable increases in productivity and cost savings, not to mention the tremendous human benefit.

While there may have been a debate several years ago as to the merit and value of employee health and wellness within the context of return on investment, this is no longer the case. Whether employee health programmes are deployed to combat chronic stress, address mental health compromise, reduce health inequality or increase productivity, they are no longer a 'nice to have' aspect of the business, but rather an absolute necessity.

Health underpins success in every sphere of life. Learning and academic potential is strongly influenced by key neurochemicals that include dopamine, norepinephrine, serotonin and BDNF. BDNF is not only influential in learning and the formation of memory, but is also associated with better cognitive function, fluid intelligence, cognitive agility and flexibility, not to mention overall brain size (which, incidentally, translates to greater potential). When we engage in health promotion activities like aerobic exercise (for 20 minutes or longer), eat the right foods (specifically a plant-based diet), take dietary supplements (ie magnesium, curcumin or Omega-3 fatty acids) or spend more time outdoors, we generate a tremendous surge in this all-powerful molecule, creating a vehicle for improved academic performance.

Knowing the immense value that health holds in the promotion and facilitation of productivity, business leaders and management should use every opportunity to provide their employees with a platform for health security and development. In light of the exponential changes that have taken place in the world in a short space of time, merely providing an environment that supports and encourages individual health promotion (facilities, healthy food options and health professionals) may no longer be enough.

> In the future, businesses will need to deliberately and purposefully protect the health of their workforce. Over and above health promotion programmes, this will require addressing organisational stress as well as offering protection from environmental hazards.

Organisations need to be proactive in guarding the health and well-being of their workforce. This will require lowering the business's stress footprint by removing unnecessary stressors, shielding employees from various external challenges that may have unfolded (ie the risk of viral infection) and even careful consideration of lesser-known environmental factors (electromagnetic radiation, toxic cleaning agents, air pollution and food choices). As complex and challenging as these fairly short-term interventions may appear, the long-term rewards will far outweigh the effort required.

WELLNESS PROGRAMMES

According to the WHO, 'A healthy working environment is one in which there is not only an absence of harmful conditions but an abundance of health-promoting ones.'

When it comes to business and organisational potential, little compares to health promotion and, equally importantly, the safeguarding of employee wellness. Yet, many work environments pay little attention to this important precept, while at the same time demanding productivity and an unwavering commitment from employees.

The impact of toxic work environments on employee health and well-being is well established. For several decades, research has shown that many workplace stressors have strong associations to mental and physical health compromise and may even play a role in drastically shortening lifespans.

> The potential of a business is deeply connected to the health of its employees.

In 2015 Joel Goh, Jeffrey Pfeffer and Stefanos Zenios published a study entitled 'Exposure To Harmful Workplace Practices Could Account For Inequality In Life Spans Across Different Demographic Groups',[6] that was able to determine the degree to which work environments can impact lifespan.

Health inequality, which encompasses inequality in lifespan, is a growing concern that impacts the social fabric of society and economies, not to mention businesses throughout the world. Health inequality is essentially the disparity in health status between different population groups. For example, the difference in lifespan between those that come from privileged backgrounds versus those that come from disadvantaged environments.

While the socio-economic drivers in health inequality are better defined, the role of toxic work environments has until recently been far less clear.

As South Africans we are all too aware of the vast inequalities that exist within our country, especially in the health sector. This is one of the reasons why the South African government is pushing for radical healthcare reforms. Current failings of our healthcare system aside, numerous South African studies show that poor education, unemployment and regional poverty are some of the strongest drivers in the national health inequality challenges.[7]

Looking beyond our borders, evidence shows that a lack of proper education is at the centre of the global health inequality challenges. A study in *Health Affairs* showed that in the US, individuals with fewer than 12 years of education have the same life expectancy as those seen in the 1950s and 1960s, approximately 11 years less than today.[8] The same article showed that in 2008, white men that came from advantaged backgrounds with more than 16 years of education, lived 14.2 years longer than black men who came from disadvantaged communities with fewer than 12 years of education. Applying these findings to life expectancy trends in South Africa, it would mean that South Africans who have not completed high school would have a 20-year (or more) lower life expectancy than those who have a tertiary education.[9]

Numerous studies have supported these findings and research has reliably shown that people who earn a higher income and have a higher level of education, enjoy better health, have longer life expectancy and a lower incidence of most diseases.

Driving positive health behaviours in those who were previously disadvantaged is not only the moral responsibly of every organisation, but it will also unleash untapped potential, promote enthusiasm, raise motivation, increase loyalty and drive productivity within business.

> Within developed nations, highly educated individuals with 16 or more years of education live, on average, 14 years longer than those who haven't had the same advantages.

I have seen the benefits time and time again of organisations whose leadership and management subscribe to the value of employee health and wellness and invest huge resources in bringing their vision to life.

I was recently contracted by a medium-size business in the professional services sector that had a strong diversity and inclusion ethos with many of their support staff from previously disadvantaged backgrounds and communities. Like so many progressive institutions, the firm placed health equality at the top of their agenda.

The wellness programme I set up for the company involved the development of a healthy food menu for the on-site canteen, health talks, wellness discussions and forums, the introduction and implementation of The Stress Code app, podcasts and regular short videos on key topics such as mental health.

From the outset, attendance and engagement in the programme by the staff was a remarkable 89%, driven largely by management's enthusiasm, but the real turning point was the installation of an on-site gym. The excitement and enthusiasm of the firm's employees resulted in staff members giving me real-time updates on their workouts every time I visited the offices. They were proud to share, in detail, their fitness accomplishments that included weight loss, greater muscle tone as well as fitness and strength. Also, stronger friendships emerged as colleagues teamed up to exercise together. The overall feeling was one of gratitude and appreciation.

Many of these employees had never had the opportunity to set foot in a gym, let alone make use of its facilities. Needless to say, stress within the company lessened, mental health improved, there was a far greater sense of community and productivity increased measurably.

In addition to driving positive behaviours in previously disadvantaged members of staff, as a leader or manager, you have been entrusted to promote and safeguard the well-being of your workforce. They trust you; they believe that you will make every effort to protect their well-being in all aspects of their lives. It is a moral and social obligation that falls within the modern leadership mandate and part of this role is to address existing inequalities such as economics, education and health.

By doing so you have the power to not only change your business and the lives of everyone within it, but the very fabric of society.

> Leaders of the future are given the responsibility to address various forms of inequality. This can be achieved through:
> - Extensive health and wellness programmes
> - Health support tools
> - Fair remuneration packages
> - Income protection policies
> - Ongoing skills development
> - Educational subsidies

Sir Michael Marmot, Professor of Epidemiology and Public Health at University College London and his Whitehall studies[10] were some of the earliest research papers to illuminate the disparities that exist within businesses due to education and other social factors. What made these studies so exceptional was that they involved the careful monitoring of 27 808 individuals from one institution – the British civil service. The study began in 1967 and follow-ups are still ongoing.

The studies showed that the lower someone's position in a company, the greater their levels of stress and the higher their risk of developing stress-related health issues.

The challenge for any organisation is that those with lower education levels are typically assigned to positions that hold less job security and very little authority. Moreover, these roles are often associated with a lower degree of support and a greater degree of organisational injustice or lack of fairness. Collectively, these primary stresses can create a dramatic shift in personal health and wellness, which in turn may reduce an employee's lifespan and indirectly affect their personal and professional opportunities. This is in addition to existing predispositions to greater health instability and vulnerabilities based on their lower levels of education and historic backgrounds.

The 2015 research paper, 'Exposure to Harmful Workplace Practices could Account for Inequality in Life Spans across Different Demographic Groups', concluded that stressful work environments that offer minimal support infrastructure such as wellness programmes, and interpersonal support can cause a 10% to 38% reduction in lifespan when compared to less stressful and more supportive work environments.

South African companies are some of the most diverse seen anywhere in the world, where disadvantaged and privileged work towards common goals and objectives. But health instability and equality due to educational disparities, poverty, historic traumas, adversity and environmental factors such as air and water quality are very real challenges that need to be addressed.

Since 2010, there has been a steady decline in productivity within our labour force that has had noticeable effects on the broader economy. While there are many reasons for this such as the high cost of doing business, a skills shortage and lack of competition, health inequality is also a strong contributing factor in South Africa's current Achilles heel.[11]

Poor health has a high price tag

A report by the WEF and Harvard School of Public Health[12] delivered strong evidence that non-communicable diseases (NCDs) such as cardiovascular diseases, cancer, chronic respiratory diseases and diabetes will cost the global economy $47 trillion in lost output over a period of two decades.

The report stressed that these NCDs not only pose a significant threat to human health, but also to the future stability of the entire world economy. While the threat of COVID-19 has been overt and the health, education and economic implications extensively modelled by governments as well as business and medical schools, NCDs (as a result of chronic stress, poverty, rapid urbanisation, health inequality, low education, trauma, etc) have an equally devastating effect on human health and future livelihoods.

However, unlike COVID-19, economic stimulus packages, social distancing and lengthy quarantines cannot contain this additional epidemic. Instead, only the prioritisation of health by individuals themselves, companies and governments can create the much-needed change for this monumental global challenge.

> Reducing the economic impact of poor employee health on companies requires a wellness programme that promotes health education, health skills development and the provision of key resources.

Unfortunately, many South African businesses are still not aware of, or able to appreciate, the impact that stress and NCDs have on their employees and even on organisational success. Fifty per cent of those who die from NCDs are in the prime of their productive years. The lives that are lost are not just fracturing families and destroying communities, but also endangering industry competitiveness across borders.

According to the report, 'The results are unequivocal: a unified front is needed to turn the tide on non-communicable diseases. Governments, but also civil society and the private sector MUST commit to the highest level of engagement in combating these diseases and their rising burden.'

Most, if not all, emerging economies like South Africa are encumbered with high levels of unemployment, rising poverty, undernourishment, health inequality and lower education levels, which all have significant health implications that affect organisational competitiveness and productivity. Businesses have the opportunity to rewrite the script through well-constructed wellness programmes and lowering their organisational stress footprint by reducing at least eight of the 12 common stresses. These include: lack of control, lack of support, injustice, conflicts, job insecurity, effort-reward balance, medical expenses, health, long working hours, high demands, sleep deprivation, financial difficulties.

Not only can this approach promote greater competitiveness, innovation and growth but it can also radically elevate communities and, in turn, contribute to the nation's upliftment.

Board members, CEOs, senior executives, managers, and all those involved in decision-making, need to appreciate that on this global stage and in these turbulent times, wellness programmes are an essential resource that can translate into a performance and competitive advantage.

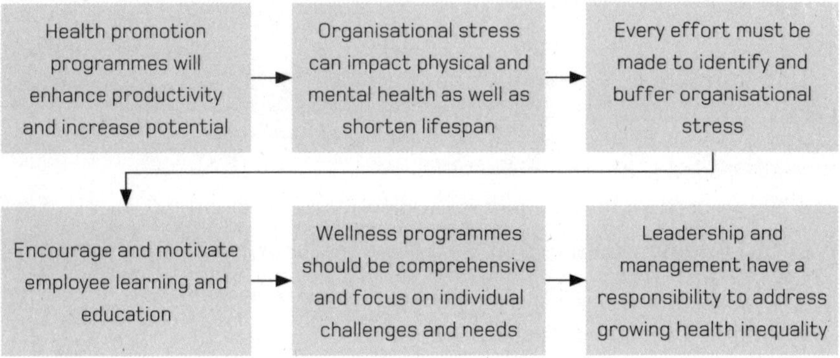

QUANTIFIABLE RETURNS

Whether your motivation as a leader or manager is to address health inequality, reduce the disease burden for the people in your care, enhance productivity or inspire your organisation to new heights, you need to be aware of what you can expect to see from a wellness programme or new health vision.

Firstly, let me tell you what *not* to expect. The ideal wellness programme will not create an obsessive and competitive culture within the organisation where employees who are not that way inclined in the health and fitness space, feel marginalised and excluded. Protein shakes and green juices won't be replacing the all-important morning coffee routine. Your teams are not likely to be wearing undersized and too-tight clothing to the point of respiratory failure. The office chat will not centre on how many times someone vomited during the last CrossFit session or that 25 000 steps is the new normal.

Instead, what you should expect from a good wellness programme is the promotion of organisational and individual potential through the use of health practices as a vehicle of enablement. Greater productivity, creativity, innovation and competitiveness should not be overshadowed by dietary and exercise preoccupations.

> Health behaviours and practices should be viewed as a vehicle through which potential is enabled.

Do some exercise so that your mind will be clearer and more focused. Eat well so that your energy levels will be sustained throughout the day. Take nutritional supplements to combat the effects of stress, pollution and electromagnetic radiation. Do yoga or meditate so that your body has an opportunity to recalibrate during periods where demands are high and your days are long. Get outdoors and enjoy nature to create emotional balance and stillness.

> Health promotion is merely a tool we use to support the business and our own personal objectives. The belief, 'Do what you have to do so you can do what you want to do', is a strong motivator.

The second focus of a proper employee wellness programme is what the programme actually entails. Treadmills are not set to replace desks and taking carbs to work will not be grounds for disciplinary action!

In the 1980s, 1990s, and even the early 2000s, the central focus of wellness programmes was reducing health-risk factors like smoking, excess weight and alcohol and/or drug abuse. More recently, stress and mental health have come to the fore due to the rising prevalence and socio-economic implications. This has meant that in order to help cope with chronic stress and the mental and emotional repercussions, wellness programmes have taken a more holistic approach. Resilience coaching, reframing, the building of stronger social connections and self-care, through meditation and yoga have emerged as the primary intervention tools.

> Corporate health and wellness programmes will typically involve:
> - Health-risk assessments
> - Self-help educational materials
> - Individual counselling
> - Classes
> - Seminars/talks
> - Group activities
> - Participation incentives

Between 2011 and 2030, the cumulative economic output loss associated with mental disorders is projected to be $16.3 trillion worldwide, making the economic output loss related to mental disorders comparable to that of cardiovascular diseases and higher than that of cancer, chronic respiratory diseases, and diabetes.[13]

In 2016 alone, stress- and mental health-related presenteeism was costing the South African economy R276 billion in lost output and productivity.[14] This amounted to 4.2% of GDP and in the aftershock of the pandemic this figure is likely to be far greater in the years to come.

Despite the growing understanding of the value of self-care, there are still many leaders and executives that question whether wellness and health promotion drives can deliver on promises and materially increase productivity and engagement, reduce presenteeism and lower organisational stress. Time and time again I am confronted with questions such as: 'Can they really be so impactful?' 'Can they really change society and correct health inequality?' The research says yes – but only if wellness programmes are well-constructed and properly applied.

There is still a division in the literature where many studies have showed profound value, while others show a marginal or even no return on investment. A 2019 randomised clinical trial involving 32 974 employees revealed that exposure to a workplace wellness programme resulted in fairly flat overall results. After 18 months, while there were improvements in positive health behaviours in those employees who participated in the programme, there were no significant differences in clinical measures of health, healthcare spending and utilisation, let alone absenteeism and job performance.[15]

By contrast, there have been countless literature reviews of studies on corporate wellness programmes that show impressive returns on investment. One of the first big meta-analyses that was done on worksite health promotion and economic returns was done in 2003 and showed that in a sample of 42 peer-reviewed studies involving more than 500 000 people there was a

25% reduction in healthcare and disability costs and a significant reduction in absenteeism.[16] The author, Larry Chapman, who holds a Master's degree in public health, comments: 'Worksite health promotion represents one of the most significant strategies for enhancing the productivity of American workers'.

> Employees who engage in properly constructed wellness programmes show a 52% lower rate of absenteeism compared to those who don't.

This review was followed by two later analyses and with each revision, the research was bigger, stricter and showed even greater returns and there were two papers in particular that were impressive from an outcomes perspective.

A Dutch study showed that those who engage in wellness programmes have a 52% lower rate of absenteeism compared to those that don't.[17] The second study focused on the insurance industry and investigated a wellness programme over a five-year period. The outcome of the study showed that within the first year of the launch of the programme, medical costs within the company dropped by 45.7%.[18] Costs aside, this means that employees were healthier, more functional and productive.

> Within the first year of a well-constructed wellness programme, medical costs can be reduced by over 45%

Get ready to be amazed

In 2010 an insightful research paper on the monetisation of wellness programmes and their value was published in *Health Affairs*[19] by two economics professors and a PhD student at Harvard. After sorting through over 100 high-quality wellness programme papers, that spanned three decades, the research team narrowed their study down to the studies that had a well-defined intervention, a well-defined treatment and comparison group and that characterised an analysis of a distinctly new intervention model (ie not merely a commentary on others' research).

By applying these criteria, together with additional stringencies, the sample size was reduced to 36 of the highest quality studies. Within this elite group, 22 studies looked at healthcare costs, 22 looked at absenteeism and eight looked at both of these aspects.

What made the data so strong was that 90% of the studies involved large organisations with over 1 000 employees and 25% of the studies centred around companies with over 10 000 workers. Municipalities, schools, universities, the pharmaceutical sector, manufacturing, consumer products and energy were all represented in the study, providing an extremely broad understanding of the relationship between health and organisational performance.

The type of health programme that was implemented was also important in understanding the return on investment. The majority of companies (80%) used health-risk assessment surveys to gather data and tailor-make programmes accordingly. In addition, health screening such as weight, blood pressure and cholesterol was often combined with the surveys. This wellness model is fairly familiar within corporate South Africa, due the big health drive by several of the country's top medical aid schemes.

The next most common wellness approach was the use of self-help education materials such as flyers or mail, individual counselling with

Review snapshot

- Over 100 high-quality wellness studies identified
- 36 studies reviewed
- 22 monitored absenteeism, 22 evaluated healthcare expenditure
- Eight focused on both
- 90% of the studies involved more than 1 000 employees
- 25% of the studies involved more than 10 000 people
- 80% of companies used health-risk surveys and health screening
- 35–40% of companies focused on self-help education materials, counselling or group activities
- A third of companies put incentives in place to encourage participation
- 75% of health/wellness programmes focused on stress, pain, nutrition, various health conditions as well as alcohol and smoking

healthcare professionals such as psychologists or social workers and on-site group activities led by health experts in activities such as yoga and Pilates. 35% to 40% of companies incorporated one or more of these interventions.

Finally, 75% of programmes focused on multiple employee health challenges that included stress management, back care, nutrition, alcohol consumption, blood pressure and preventative care, in addition to smoking and obesity.

At least a third of the wellness programmes used incentives for participation that included bonuses and reimbursements. Although most of the wellness programmes were active over many years, the average duration of research evaluation was three years

The meta-analysis showed that large employers who take on well-constructed wellness programmes see substantial returns, even within the initial stages of adoption. For every dollar spent the return on spending was $3.27 in medical savings and $2.73 in absenteeism reductions. Together, the return on investment was a tidy 600% and this is not taking into account the other benefits of the programme such as reduced presenteeism, reduced staff turnover, better overall engagement and enhanced productivity.

As a general rule, the return on investment could actually be considerably higher, as these studies were done over a fairly short period of time and wellness programmes tend be front-loaded – or more costly at the start – while health benefits are likely to accumulate gradually.

WHY WELLNESS PROGRAMMES OFTEN FAIL

Some wellness platforms are able to rapidly transform an organisation while others have no impact. The drivers in unprecedented success or utter disappointment are complex and multifactorial with many converging layers such as culture, budget, size of the workforce and environment.

What *won't* work, however, is offering an annual (poorly attended) health

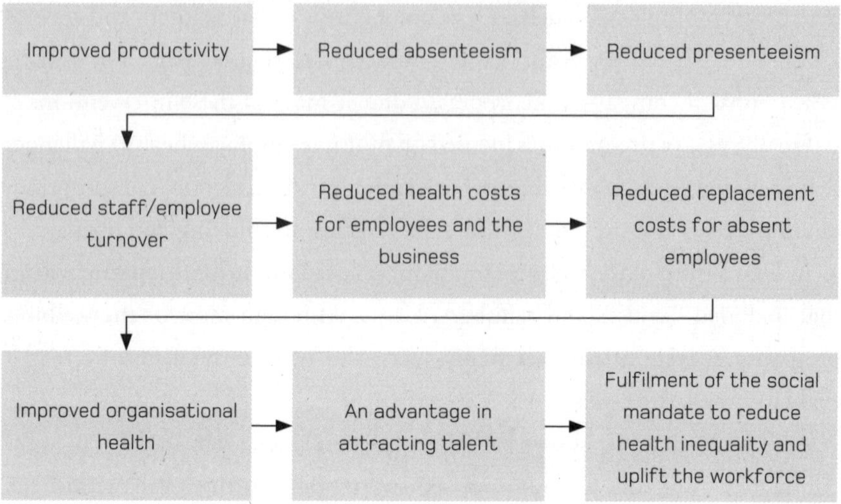

Benefits of wellness programmes

screening, a poster in the bathroom encouraging employees to have a flu shot or a subscription to a remote counselling service that the workforce don't connect to, let alone trust. Average effort simply won't translate into an exceptional outcome but neither will a multimillion rand investment in state-of-the-art gym equipment or bringing on board a team of the country's best health professionals.

New wellness visions fail to achieve their intended outcomes due to a number of reasons but the primary reasons include time limitations, not addressing the root cause of the problem and underexposure to the new vision.

The time factor

Exercise, meditation, yoga sessions, trips to the health store, seminars (digital or live), workshops, preparing healthy meals and seeing a physical therapist all take time – and loads of it. With so many businesses downsizing and restructuring, fewer employees find themselves fulfilling the roles that were historically performed by many. While technology and automation has certainly improved some professional efficiencies, many of us find ourselves fulfilling multiple roles or even new and vastly expanded portfolios. The challenge the world's workforce is facing is that even when the economic fallout of the coronavirus pandemic has started to recede, businesses are likely to continue to use fewer employees than before.

Add a family to the average person's time-strapped day and it is not surprising that employees just don't have the time to participate in the company wellness programme. For many, their day will look like this: Get up at 5am (or earlier if you have very young kids or a long commute), dress the kids, give them breakfast, rush them to school (or sit down with them for home schooling), rush to work (or sit at your home workstation), fetch the kids from school (or monitor their learning progress throughout the day), go back to work (or sit back at your home workstation), organise lunch, coordinate extramurals (or additional skills development), get home from the office (or step away from your home workstation), help with homework (or additional schoolwork), make dinner, bath the kids and, finally, into bed, eat your own dinner, respond to a few emails, watch a few minutes of TV and the whole cycle repeats itself the next day. Time is the biggest consideration in every wellness programme and initiative introduced in any company.

According to a 165-page report compiled by RAND Health Care, part of the RAND Corporation, a non-profit institution that helps improve policy and decision-making through research and analysis,[20] nearly half of US employers with more than 50 employees currently offer some sort of wellness programme. This popularity has enabled researchers to access a wealth of information in many core areas, including participation trends, which are mostly voluntary as opposed to mandatory. According to the report, only 47% of employees actually participate in annual or biannual screening assessments. The primary reason given for such low engagement was insufficient time due to work-related demands and responsibilities.

Most screening protocols take only a few hours, no more than once or twice a year so if a workforce can't afford (or is unwilling) to make time for these basic screenings, the other more rigorous and time-intensive activities would fare really poorly, according to this report. Participation levels in regular exercise and disease management programmes (ie wellness education, counselling, podcasts, etc) within US companies is a mere 16% to 21%.

> Without the right wellness approach, employee participation in exercise and health management programmes can be as low as 16% to 21%.

The message here is that a successful wellness vision must factor in inherent time constraints, especially with all the changes that have taken place around us. Key action steps to help overcome some of these time constraints include:

- Employees should be able to engage in a wellness programme at a time that suits them. For this to happen, consider the following:
  - Extending hours for engagement and participation, ie gyms that are open 24/7, online surveys, apps to engage with
  - Create convenient access to assessment and consultancy teams either after hours or on weekends

- Bring the wellness programme to your teams.
  - Innovation and technology have brought about exponential change and in the health and wellness arena they can offer immeasurable value. Health and wellness apps can greatly increase wellness programme participation.

- The pilot study of The Stress Code app involved 117 lawyers over a period of a year and the programme participation rates were 89%. To achieve this, the technology needs to offer a range of services such as:
  - Stress, health and resilience self-assessments
  - Relevant health-orientated podcasts (ie immune-boosting

strategies, stress, resilience, etc)

- Short videos related to trending and relevant topics such as burnout, sleep, etc
- Online shopping services for nutritional supplements, health foods, etc
- Relatable health advice and stress-management solutions

- Keep health activities and engagements short and purposeful. Programmes must be able to continually provide answers to questions and pressing issues, in real time with minimal drag.

- If space and budgets allow, offer key resources on-site. Providing healthy food options, counsellors, therapists and even training facilities, will effectively support and propel any wellness and health vision in the right direction.

Playing for time

Make wellness programmes and facilities available after hours and on weekends	Technology should be at the forefront of health promotion programmes	Keep health-related engagements short and purposeful	Provide easy access to health resources (healthy food options, counselling services, training facilities)

Not addressing the root cause

Many wellness programmes fail to deliver on expectations because they don't address the primary issues, such as organisational culture and management practices, that impact employee health and well-being.

Stress in the workplace is as harmful to our health as second-hand smoke, a known and regulated carcinogen. The most common assumption in the corporate world is that stress occurs when the typical work demands and pressures of the job are not equally matched by an employee's knowledge and abilities. This may be true in a handful of cases, but what more and more research is showing is that our work environment has the potential to impact our mental and physical health on a level that is unmatched by any, if not all, other circumstances.

High-stress work environments are the fifth-largest contributor to premature mortality.

In 2016 the journal, *Management Science*, published a report that was able to measure the collective effect of how US companies manage their workforce in respect to employee health and its impact on national medical expenditure.[21] The outcome of the study showed that more than 120 000 deaths result every year from high-stress work environments, making this the fifth-largest contributor to premature death in the US. What's more is that the report showed that the annual cost of harmful work environments exceeds $190 billion which equates to 8% of annual healthcare expenditure in the US.

In his book, *Dying for a Paycheck: How Modern Management Harms Employee Health and Company Performance – and What We Can Do About It,* Jeffrey Pfeffer points out that at least half of these deaths can be prevented and the healthcare burden reduced by more than a third through changes in a management ethos and organisational culture.[22] This pattern of toxic work environments resulting in compromised human health is not confined to the US and affects each and every business, in every country, around the world.

Through my own research and extensive data collection, I have observed that the vast majority of stress that is experienced within organisations stems from the collective contribution of poor organisational justice, employees feeling undervalued and underappreciated, internal conflicts, limited control and authority within

If managers and leaders create positive changes to their organisational culture, they will be able to save lives and reduce the healthcare burden.

the work environment and more recently job insecurity and a lack of support. While the demands of the job are frequently reported as stressful, the relative contribution to the stress matrix seldom exceeds 12% to 15% of the total stress experience.[23]

By contrast, well over 50% of organisational stress relates directly to factors that can be effectively addressed by modifying and refining management and leadership practices. People are a business's biggest asset and they need to be nurtured and valued.

Toxic work environments result in over 2.3 million deaths every year worldwide.

For a wellness and health vision to be effective, it must not only manage the typical stress symptoms, ie mental and physical health issues, burnout, emotional fragility, pain and NCD prevalence, but also the root cause of the stress. In many instances, it is the very environment and culture people work in that creates the stress and illness set.

A key Australian review that spanned 15 years of research and involved 90 leading studies from around the world, compared the effectiveness of programmes that address culture (ie primary stress cause) versus reactive measures (ie symptoms) to work-related stress.[24] The authors were able to clearly and distinctly define and categorise the various interventions and the analysis identified three different management approaches to workplace stress and the degree of effectiveness on an individual and organisational level.

Through the refinement of management practices, more than 50% of organisational stress can be reduced if not altogether eliminated.

This review was instrumental in changing the way I ran my intervention programmes and is largely responsible for much of the historic successes I have had. In the early stages of my career I would dedicate much of my time and resources to reactionary measures. In simple terms this would entail managing the effects of chronic stress (ie physical pain, digestive issues, emotional and cognitive decline, overall performance compromise, etc) within teams (sports and corporate) and on an individual level. However, through a greater understanding of stress and the cause-effect relationship, my emphasis changed to prevention and amelioration strategies.

It is often thought that reacting to and addressing existing issues is more challenging than prevention, but this has not been my experience. In many respects, stress prevention can be more difficult and complex due to individuality and the relationship to the environment.

A few weeks into the South African lockdown a small team of very senior executives approached me to assist them with their stress and resilience during the coming months. The group was all too aware of the challenges that lay ahead, the need to be able to cope with exceedingly difficult circumstances, the fact that their roles were likely to change, not to mention that setbacks and disappointments were inevitable. It is not often that one gets an opportunity to develop a programme purely on a proactive basis, but this team was extraordinary in their self-awareness and camaraderie.

The programme began through a deep exploration of individual resilience characteristics. An assessment of existing levels of resilience, perceived levels of stress, self-rated mood disposition together with genetic testing was able to provide remarkable insights for the journey that lay ahead. Biological factors that could contribute to reduced mood, worry and anxiety, compromised mental acuity and agility under stressful conditions was uncovered on an individual and group level. At the same time the emphasis was not only focused on potential weaknesses that could be neutralised, but also on strengths that could be better realised. These 'resilience tools' when identified and nurtured can lead to greater tolerance to stress, more optimism and fearless in difficult situations and so on. Many of the core differentiators relate to several neurochemical systems (dopamine, serotonin, oxytocin, etc). The choice of foods, nutritional supplements, the timing and intensity of exercise, the use of meditation, yoga and therapists was masterfully coordinated on a group and individual level.

At the same time, the stress landscape would require careful management. Considering that the demands were going to escalate due to greater uncertainties and mounting challenges, the work days set increase (by hour and number), professional roles become more unclear and greater conflicts arise, environmental control was of the utmost importance. Support, care, trust, honestly, value, respect needed to be infused into a remote set of working conditions, which it was through trainings and engagements.

The team grew stronger, became fiercely protective of one another and thrived under the new conditions. It is not to say that the dynamic circumstances did not require additional support and reactive measures, but the foundation was strong which reflected on the team's sustained health and exceptional performance.

Over the years, I have applied various approaches to businesses and organisations based on their unique circumstances and requirements. Businesses have the option to introduce three basic health and wellness models. They can be used in isolation or collectively and are based on a primary, secondary and/or tertiary level of intervention. The stress reduction programmes have specific and unique targets and different effectiveness ratings.

- A primary intervention plan is based on a preventative approach that works to reduce organisational stress and empower employees with skills and ongoing knowledge pertaining to their health and well-being.
- A secondary intervention plan is an ameliorative model that teaches employees to cope better with their stress and provides tools and resources for improved individual health.
- A tertiary intervention plan has a reactive focus and offers stressed employees counselling and medical services, assists in return-to-work programmes and is very much focused on crisis management.

Type of stress reduction programme	Description	Targets	Effectiveness rating
Primary intervention	**Preventative** Altering the stressor before the workforce experiences stress-related symptoms or disease	Skills development Support Communication Conflict management Effort-reward balance Greater sense of control and authority	Very high
Secondary intervention	**Ameliorative** Help equip the workforce with knowledge, skills and resources to cope with stressful circumstances	Change in perception of stress, behaviour modification in response to stress, meditation, breathing, yoga, exercise, nature exposure, supplements and diet	Moderate
Tertiary intervention	**Reactive** Treat the symptoms of stress	Medical intervention, occupational therapy, return-to-work programmes	Low

The Australian meta-analysis showed that there is a recent global trend towards wellness programmes that equip employees with the skills to manage their stress and health challenges more effectively. Moreover, this is now being coupled with a strong drive towards improving the culture and adapting management styles.

While this combined approach of programmes is not the norm yet, what has been clearly identified is that a reactive approach to stress management as a wellness intervention plan, has limited effectiveness. Any model that principally deals with individuals only *after* they have succumbed to the adverse effects of stress, does little to promote a healthy, productive, innovative and thriving organisation. Health programmes that only focus on issues once they have materialised, will do nothing to promote organisational improvements and growth.

According to the authors of the study: 'Individual-focused, low-rated approaches are effective at the individual level, favourably affecting individual-level outcomes, but tend not to have favourable impacts at the organizational level'.

What this, and many other more recent studies are showing, is that by helping people manage the consequences of chronic stress, leaders are able to make a significant difference in their lives. And they have a moral obligation to do so. At the same time, research acknowledges the need to prevent these scenarios from unfolding in the first place. By doing this, leaders will not only be able to positively impact the people in their care, but also the business and all the performance metrics more successfully.

During 2009 and 2010, I worked with a professional tennis player by the name of Li Na, who typified this model of the value in addressing cause and not simply effect. She had incredible talent and unparalleled athleticism, but her barrier to stardom was a reoccurring and debilitating right knee injury. To keep her dreams alive, she underwent three knee surgeries within a period of a few years but sadly, the interventions only provided short-term relief, limiting her ability to compete in only a few key tournaments during the year. Despite not playing 75% of the yearly events, she still managed to keep her ranking at number 25 in the world. Yes, she was that good.

We started working together six weeks after her third knee surgery, which was performed by a highly acclaimed team of doctors in Germany. The mood in the team was not overly optimistic based on historic trends, but a strong work ethic compensated for the existing fears and concerns for the future of her career.

In my initial evaluations with Li Na, I picked up on structural issues pertaining to her spine and pelvis that I felt could have been affecting the knee. But as I investigated further, I soon discovered what later proved to be the root cause of her historic injury challenges. From all the years of intense training that included plyometrics (a highly explosive and intense form of training that serves to create greater speed and power), she had developed a second-degree kidney prolapse. When this occurs, the kidney migrates lower in the abdomen and can compress the primary nerve systems that supply the knee. This results in muscular weakness in and around the knee, poor coordination and compromised structural integrity, together with accelerated wear and tear on the knee joint due to reduced intrinsic controls.

I spent the next 10 weeks in the far South of China working with Li Na and her team focusing on addressing the prolapse, using visceral manipulation,[25] re-educating the movement patterns and enhancing functional strength, which had been corrupted from the long-standing nerve compression. By the beginning of the next year, she was fit and healthy and ready to hit the tennis circuit running. At the second tournament she competed in, the Australian Open, she reached the semi-finals after beating Venus Williams convincingly and in doing so, became China's first ever Top 10 singles player. That was just the beginning of her meteoric rise at the age of 28 and she went on to win two Grand Slams, one in 2011 and one in 2014, and achieved a number 2 world ranking, despite her fairly advanced age.

Five years after her retirement in September 2014, Li Na was inducted into the International Tennis Hall of Fame, becoming the first Asian-born player to receive this honour.

The value and importance of identifying and addressing the underlying cause of Li Na's issues, as opposed to merely reacting to the more obvious symptoms, made all the difference to her career trajectory.

The same concept holds true for health and wellness programmes. Merely managing the after-effects of stress on the workforce does not create meaningful change, or give the business and its teams the best opportunity to thrive and grow amid the challenges we are all confronted with.

When you buffer the organisational stresses and arm your workforce with tools and resources that develop resilience, incredible transformation occurs. This proactive model will result in a reduction in stress-induced depression, anxiety, burnout and employee disengagement. While at the same time increase productivity, innovation and creativity. Through this methodology, businesses can realise significant returns on their investment across all domains.

Over the last five years, I have noticed a strong shift in medical thinking and practice. The traditional paradigm of simply treating the symptoms is slowly being replaced with a preventative approach, largely through developments in medical technology such as genetic and other highly sensitive testing methods.

One of the best neurologists in South Africa is a young, highly driven woman who is admired and respected within the medical community. What gives her the 'edge' over her colleagues, is not only an in-depth and intricate understanding in her specific area of expertise, but also her passion and commitment to understanding the interconnecting parts. Her professional ideology is to proactively and continuously search for answers. Accepting a condition at face value and reactively managing the symptom set is simply not her style.

The same holds true in corporate health and wellness. By the time employees have been impacted by stress, the damage has already been done, lives have been affected and families impacted, sometimes forever.

Future-proofing for economic uncertainty, exponential change and even rapid advancements, requires a strategic vision and a commitment to understanding chronic stress, a condition known for its impact on mental and physical health compromise, chronic disease manifestation and, in some cases, premature mortality.

A sound strategy and a deeper understanding of how stress and employee health impacts you or your business is nothing without an action plan. To add even deeper complexity, because of the unimaginable changes taking place in the world, action plans need to be flexible, agile and seriously creative.

Addressing stress at its source and giving people the tools and skills to overcome adversity, will define success in both our personal and professional lives. In order to do so, the following action steps can be taken:

- Assess the landscape; knowledge of the current stress set and its degree of impact is invaluable in a prevention programme. This can be achieved through surveys, personal or team engagements and by using technology.

- Alter the stressor before the workforce experiences stress-related symptoms or disease. Focus on enhancing and growing support, showing appreciation and care, invest in growing individuals, be transparent, increase communication and endeavour to rapidly resolve conflicts within the workplace.
- Equip yourself, your teams and the entire workforce with the knowledge, skills and resources to cope with stressful circumstances.

Address the cause, diminish the effects

Perform a thorough assessment of the organisational stress, health and resilience landscape	Identify which stresses are having the greatest impact on organisational health and performance	Develop a strategy to address existing stresses
Encourage leadership and management to take responsibility for stress mitigation and buffering	Enhance and grow support, show appreciation and care, invest in growing your teams, be transparent, increase communication and resolve conflicts	Equip your teams with knowledge, skills and resources to better cope with stress

Underexposure to the new vision

While spending time with Maria Sharapova at her Los Angeles home, I was introduced to the work of an organisational psychologist by the name of Adam Grant. Adam was a great mentor to her and a highly accomplished author who has written several bestselling books and hosts a successful podcast, WorkLife with Adam Grant.

His book, *Originals: How Non-Conformists Move the World*, answers a question I've often wondered about as to why, so often, the new visions that companies introduce to the workplace, often fail to achieve the intended outcome, despite providing solutions to existing and important problems.[26]

A strong wellness vision may sometimes fail because the new narrative is grossly under-communicated within the organisation. The team who have created the vision, done the due diligence and who have been working on the project for weeks, months or even years, assume that the same level of understanding exists throughout the business and its workforce. This is incorrect.

Think about when you have had a topic on your mind, running through different scenarios and the moment your partner walks in the room, without any communication or explanation, you ask them their views on the topic. They have no context and will typically give you a confused expression and blank stare. But usually, after lengthy clarification, you will generally get the feedback you wanted.

According to John Kotter, a professor of leadership at Harvard Business School, in a three-month period, employees might be exposed to up to 2.3 million words or numbers. To put this into perspective, a 30-minute seminar on health behaviours, stress reduction or leadership practices, will expose the audience to only 13 400 words or numbers, at most.

> In a three-month period, we are typically exposed to 2.3 million words and numbers in our work environment. When a new vision is introduced, it seldom exceeds 13 000 words or numbers. This underexposure to a new idea results in limited uptake of the new vision and disappointing results.

Regardless of how well the narrative is delivered, how commanding the argument or how valuable the content is, more than 99% of the communication that the workforce has encountered over the past three months does not concern the new wellness vision and resilience strategy being implemented at the company. Employees cannot be expected to understand, let alone internalise or apply, the vision with so little explanation or communication.

Kotter, who has authored 12 bestselling books on business and organisational success, believes that to introduce a new vision or culture and for it to be successfully integrated in an organisation, the narrative needs to be communicated to a factor of 10, 100 or 1 000, depending on the organisational landscape.[27]

This doesn't mean that there needs to be a seminar twice a day for the next three months, however it is important to consider that effective communication requires more than sending an email, a short presentation or handing out a flyer. Complex language, non-relatable content, limited communication forums, leaders who don't embody the vision, inconsistencies and one-way communication will cause the programme to implode before it has even started. A perfect example of what *not* to do:

> *Dear Andy*
>
> *In response to the current health threats and challenges, we are delighted to announce our new health augmentation programme. The programme is designed to facilitate biological responses and neurochemical changes that may create improved emotional stability, mental integrity and a better physiological suite. We invite you to participate in various scheduled events that encourage nutritional decision-making, increased respiratory demands and environmental adjustments. Unfortunately, management won't be able to attend due to a busy schedule and meetings, but we do expect staff members to participate. Please see the poster in the bathroom, canteen and other communal areas, for more details.*
>
> *Regards*
> *Human Resources team*

This all-too-common delivery is completely unrelatable, detached and shows no commitment by leadership to champion positive change.

Instead, the communication vision needs to cover a few areas and be multidisciplinary in its approach.

- It needs to be simple and relatable
- It must make use of a number of forums

Spread the word through as many different channels as possible. Use email blasts, WhatsApp groups, short talks, podcasts, short videos on relatable topics, online engagement, group activities and maybe even the odd poster in the bathroom!

- Use repetition

New ideas have to be communicated as often as possible. In order not to overwhelm the workforce, knowing many of your teams, their communication style and the demands that they are under, will help fine-tune the level of this exchange.

- Communication must be leadership-driven
  - The figureheads of the new vision must be in leadership and management roles and respected employees within the organisation. This creates an authentic communication that can be trusted.
- Have a two-way dialogue

No one wants to be dictated to, no matter how great the opportunities are for the future or the value of the vision. Listen to what your teams have to say.

A definitively better approach of how to communicate with the company would be:

Dear Andy

We know that this has been a particularly difficult time for everyone and it has motivated us to focus on health and wellness here at the Firm. We would love to hear from you in terms of your needs and views so please send through some ideas when you get a chance.

We will be holding a Zoom call later this week with a leading health expert focusing on relevant stress and health topics. Be sure to check your WhatsApp group for an informative podcast focusing on exercise and diet.

Our management team is excited to be standing shoulder to shoulder with you on this journey.

Thanking you for all your hard work and effort

Sarah (Group CEO)

It's not always what you say, but how you say it

Make sure your health and wellness vision is simply communicated	Make the health vision relatable and relevant	Make use of a wide array of communication platforms
Repeat and reinforce the health vision as often as possible	Leaders and management must champion the change	Create the opportunity for regular dialogues and two-way communication

A WELLNESS PROGRAMME THAT WORKS

For any new vision to promote the desired change within a business or organisation, it is important to direct the focus on the most prominent and influential levers. Enhanced organisational health, well-being, happiness and productivity can only truly be realised by reducing the organisation's stress footprint. This means creating an environment where the unnecessary stresses are controlled, moderated and, in some instances, even removed. This kind of environment empowers, enables and inspires employees, but most importantly they are able to tap into the vast resources of discretionary energy that we all have.

This discretionary energy could be devoted to work, but many people are not in the right environment that allows or inspires them to do so. Creating a largely stress-controlled environment where employees feel safe, valued and rewarded creates a far greater degree of job satisfaction.

According to Michael Mankins from Bain & Company, this greater satisfaction can increase productivity by up to 40%[28] and means that 40-hour working weeks transition to 56 hours, with potentially no additional time spent in the office due to greater dedication, proficiencies, efficiencies and urgency. This productivity upturn within the context of an entire month means a typical 160-hour work month transforms into 224 hours, bringing with it the potential for greater growth realisation.

> Greater job satisfaction increases productivity by 40%.

To create this competitive advantage, leadership needs to reduce and control key organisational stresses. The creation and promotion of a professional environment where people feel that their efforts are appreciated and rewarded, where they feel supported and cared for, is the first step in the buffering process and actualisation of job satisfaction.

> Showing appreciation, support and providing opportunities for growth will increase employee satisfaction.

By creating an effort-reward balance and offering greater support, you are merely scratching the surface of an individual's or an organisation's potential.

Endeavouring to make your workforce feel that they are part of an extraordinary team, that they have autonomy to do their jobs, and giving them the opportunity to learn and grow in their job scope, you are likely to see a dramatic rise in engagement. This increase in engagement can result in an 88% increase in productivity. Imagine what your business would be capable of achieving when 40 hours of work is transformed into 75 hours of creative and innovative output.

> Engaged employees are 88% more productive than those who are unsatisfied.

Giving more control and authority to employees, providing them with skills development to reduce the fears of unemployment and making them feel that they are part of a powerful collective is imperative for full engagement, but there is more that can be done and more that can be achieved.

One of the keys to exceptional leadership, especially at this point in human history where productivity, creativity and innovation are the primary success differentiators, is the ability to inspire.

Inspiration is energising and gives us all meaning. The 2019 Rugby World Cup was a true showmanship of leadership for our country. Over the last eight years, South Africa has been afflicted by corruption scandals and brought to its knees by socio-economic challenges and ongoing political turmoil. We have all been impacted, whether knowingly or unknowingly, and this has eroded our intrinsic belief in the future, stifled positivity and taken away confidence and trust. But in November 2019 something incredible happened when 31 men and their support staff, who represented where we had come from as a country and where we wanted to go, changed everything. Within 80 minutes, the Springboks united a nation and made us believe and dream again.

It wasn't just that they won the World Cup that day, but how they did it. On the field they were truly a united team who showed courage and fearlessness and urgency, but their greatest strength was that they were inspired. The moment the final whistle blew each and every South African felt that anything was possible. It felt like a new chapter had begun and we were energised and unstoppable as a nation. This is the power of inspiration and something we need to be reminded of all the time.

When teams and employees are able to derive meaning and inspiration from the company's mission (ie trust) and are sufficiently motivated by its leadership (ie that they have their best interests at heart), extraordinary things happen. According to Mankins, under these exceptional circumstances, an enormous amount of discretionary energy is liberated within the workforce. Inspiration to this degree can increase productivity and innovation by 125%, when compared to an already motivated and satisfied employee.

> When we are inspired, we are able to perform the work of three people.

For every truly inspired employee, you will need more than two satisfied employees and almost three unhappy employees to perform the same amount of work in a week, during a month and over a year.

To create a happy workforce I need to:

- Reduce their stress
- Show my appreciation more
- Properly reward their efforts
- Show more support
- Show that I care on a personal level
- Provide opportunities for career growth and development

→

To create a committed and engaged team I need to:

- Give my team a voice in the decisions that affect them
- Allow for a certain degree of autonomy, but be sure to create accountability
- Provide ongoing learning opportunities
- Emphasise the importance of skill development
- Make my team feel that they are part of a powerful collective
- Remind my team of the value of their role and their importance to the business

→

To create an inspired team and organisation I need to:

- Create an organisational mission
- Both leadership and I need to be aspirational
- Both leadership and I need to be an inspiration to our teams
- Create an environment of meaning and purpose
- Strive to be the best at what we do

A story of leadership

Often a professional athlete is seen as an individual who merely possesses exceptional talent in their chosen sport. While this is the original precursor to their achievement at stardom, in reality, an athlete at the highest level is a micro-enterprise. They employ agents, marketing staff, social media staff, a financial team, coaching staff, medical staff, training staff, travel coordinators and other staff that contribute to their career on some level. The same governing principles that apply to a business's success, applies to them. Following a breakthrough success, this transition often happens overnight, with many athletes failing to recognise the recalibrated role. In many ways, it is not dissimilar from a business starting out as an entrepreneurial venture and maturating into a mechanised organisation. Athletes are not only selling entertainment, but also aspiration and inspiration and that is why clothing brands, luxury cars and watches, beverage companies and other lifestyle products are part of the endorsement journey.

A few years ago, I received a call from Kevin Anderson, a South African tennis player living in the US. He had sustained a significant injury that promised to end his career and, at the time, Kevin was in his late 20s and had only just found his stride. He ranked approximately number 30 in the world, which wasn't a reflection of his ability, but rather a consequence of his physical limitations through repeated injuries.

His injury was complex and the statistics showed an extremely low probability of recovery. While talking to him, it was clear that he was committed to my involvement in his journey to recovery, regardless of the direction, whether conservative or surgical. Without hesitation, I accepted the challenge and joined his team.

The first and biggest decision we needed to make was whether surgery was necessary. Kevin had assigned me a significant amount of authority and I would ultimately have to guide him in making this decision.

A decision of this magnitude cannot be made without consulting the best medical minds in the world. Several leading orthopaedic surgeons, from Europe, the US and South Africa, all provided their insights and advice and, from their input, the decision was made to pursue a conservative approach in Kevin's rehabilitation and recovery, owing to the existing physical set. Within days of the decision being made, Kevin and his entire team arrived in South Africa.

Being given such a degree of authority within the context of Kevin's situation and knowing how high the stakes were, was a huge responsibility. It was extremely stressful, but it created a full and inspired commitment on my behalf to find a solution. I spent hours and hours researching various approaches and ideas, looking for solutions to the extreme hurdle that Kevin needed to overcome.

The team culture that Kevin had created was remarkable and there was a tremendous amount of mutual support. His physiotherapist, sports physician, coach and family members provided constant encouragement and offered their assistance. The intervention sessions felt like community gatherings and were positive and motivational.

Another positive quality within this professional dynamic was the reliability of Kevin and his team and their consistency in their treatment of one another and of me. It was a demanding environment that had high expectations and I was held accountable for outcomes, but at the same time it was predictable and safe, which gave me great comfort.

Despite Kevin's fears and uncertainties about his future, he always treated his team and those around him with the utmost respect and dignity, which can be difficult considering the emotional toll of the circumstances.

The impact COVID-19 has had on you, your business, your family and your financial and employment security is similar to what an athlete, in the prime of his career, who has sustained a career-limiting injury, experiences. This may happen repeatedly over their short careers, creating enormous financial and career uncertainties. Often they don't have the means to sustain themselves for months, let alone years, or have no tertiary education to fall back on. The fear and vulnerability can be unprecedented.

Kevin had a remarkable ability to acknowledge his team's effort and input and would thank everyone for their ongoing contribution, tell them how much he valued their commitment and hard work and not miss an opportunity to remark on every positive milestone. Kevin was an inspirational leader and, as such, inspired his entire team to achieve personal and collective greatness and, by bringing the best out of his team, he was able to harness his own potential.

Incredibly, within several weeks, Kevin made a full recovery and 18 months later, reached a career high of number 5 in the world. He showed brilliant leadership in very difficult and demanding circumstances and had the courage to relinquish control, the confidence to give his team a voice and valued the role of support. He also promoted an environment of stability, strived for fairness and fully appreciated the value and worth of every person who was part of the challenging journey. In October 2020, Kevin was named President of the ATP Player Council, succeeding World Number 1 Novak Djoković.

A year later I was put into a very similar position, but this time the outcomes were vastly different. I received a call from a sports agent representing an athlete who was plagued with health and injury issues and needed to find solutions to revive her career. I had always admired the player as she had won all the Grand Slams throughout her career (some more than once) and was a force to be reckoned with.

She employed a large health team and had recently recruited the best nutritionist, physiotherapist, sport physician and trainer. My role was to 'connect the dots', so to speak, and form the final piece of a collaborative model. I jumped at the opportunity to work with some of the best people in the industry in such a collaborative fashion and to be part of a recovery plan for this iconic athlete. The only catch was that I had to spend most of the year travelling, but it seemed a small price to pay.

A few days later I was on a plane and within my first 48 hours on the job, it became apparent that it was not a collaborative exercise. Every engagement with the rest of the team seemed to be a fight for position, with each member having to continuously justify their role. Conference calls were meant to coordinate the team and provide a platform to present ideas, but instead they became defensive and a forum for lecturing. We were all micromanaged and no one had a voice or a say, let alone any decision-making authority within their area of expertise. This lack of control lowered overall motivation within the team and created an emotionally charged and highly agitated dynamic.

It was the most disjointed environment I had ever worked in. There was no mutual support and none from the athlete herself. During one particular conference call, the trainer overtly blamed the athlete's lack of progress on other members of the team, which created resentment within the team that would ultimately never get resolved. That time could have been spent productively and creatively as opposed to finger-pointing and fostering animosity among the team.

Support systems in any business or team always stem from its leadership and filter down from there, and so the distrust and lack of mutual support within the team was actually a symptom of failed leadership. This was just one of the many fundamental challenges. Another daily frustration was the unpredictability of the professional environment. No two days were the same, not only because of the travel schedule, but because team decisions were made unilaterally, inconsistently and illogically.

Strangely enough, all of these challenges and obstacles were quite manageable, but what was the most upsetting was the lack of acknowledgement for the effort and commitment we all put in. Every team member made significant sacrifices to be part of the athlete's return to form, but no acknowledgment of this was ever made. Families were separated, relationships jeopardised and all personal goals were put on hold. We all believed in the player and were motivated to be part of the change vision. Throughout the time I spent with the athlete, there were steady improvements in her health and performance. Many historic health issues faded away, injuries disappeared, yet she didn't acknowledge the role that I, or anyone else, played in her journey. Appreciation was not part of the team's vocabulary as it was overshadowed by an all-consuming expectation that it was just part of the job.

Despite a consistent level of progress and a really good personal relationship with the player, I resigned after six months. The dynamics within the team were far too strained and growth-limiting and, shortly after I resigned, several other team members followed suit. Sadly, the player was never able to regain her form and return to the podium.

My time with this athlete was one of the greatest lessons in leadership I have ever been taught. So often we believe that our success is independent of others, yet at the highest level nothing is further from the truth. The people around us are an integral part of our (or the business's) success and to move forward we need to empower people, inspire them and nurture them.

> The people that surround us are the reason for many of our successes. We need to do our utmost to nurture and develop these relationships.3

This can be effectively achieved when the stress footprint is reduced. There are stresses that are inherent to the circumstances but there are stresses that can, and must, be avoided. Micromanaging others, removing their voice, being unsupportive, pitting business people against each other, unfairness in decisions and actions and lack of appreciation and value for people's roles will corrode job satisfaction and engagement, but most importantly will diminish inspiration.

WELLNESS PROGRAMME FUNDAMENTALS

For a wellness programme to be effective and provide a competitive advantage to a business, it must be focused on stress prevention and moderation, as opposed to a reactive philosophy and model.

To roll this out, leaders and management teams should approach stress prevention in a number of ways in order to get the best results.

Give more control and authority to your team

This doesn't mean that leaders need to allow people to work in isolation, without a safety net, and encourage them to work where and however they want to. Rather, work autonomy centres around allowing for individual choices within established parameters, accepting that mistakes are part of the growth journey, building trust, allowing for individual ownership of projects and providing a stable environment for interaction for employees.

> In order for wellness programmes to provide businesses with a competitive advantage, they must focus on stress buffering and prevention, as opposed to the reactive management of stress-related health and performance. disorders

Creating choices within established parameters

What makes the game of tennis so impactful is that players have to hit the ball within established lines and they can hit the ball at any speed, in any direction, at any depth or any level of spin. The sport is enjoyable to watch and play because remarkable things are possible within these boundaries and so players have to constantly refine their skills and come up with creative solutions to stay in the game, let alone win a match.

> To bring the best out of your people, provide them with the necessary skills and resources as well as control and authority. At the same time, create a safety net that demands accountability, which is contained within clear parameters.

Imagine all the lines on a tennis court are removed and players are allowed to hit the ball haphazardly, in any direction and without any target. The entire game, and all its enjoyment, would cease to exist. That same principal exists within the workplace and in all professional endeavours. Freedom of choice and the ultimate expression of potential are best achieved in an environment of defined parameters, where accountability is important. The onus on leaders is to first establish the boundaries and then provide employees with a maximum amount of decision-making latitude.

Allow for mistakes

Being overly critical of employees not only reduces engagement, but also initiative. For businesses to grow, initiative and creativity must be nurtured. Working in an environment of fear stifles creativity and innovation. I often get asked how I was able to achieve some of my career milestones at such a young age. This is always followed by the person giving answers on my behalf: 'It was drive, wasn't it?' or 'Grit and determination, hey?'

While they are right in many respects, I put it down to the countless failures, or what I like to term 'learning opportunities'. My biggest growth curves resulted from making mistakes or through some form of failure. While I didn't enjoy those painful experiences, they did force me to relook and, in many instances, overhaul my approach to the task or activity.

In an ideal world, we learn from other people's mistakes, but in my experience, the only lessons that tend to promote growth and necessary change, are the ones we live and experience ourselves. As we grow, our ability to learn is achieved by observing the connection between actions and their consequences. To work in an environment where there is fear of taking action due to the negatively anticipated consequences, does not allow for individual, let alone organisational potential, to blossom.

Leaders must give their teams the opportunity to grow by being there when needed, but allowing them the scope to make the odd error.

Don't micromanage

This is one of the biggest leadership errors and is far more common than people think. Being micromanaged is extremely stressful for anyone, regardless of seniority. It strongly undermines a person's sense of self-worth and personal value as well as their health and well-being. Research shows that people feel exhausted and less fulfilled when placed in these micromanaged environments.

A few years ago I worked for a top-ranked athlete who held some of the biggest endorsement deals ever made in sport. She was the ultimate success story and an inspiration for millions of people around the world. What made her so iconic was that she had come from humble beginnings and rose to stardom through sheer will and determination. Sadly, nothing comes without a price and somewhere in her journey to success and stardom, she lost faith in people and stopped trusting them. Admittedly, it is hard to be trusting at that level because many of the people encountered along the way have very specific personal agendas within the context of the broader relationship. This is a sensitive way of saying that when you are at the top, everyone wants a piece of you. This is the reason why so many great athletes and performers stick to their core teams, despite the fact that they could sometimes derive benefit from outside expertise. A breakdown in trust, whether it is a recent development or more of a historic trend, creates the most ardent micromanager.

I had very seldom been confronted with the degree of micromanagement I experienced with this athlete and it took a huge emotional toll. Within weeks, I started doubting myself, felt down, despondent and drained and lost the ability to think creatively and I definitely didn't access the vast reserves of discretionary energy I had within me. My days were full of self-dialogue, in an attempt to lift myself out of the state I was in. Although I had a great working relationship with the athlete and it was a successful work partnership, I had to access every stress-management resource I knew in order to maintain my sense of self and personal value.

> A leader's primary role is to support their team and help remove obstacles and roadblocks.

Research shows that the amount of choice you have to determine what you do and how you do it, is one of the most powerful predictors of job motivation, satisfaction and performance. A leader's role is to support their team and help to remove obstacles and potential roadblocks. Dictatorship is not part of the mandate.

Create an environment of mutual support

Support in your personal and professional life is one of the most significant predictors of health, well-being, performance and ultimately, potential. This was one of the first lessons I learnt in my professional sports career. There have been a handful of occasions when I have been part of a team that was believed to be unstoppable. On paper, we had the best players, coaches, facilities, training methods, nutritionists, medical staff and psychologists, yet, as the season unfolded, expectations weren't met and the reality was vastly different. A run of flat and poor performances combined with in-fighting and the apportioning of blame, would be the undoing of the elite group. Bit by bit, players and support staff moved on and within a season or two, a new team would emerge, and the rebuilding process would start again.

Immense talent can be grossly overshadowed by organisational fragmentation, discord, a lack of mutual and upward support, and this all simply amounts to poor leadership. This scenario plays out time and time again in sports teams and businesses throughout the world.

Conversely, emotional and instrumental support, care, empathy and mentorship can transform teams and businesses. The inspirational 2019 Springbok rugby team personifies the importance of this level of support.

They began their preparations for the 2019 Rugby World Cup to be held in Japan, in 2018. This meant building the right squad from the ground up and former player, Rassie Erasmus was named head coach and the charismatic Siya Kolisi was named captain. In their 2018 build-up, the Springboks played 14 matches and lost half of them. The public was outraged and the critics vocal. However, throughout this time, both Rassie and Siya remained united and true to their vision and ultimately to their soon-to-be winning partnership.

Their long-term vision began to unfold after winning the Rugby Championship (formerly known as the Tri Nations). Incidentally, the last time South Africa won this event was back in 2009. The first match of the 2019 World Cup was against arch-rivals, New Zealand. South Africa lost their opener and the public's hopes of success for the team were crushed. However, instead of letting the loss fragment and destabilise the team, it galvanised and brought them closer together. The pressure was on, but more than any time before in the team's history, they weren't playing merely as a group of talented individuals, but rather as a united collective force. They weren't only playing for themselves, but also for each other and for the country and to inspire the next generation. They had a mission and every player was aligned to it.

Five impressive and successive wins followed, fast-tracking the team to the final. Despite the team's success, two of its star players, Faf de Klerk and Willie le Roux, were experiencing a challenging World Cup in their personal capacities. The criticism of the players was callous; 'Out of form', 'Scarily unpredictable', 'Fundamentally flawed' were some of the headlines used to describe these players. It was the trending topic and everyone in South Africa had a say. The public and critics demanded that the players be dropped from the squad, but Rassie, Siya and the rest of the team backed them.

The final was played against an in-form English team who defeated the All Blacks convincingly in the semi-finals, who, up until their English defeat, had not lost a single match at the World Cup in 12 years and were clear favourites for the tournament. Eddie Jones, England's coach, is one of the most formidable in the game; his ability to read teams and tactics is unprecedented. South Africa lost to New Zealand in their opening match and were then faced with a team that had given the iconic All Blacks, a rugby lesson.

Eighty minutes was the decider as to who would be the champions. Over and above Rassie's tactical decisions, South Africa had a secret weapon – the two so-called out of form players. That day, Faf de Klerk and Willie le Roux played the match of their lives and were flawless, as was the rest of the team. Jones's tactic to target them failed, and instead he was playing to the Springboks' strength, not their weakness. South Africa destroyed England in one of the best rugby performances in World Cup history and to me it was one of the greatest displays of trust, unity, loyalty and support. Individuals, leaders and businesses can learn from this kind of support shown between team members.

Support encompasses listening to and encouraging others, providing professional guidance, skills advancement and assistance on work matters.

We often confuse support with emotional comfort but support is far broader and more complex. Essentially, support is divided into emotional support – listening and encouraging others, and instrumental support – providing professional guidance, skills advancement and assistance on work matters.

Set a supportive precedent

It is widely known that feeling emotionally and materially supported can significantly reduce the psychological and physical burden of chronic stress. A 2019 meta-analysis in the *Journal of Occupational Health Psychology* investigated the concrete value of high levels of support within companies and their teams.[29] The review involved nearly 150 000 people and focused on the buffering effects of support in relation to key aspects of job stress that came from job strain as well as stress-induced shifts in employee attitudes and behaviours.

We are all very familiar with job strain and its many triggers and for some people, professional roles are fraught with conflict. The more you focus on one aspect of your job, the more another aspect can be compromised. In my professional life, the more I am involved in speaking engagements the less time and effort I can invest in individual consultations.

For others, job strain means the professional role uncertainty that has accompanied all the changes that have transpired in the world. For example, an occupational therapist who previously spent one-on-one time with her patients, now has to reinvent her profession. Telephonic parent consultations, Zoom sessions and at-home programmes have replaced the previously established model. None of these new methods are familiar, let alone proven, and this does create a significant degree of stress.

This level of uncertainty can be likened to your first day at university or the first day in a new job. It wasn't stressful because of pressure to meet a deadline or competing demands, but it was stressful due to the uncertainty of not knowing what your role was in that moment, in that specific situation.

I have consulted to many professionals who have taken on new roles, even dream jobs and by the end of the first week (in a few cases only one day), I receive a call from them with what has now become a familiar, 'I think I have made a mistake' or 'This may not be for me, I'm not sure what to do'. These feelings usually pass once uncertainty has been replaced with familiarity.

Job strain also stems from relentless demands and sheer overload. This is all too common at this time with every business trying to survive the economic fallout of COVID-19 and having every resource in a state of hyper-vigilance. According to a few recent reports, the average employee has been working two to three hours longer every day over this period.

Regardless of the source of job strain (role conflict, uncertainty or demands) the consequences on our mental and physical well-being are immense, not only impacting us on an individual level, but the broader workforce too. No one is effective when they constantly feel emotionally exhausted, disconnected from their own lives and regularly experience a low sense of accomplishment due to job strain-induced burnout. No emotional experience is without physical reactions and digestive issues, pain and sleep disorders amplify the stress already being experienced.

> Job strain can arise through role conflicts or uncertainty or due to high demands and long working hours.

Within a short space of time, job strain can negatively impact our attitude to work and projects, creating reduced satisfaction and commitment. This can progress to starting to look for new opportunities or, at the very least, affect overall job performance. In this elevated state of strain, the ability to access discretionary energy and perform beyond the basic job requirements is unlikely.

Sadly, this scenario is all too common and is playing out in businesses everywhere, every day. But there is a solution in that support, both emotionally and instrumentally, can prevent or reverse this scenario.

The concrete value of high levels of support within companies and their teams investigated in the large meta-analysis, showed that greater emotional and instrumental support reduced exhaustion, depersonalisation, increased sense of personal accomplishment and reduced all physical symptoms associated with chronic stress. It was also associated with greater job satisfaction and organisational commitment and with less turnover intention and better task performance.

> Creating a supportive environment will reduce employee exhaustion and stress-related health issues. Support will also promote job satisfaction, commitment and performance.

Support is transformational and central to every business's success but the type of support behaviour must be the right fit for your personality and match your skill set. Some of us have an affinity for emotional interactions and are able to connect with people on this level fairly easily. For others, this is very difficult and may be uncomfortable and fortunately, instrumental support such as mentorship, professional advice and practical assistance goes just as far.

The following self-assessment may help identify how you are faring in terms of providing support to others, and is also a means of identifying the possible ways support is being delivered throughout your organisation.

The assessment requires you to rate yourself on a scale of 1 to 5 on both an emotional and instrumental level. Add the total score on both sections; the outcomes might just surprise you!

Once you have completed both the assessments, add up your total score. A higher score suggests lower stress and high potential environment, whereas a lower score suggests an increased organisational or team stress and a possible health burden in the future.

- A score of 65 to 100 suggests exceptional leadership. You have a low stress footprint and are providing an environment for your team to thrive and grow.

Emotional Support	Definitely not	No	Sometimes	Yes	Very much
I provide others with regular encouragement	1	2	3	4	5
I gladly offer emotional support to those who need it	1	2	3	4	5
I encourage others to share their personal problems	1	2	3	4	5
I regularly show people my appreciation	1	2	3	4	5
I like to create positive narratives in the office	1	2	3	4	5
I show empathy for people's feelings and concerns at the office	1	2	3	4	5
I feel it's my responsibility to support my colleagues	1	2	3	4	5
I frequently make an effort to have a coffee or meal with my team	1	2	3	4	5
I feel I am trustworthy	1	2	3	4	5
I view my work colleagues as friends	1	2	3	4	5
Total score					

Instrumental Support	Definitely not	No	Sometimes	Yes	Very much
I frequently provide practical advice and assistance to my team	1	2	3	4	5
I regularly share knowledge and expertise related to work projects	1	2	3	4	5
I provide opportunities and directions that enable my team to grow	1	2	3	4	5
I try to engage in regular feedback sessions	1	2	3	4	5
I strongly subscribe to upskilling my team	1	2	3	4	5
I keep my team in the know pertaining to career advancement opportunities	1	2	3	4	5
I regularly mentor my team and do my utmost to support their professional growth	1	2	3	4	5
During difficult periods I provide material assistance to my team	1	2	3	4	5
I am always available to help find solutions to work-related challenges	1	2	3	4	5
I strongly champion my team's journey towards potential	1	2	3	4	5
Total score					

- A score of 40 to 64 suggests a fair degree of support within the office but there is room for improvement if you want to see your team fly.
- A score of 20 to 39 implies that there is a fair amount of stress within your team and/or organisation. By creating a more supportive environment, health and productivity is likely to increase.

The next aspect of the test is to get one or more of your team members to rate *you*. Often, we assume that the world sees us in much the same way as we view ourselves and this is frequently not the case. Objectivity, and the experiences on the other end of the table, so to speak, are vitally important in identifying inherent strengths and weaknesses. Incidentally, this can also serve as an exceptional trust-building and unifying exercise. While improvements can and should be made in areas that are lacking, it is equally important to further amplify your existing strengths.

Listen, always be fair, consistent and authentic

Organisational justice (or any justice) refers to the extent that individuals working in a business perceive that they are being treated justly and properly. It has been postulated that it is one of the largest contributors to any business's success. Fairness and justice are so important because injustices trigger strong feelings of anger and resentment which, from an ancestral perspective, signalled a threat to our survival and/or imminent danger.[30]

> From an ancestral perspective, feelings of injustice and a lack of fairness makes us want to remove ourselves from the offending environment. This may happen on a physical level (resignation), emotionally (disengagement) or in both capacities.

Research shows that justice perception guides us in the selection, interpretation and reaction to stimuli. It encourages us to approach rewarding life situations and remove ourselves from noxious environments.[31]

Research shows that when leaders and decision makers make decisions that promote unfairness or a sense of injustice, it triggers a decline in productivity, disinterest, physical and mental exhaustion, increased conflict, higher turnover intentions as well as higher levels of anxiety and stress.

> Organisational injustice results in reduced productivity, disinterest in work, physical and mental exhaustion as well as increased stress and anxiety.

However, the biggest danger that any business faces as a result of ongoing injustices is the threat of unethical behaviour from its employees.

The psychological impact of perceived unfairness is perfectly illustrated by South Africa's response to the lockdown in response to the COVID-19 pandemic. We can all agree that South Africa's response to the COVID-19 pandemic, under the leadership of Cyril Ramaphosa, has been nothing short of exceptional. The country's rapid and extreme measures radically curbed infection rates, allowed time for our healthcare system to get prepared and has undoubtedly saved an untold number of lives. However, it was not without its challenges. Even though there was an extension, the first 35 days of 'hard' lockdown were clearly defined. Only essential services were able to operate, with little to no exception, and despite the difficulties, the nation, for the most part, showed adherence and commitment to stopping the spread of the deadly virus. However, following the initial 35-day lockdown, as the nation moved into Level Four, many 'grey areas' outlined in the restrictions began to surface. The restricting of the sale of books, toys, sporting goods, clothing, alcohol, etc, created frustration, widespread animosity and public outcries. One of the biggest resentments stemmed from the three-hour time restriction that limited walking, cycling or running outdoors to between the hours of 6am and 9am. Parents with young families and many professionals simply couldn't make use of that time. Moreover, as the country approached winter, two-thirds of this 'outdoor time' was either spent in the dark, in the cold or a combination of both. Irritation and resentment grew, as the country began to question government's decisions and actions. The perception of injustice, inconsistency and unfairness induced significant stress in those affected.

> Strong organisational values and a commitment to fairness/justice will build loyalty and unwavering commitment among employees.

A recent research paper, 'The Impact of Organisational Justice on Ethical Behaviour',[32] highlights the undoing of many large multinational organisations due to poor organisational justice. The study points out that injustice leads to dissatisfaction within the workforce and has the potential to degrade into unethical behaviour in some employees. Arthur Anderson, British Petroleum, Enron, Toyota, Tyco, WorldCom and, more recently, VW, are some of the organisations where injustice translated into unethical behaviour. While these are some of the more extreme examples, this phenomenon is playing out in countless businesses around the world every day.

By contrast, when truth, strong values and moral practices form the core fabric of a business, employees will be loyal and will make significant personal sacrifices for the better good of the organisation.

By promoting fairness and organisational justice, leaders and managers will be able to augment organisational health and well-being and uplift lives.

High levels of justice and fairness impact the workforce in the following ways:[33]

Lower the risk of mental health compromise by ±60%	Lower the risk of physical health compromise by ±35%	Lower the risk of chronic disease diagnosis by ±55%

The promotion of fairness and justice can be organised into the four key areas of distributive, procedural, interpersonal and informational justice.[34] By paying close attention to each of these areas, managers and leaders can significantly improve productivity, engagement and overall employee commitment, while at the same time reducing anger and resentment within the workforce.

Distributive justice requires that your workforce believes that outcomes for their efforts are equitable (ie effort-reward balance). This would mean:

- Ensuring fair compensation and future opportunities for career/personal growth
- Equal pay
- Regular and proportionate recognition of your team's inputs and efforts

Procedural justice centres on fairness of the decision-making processes within the business. In order to promote this feeling among employees, you will need to take the following steps:

- Encourage your team to voice their opinion and listen
- Procedures and organisational processes must always be fair and consistent, no matter what position you hold in the company
- Truthfulness must be a set priority
- Always be ethical. Do what's right, not what's popular
- Stamp out bias and prejudice. This includes differences in race, religion, gender, sexual orientation, age, socio-economic status or physical disability

Interpersonal justice requires that the workforce is treated with respect, dignity and sensitivity. The focus for leaders and management should be on:

- Encouraging all employees to treat each other with respect and courtesy
- For management to treat all employees with politeness and respect
- The abuse of a position of authority should not be tolerated and should be dealt with swiftly

Informational justice centres on the ability to provide clear explanations and insights on current trends and issues impacting the business and its people. Leaders will need to:

- Be transparent and truthful
- Offer insights and explanations in real time
- Be clear and avoid vagueness

It is often assumed that justice and fairness within a business is a given, but it isn't and like many areas in life, requires hard work and tremendous effort.

In response to the global lockdown, many businesses reduced staff salaries and, in some instances, even had to lay off employees. Due to the general feeling of panic and urgency many organisations have been clinical and detached in their approach to cost-cutting. Blanket and impersonal communications such as emails and large group meetings outlining spend freezes and 50%, or greater, pay reductions with immediate effect, have been common practice. While these measures may be necessary, employees are expected to perform the same job (in some instances, with increased responsibilities) on a reduced salary, which in itself constitutes a form of distributive injustice. On its own this situation should not be an issue as there is a collective realisation that everyone needs to make some sort of sacrifice at this time. The primary challenge lies with the manner of communication, ie procedural justice. Research shows that when a message is communicated in an insensitive way, without regard for the feelings and the views of your teams, it has the potential to ignite thoughts of inequity and even unethical behaviour.

There are, however, businesses that have been confronted with the same circumstances that have excelled in this domain.

The CEO of McDonald's South Africa, Greg Solomon, recently got in touch with me. From a leadership-in-crisis standpoint, he checked every box. He made rapid decisions under pressure, adapted quickly to the new business reality, took ownership for shortcomings and strongly amplified positive messages, no matter how big or small.

His business employs almost 15 000 people, serving nearly 8 million customers a day. Being forced to close their doors for 66 days, followed by only being able to operate at 10% of capacity in the following weeks, was taking an enormous toll on the group. Survival in the future was a real concern; something I never imagined possible for this chain and that highlights the extreme challenges that exist at this time.

It reached a point where Greg and his management team were left with no choice but to cut expenditure in order to survive, which meant reducing salaries. Following clear and well-communicated personal conversations, supported by small group meetings, wage reductions were agreed upon. However, the scale of reduction was based on an employee's position in the company, with the CEO taking the biggest cut of more than 30% and the people on the ground only being impacted slightly. Not only was the survival message communicated sensitively and authentically, but the CEO showed additional solidarity with the struggle and allocated the entire advertising budget for food and care parcels for his workforce and their families. This was an unprecedented move that sent a powerful message of solidarity. By the end of October 2020, business was back to 95% of pre-COVID levels and growing every day.

Greg's leadership showed how, through challenges, we are given the unique opportunity to grow trust, build relationships and loyalty and shine on an individual level. Justice, fairness and doing what's right are the vehicles through which this can be achieved.

Fairness can be a state of mind

The perception of justice is both a subjective and objective experience. An extensive meta-analysis done by Australian researchers[35] showed that being happy, healthy, energised, motivated and generally active is associated with reduced feelings of injustice perception, regardless of the actual circumstances. Simply put, nothing fazes us if our mindset is positive.

Conversely, being stressed, angry, guilty, fearful, worried and nervous will increase a person's perception of a lack of fairness. At its core, we perceive that the world is against us and our back is up against the wall. We have all experienced this in some way when we are down, anxious or simply worried, the world appears unjust. We perceive the people around us to be insensitive and uncaring and life seems unfair. But then something happens that lifts our mood and these perceptions fade and a new reality replaces this negative illusory universe. Not to say that there aren't times when there is merit in the assertions, but as a general rule they get inflated when we're stressed, emotional and upset.

The value and power of health promotion, both on an individual and organisational level is vital. Every effort has to be made to ensure your teams have access to both knowledge and resources that can promote their well-being, especially during challenging times. If not, the consequences can be catastrophic, not just from a health and wellness perspective but from an injustice perception standpoint.

Diversity and inclusion

Even before the tragic killing of George Floyd and the much-needed awakening, the global justice movement and diversity and inclusion (or D&I), had become one of the most important organisational focus points within South African companies. Considering the country's complex social history and that we still have a very long way to go, we have made good progress over the last two decades. According to a 2018 McKinsey and Company report, South Africa has some of the highest levels of ethnic and cultural diversity in leadership roles seen anywhere in the world.[36] Organisational and societal discrimination or bias based on race, differences in religion, gender, sexual orientation, age, socio-economic status or physical disability, impacts all four pillars of justice, creating increased stress and anxiety throughout the entire business.

There have been a number of situations where I have been exposed to prejudice and bias on some level, and while the realisation of one of my lifelong dreams is an achievement I am proud of, it also resulted in me truly experiencing a level of discrimination I had not experienced before.

Ever since I was a child, I dreamt of walking through a full stadium at the opening ceremony of the Olympic Games, either as an athlete or as part of the support team. Growing up, I watched the opening ceremony every four years, saw the teams waving and smiling as they walked into the stadium and wanted to one day be part of that ultimate show of unity and recognition of an individual's value as well as the results of hard work.

'Rich, what do you want to be or do when you grow up?' I would be asked and every time I responded with my true aspiration, ie sport, people would laugh and I was told on countless occasions to choose something more 'realistic' or conventional – whatever that meant at the time.

I soon realised that I didn't have the physical aptitude to be a professional athlete and so I chose to be part of the coaching team. I studied by day and worked to support my studies at night and after many years, in the year 2000, I began working with a handful of professional athletes. Through passion, determination and unwavering commitment to their development, I went from national to international level and in 2007 I was offered a position as the athletic director for the Chinese Olympic team. The role required that I oversee a select group of athletes across different sports who were strong medal contenders. To be able to work with a team that could actually win medals at the Olympic Games was a dream come true and I accepted the position and moved to the Chinese capital, Beijing, and was based at the Olympic Training Centre.

The initial stages of this chapter of my life were not easy and the athletes and administration were not warm and welcoming and it was a very solitary and lonely existence. The first six months were particularly stressful. I didn't have any social support or a voice within the team due to a historic distrust of outsiders by the coaching staff and athletes, or any control over the decisions that had a direct impact on me owing to the 'iron fist' the administration wielded over the national programme. Added to this were the high demands and expectations, seven-day working weeks and no recognition for my role within the broader team. My emotional well-being and physical health really suffered during this period.

As time passed and I met inspiring people and was exposed to various introspective events, I realised that in order to change my reality, the onus was on me to change, which I did. I reframed my new circumstances as a profoundly positive experience and invested heavily in building trust and developing my relationships with the coaches, support staff and athletes. I fully immersed myself in Chinese culture and these shifts created a remarkable turnaround and I soon realised that I loved living in Beijing, loved my role within the team and was so fortunate to work with the athletes every day. In a nutshell, my life completely changed but *I* had to make that change.

However, the team's senior administration were not easy and were highly intolerant, dictatorial, abrupt (or just plain rude) and hard to engage with, but it was a universal experience for all team members, so we shrugged it off and stuck together.

The months flew by and as they did I felt more and more at home in China. The people were caring, authentic and warm and the athletes became my close family. They collectively undertook to teach me Mandarin and by the end of the first year I could communicate (albeit poorly) the basics like, 'What on earth is this that I'm eating?!' and this further built trust and solidified the existing unity within the team. It was one of the most special and meaningful points in my life and the best was yet to come – the Olympics!

As the games drew nearer, all the injured athletes had recovered and found their form and my role within the team was fully valued and appreciated. About four weeks before the opening ceremony, we were shuttled to the tailors and fitted for our Olympic kit. It felt like a large-scale synchronised swimming event, where countless tailors and hundreds of athletes were engaging in perfect harmony. Despite the official outfit being downright hideous and resembling a flamboyant and futuristic cartoon character, I couldn't contain my excitement and soaked up each and every moment of what was somewhat of a surreal experience.

Two weeks later, my kit was dropped off at my room and I rushed to try it on. The pants were oversized, the belt would only fit a 3-year-old, the shirtsleeves were asymmetrical, the shoes needed six pairs of socks to stop my feet from slipping and the hat covered everything except my nose. Yet, I couldn't have been prouder or happier and I quickly ironed it and hung it up in anticipation of the big day.

A few days before the opening ceremony, one of the administrators asked me and another foreign member of the team to join him in his office. He told us that the administration had decided that we would not be staying with the athletes at the Olympic village and there was no further explanation provided.

We both walked out of his office feeling incredibly disappointed and knew we were going to miss out on a large part of the atmosphere and excitement, but we accepted the decision graciously, but asked one another what the reason might be and eventually put it down to size of the team and that accommodation was limited. At the back of our minds we suspected it was because we were foreign, but there was nothing we could do about it so we shrugged our shoulders.

Finally, the day arrived. The day dawned a bit overcast and there were fears of rain but that didn't overshadow the heightened emotions of the day. This was the day that gave meaning to all the years of hard work, sacrifice, effort and discipline.

At around midday, my teammate and I were again summoned to the administrator's office and I initially thought that they had decided to move us to the village and this would be confirmation thereof and a briefing pertaining to the logistics. As it turned out, this was not the case. The 'boss', as everyone called him, was with our close friend Brian who was our translator. Brian looked very stressed, which seemed odd considering that all the work had been done and the team was well prepared and ready.

As the door closed, Brian looked at us and said, 'My boss … um … has … um … decided that you will not be in the opening ceremony – sorry.' I was shocked. Surely this couldn't be happening! I quickly asked why and Brian smiled nervously, looked at the 'boss' and said, 'Because you are not Chinese, and we don't believe our government will appreciate having you walk with our athletes.' Brian's eyes welled up as he saw our reaction and he knew the injustice of the circumstances and the impact it had on me. He then quietly said, 'I am so sorry, if it was up to me, I would not let this happen but there is nothing we can do.' I knew this to be true as Brian had proven to be one of the 'good' guys. The 'boss' in his usual rude and dismissive manner then told us to leave.

I never knew whose decision it was – the 'boss' or a direct government instruction, but my dream had been shattered. I was hurt, angry and resentful. There was no merit in the decision, only nationalism and prejudice and I knew that the day the games were over, I was going to resign well before my contract was due to expire after the London Olympics in four years' time.

When I told some of the athletes about what had transpired, they were upset on my behalf and did their best to console us. That level of authentic care and support helped me put aside my feelings, pick myself up and throw everything I had at the games. I was no longer doing it for myself, but rather for the team and that turned out to be a very powerful motivation.

The outcome speaks for itself and that year, the team won 51 gold medals and over 100 medals in total.

I stayed in China for another year or so after that and enjoyed my time with the athletes and the people of the country. A piece of me is still there but the injustice never left my subconscious; the overt prejudice affected me so severely that I could not let it go so I made a decision to not continue in team sports following my resignation at the end of 2009. Incidentally, I still have my Olympic kit and from time to time, I put it on; laughter always ensues!

The business case

During 2019 and 2020, I was part of a panel that rated the country's 20 best HR directors, drawn from top-listed companies and non-listed entities. Over a period of several months, I performed lengthy individual interviews with this impressive group of individuals. The structure of the interviews centred on key themes that included:

- Strategy and leadership
- Transformation and empowerment
- Technology and HR
- Learning and development
- Talent management
- Employee value proposition

Despite clear delineation within the interview process, the topic of diversity and inclusion came up in every category that formed the basis of the interview. The D&I movement has its roots in the US civil rights struggle dating back to the 1960s and began with affirmative action legislation designed to remedy discrimination; not dissimilar to South Africa's journey in the mid-1990s.

Over time, the concept of D&I has evolved from simply a compliance focus to a much broader moral mandate where many aspects of diversity and inclusion are now valued and strongly considered. These encompass differences in race, religion, gender, sexual orientation, age, socio-economic status or physical disability as well as the feeling of belonging, respect, acceptance and participation from all members of the business.

Companies with greater diversity in their leadership teams are 21% more likely to perform better from a profitability standpoint.

D&I is increasingly being recognised as not only a societal responsibility, but a business imperative too. Are business leaders and managers finally appreciating the value of justice, the fundamental importance of fairness and the broader significance of equality? This is true to a degree, and it may have started out that way, but when companies begin to identify the enormous return on investment, the motivation becomes far stronger.

D&I promotes growth and value creation, regardless of the location, size and nature of the business. For example, during a 10-year period, the Top 50 US companies in the diversity space outperformed the Dow Jones Industrial Average by 22%.[37] In 2018 McKinsey & Company published a report on how diversity delivers fiscal returns. The report reaffirmed the global relevance of the correlation between diversity in leadership roles of large companies and positive performance. The research looked at 12 countries (including South Africa) and involved 1 000 companies and the primary measures of outcome were profitability and value creation or economic profit.[38]

Companies with higher cultural and ethnic diversity within executive teams are 33% more likely to have industry-leading profitability.

What the researchers found was that companies in the top quartile for gender diversity on executive teams were 21% more likely to outperform on profitability and 27% more likely to have superior value creation. The highest-performing companies also had more women in income-generating executive roles. The report also found that gender diversity was not the only driver of exceptional business success. According to the authors: 'Companies in the top quartile for ethnic/cultural diversity on executive teams were 33% more likely to have industry-leading profitability'.

Not only are there positive associations with D&I, there are also negative ones should you choose to sit by idly and not champion the long-standing social cause. According to the McKinsey report, companies in the bottom quartile for both gender and ethnic/cultural diversity were 29% less likely to achieve above average profitability compared to a collective of companies reviewed in the data set. If as a decision maker you do not drive D&I, not only are you not fulfilling your moral responsibility, but the company may fall behind and success may be limited.

The companies with the most culturally and ethnically diverse boards are 43% more likely to experience higher profits.

Many leading businesses in South Africa, and around the world, have been strongly committed to transformation, but while the numbers may look good on paper, further analysis of the different stratifications within a business reveals that the gaping hole often tends to be at the executive level. This is a huge mistake in many respects as not only does it suggest procedural and disruptive injustice, which will impact trust and lower morale, it will also have a direct bearing on organisational success.

Over and above the promotion of organisational justice and subsequent reductions in stress and anxiety, together with increased productivity and employee commitment, the value of D&I includes access to greater talent, enhanced decision-making and tremendous depth of consumer insight.

Although cultural and gender diversity is now firmly on the agenda for many of the world's leading companies (largely as a consequence of the recent global uprisings and growing awareness) the 'inclusion' part may still be lagging. According to another McKinsey & Company report entitled 'Women Matter, Taking the Lead on Inclusion', senior male managers are twice as likely to become members of the executive committee when compared to their female counterparts.[39] Plus, if women do make it to executive level, males are 500% more likely to become CEOs than their female peers.

The same report highlights that compared to men, women need to constantly provide more evidence of their competence, are more prone to having their judgement questioned, are addressed in a less professional manner and considered to be more junior than they are and subjected to demeaning remarks. Such bias and prejudice should not and cannot exist.

There are several action steps and ideas to better promote organisational inclusion that include:[40]

- Acknowledge that diversity and inclusion is not only a moral and social responsibility central to promoting fairness and justice within a business, but also an essential tool in driving its success. Diverse teams have a far better understanding of market trends and consumer needs, which ultimately creates better growth and innovation opportunities.
- Eliminate all forms of bias. Not only does this require that you and your team lead by example, but it may also entail additional training,

specialist guidance and well-positioned mentorships.

- Create a safe team environment where all employees can voice their opinion, be heard and feel welcome. Embrace different opinions and ideas and work to promote collaboration among diverse staff and try to provide actionable feedback.
- Prize authenticity over conformity. Some (in all probability, many) of your greatest opportunities will come from the non-conformists within the group.
- Don't penalise failure, allow room for experimentation and most importantly, create a platform for less orthodox solutions.
- Hold yourself and your leadership team accountable for improvements in D&I. Set attainable goals, create weigh-in opportunities and be prepared to change the game plan if the existing model is not producing good enough returns.

Interpersonal injustice and bullying

It was a Friday at 2pm and I had just completed a talk on organisational stress and personal resilience to a team of high-performing executives. At the end of the session, one of the attendees approached me and asked if she could have a few minutes of my time to discuss some challenges she was facing. She was the star performer of the highest-performing team at the company and, according to HR, she was able to do the work of two people, never dropped the ball and showed unparalleled commitment. She lived for her work and was really good at it, but her work environment was becoming increasingly strained, as she had become a victim of workplace bullying, a form of interpersonal injustice. Personality clashes within her team (ie intolerances for individual differences) and workplace stress were the primary drivers. The bullying was relentless and occurred covertly, as bullying so often does), without the knowledge of her superiors or anyone else at the company. She was on the receiving end of daily hostility, social undermining and total exclusion.

As we started speaking, she broke down. The tears streamed down her face and she was inconsolable. Within a few months, the hostile work environment had triggered major depression and generalised anxiety, to the extent that she was seeing a psychiatrist and had to be medicated. Despite these steps, she had reached breaking point and decided to take some time off to reassess her career.

The harassment had not only injured her as a star performer and as a member of her family, but also the organisation. Our conversation was not intended to gain my input or advice but was a safe space for her to share her experiences and try make sense of the circumstances.

With her permission, I called for a meeting with the head of HR who was a powerhouse who took everyone's personal well-being as her own responsibility. Once the organisation was made aware of the circumstances, they were able to provide the employee with the necessary support and address the issue. As uncomfortable as it was for all the parties involved, the matter was thoroughly investigated and effectively dealt with. Several months later, the offending individuals left the organisation, seemingly of their own accord. Fortunately, after an eight-week absence, the star performer decided to return to work and resumed her position.

Unfortunately, the profound impact that interpersonal injustice can have on people, their families and a business is, sadly, a far too common occurrence.

Bullying in the workplace is difficult to contain and monitor because it is normally something that takes place clandestinely, out of sight of leadership and co-workers. Despite this, the prevalence is still reported to be exceptionally high. According to a meta-analysis published in the *Journal of Occupational and Organizational Psychology*, 15% of the world's workforce (495 million workers) are currently subjected to some form of occupational abuse and/or bullying.[41]

Research shows large regional and socio-economic differences in bullying prevalence. A 2013 study involving 44 836 employees in 44 countries, showed that employees in poorer countries reported greater degrees of abuse and victimization.[42] Another prevailing trend is larger, male-dominated companies show higher rates of interpersonal injustice.

With the knowledge of the personal and organisational implications, leadership and management need to effectively prevent this form of injustice from impacting their business. Because this pattern of behaviour is so complex and involves many personal character traits and group dynamics, it makes it very different to address even with a team of highly trained organisational and clinical psychologists.

But the research does show that there are strong associations between workplace bullying and the prevailing job circumstances together with the social environment within an organisation. High stress at work, combined with an intolerant and unsupportive culture results in interpersonal injustice. A large review published a few years ago described several core stresses that trigger workplace bullying:[43]

- Role conflict – having too many responsibilities
- Workload – having too much work all the time
- Role ambiguity – uncertainty regarding your role amid all the changes
- Job insecurity

If you consider these stresses on a personal level, it is easy to appreciate how strong the relationship is. When we feel that we have too many responsibilities at any given time, are overwhelmed, are uncertain about our roles and feel that our financial well-being is threatened, more often than not, our default response is to lash out at those closest to us. Abrupt communication, shorter tempers, general intolerance and lack of consideration, all become more commonplace, despite our awareness and best efforts to curtail these behaviours.

While leaders and managers can't always control or influence many of the individual and team characteristics that contribute to workplace bullying, the organisational stresses can be successfully managed. It is the responsibility of every leader to ensure the safety,

It is the responsibility of every leader to ensure the safety, and to protect, the well-being of their workforce.

and to protect the well-being of his or her employees, which is why addressing abuse, victimisation and exclusion is so important.

Workplace bullying increases the risk of developing depression, anxiety disorders and stress-related psychological complaints.[44] Moreover, it also has a dramatic effect on illness-related absenteeism, increasing the prevalence by 58%.[45] Not only can workplace bullying increase the risk of mental and emotional disorders, but it can also result in physical health compromise. For example, in 2018 a large multi-group study involving 45 906 individuals showed that being on the receiving end of interpersonal injustice in the workplace increases the risk of developing Type 2 diabetes by 46%.[46]

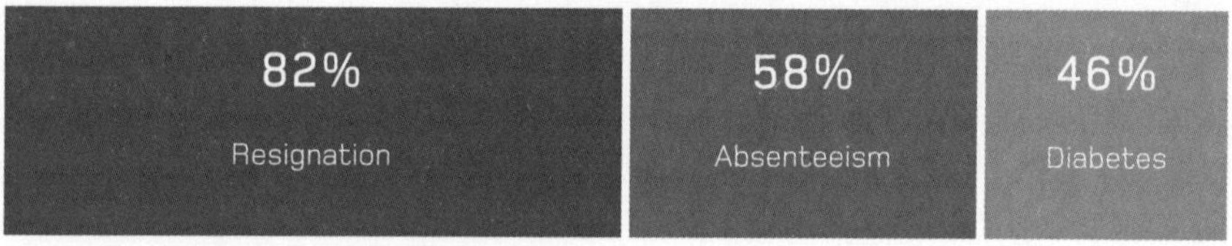

The impact of bullying and abuse of position in the workplace

Depression, anxiety and physical health compromise will often result in absenteeism, presenteeism and reduced productivity. However, interpersonal injustice also comes with the risk of employee resignation. According to one study, 82% of harassed employees left their workplace.[47] The primary contributors to their departure were related to acquired health issues (38%) as well as poor performance appraisals (44%).

Over and above the overwhelming human cost there are significant economic implications of interpersonal injustice for the company relating to lost productivity and employee turnover.

Leaders have to rigorously reinforce a work culture that promotes fairness and justice. Moreover, they have to take every possible measure to control role conflict, excessive workload, role ambiguity and job insecurity.

These stresses can be effectively reduced or mitigated by using the following strategies:

High demands and excessive workload

- Help equip your workforce with knowledge, skills and resources to better cope with stress and manangement of their health
- Keep your finger on the pulse and adjust workload if/when necessary

Job insecurity

- Encourage and facilitate ongoing skills development and training
- Create/provide income protection plans
- Involve your workforce in unfolding events, ie be transparent
- Provide support (emotional and instrumental) to employees

Role conflict

- Make sure that your employees' values are not jeopardised by the roles that they are required to perform
- Be flexible and understanding of family demands on employees
- Try not to let work responsibilities be all-consuming where they interfere with basic personal responsibilities

Role ambiguity

- Set and define clear and achievable goals
- Define the parameters of autonomy and authority
- Be decisive
- Encourage innovation and new idea sets
- Build and develop self-worth/belief within your team
- Encourage resilience training
- Encourage time away from work-related activities to allow for regrouping
- Promote trust and fairness

Nurture an effort-reward balance

If you want to bring the best out of your team, it is important to maintain a strong effort-reward balance. We often assume that this balance is solely associated with monetary gratification, but this is not true. While paying your teams fairly is a qualifier for engagement, and is central to an effort-reward balance, there are other avenues of reward that need to be considered. These include:

- Providing opportunities for career advancement
- Providing an environment, that allows for the promotion of self-esteem and respect
- Ensuring job security

Putting the effort-reward balance into simpler terms, means being respected and appreciated for the role that you play both in your professional and personal life.

This is not surprising, considering that we all want to feel valued. For any of us to be truly happy, we need to feel that we are unique and that we have a strong purpose in life. This sense of purpose can be realised through many different avenues, one of which includes succeeding in our chosen profession.

As children, it is the activities that we do well at and receive praise for that later become our identity and possibly even our life's mission. It is therefore so important to be recognised and valued for these skills and abilities as an adult.

Coronavirus and deeper progression into the Fourth Industrial Revolution has changed the world. Most of us are simply trying to survive and get through the exponential changes so carving out our own unique space and excelling at something has become increasingly difficult, if not impossible. With less opportunities, together with greater competition in all areas, we have had to push ourselves harder and harder to set ourselves apart and gain much-needed recognition, often risking burnout in the process. Not being appreciated, recognised and valued for the role we play at work has a profound effect on our mental and physical well-being.

> An effort-reward imbalance increases the likelihood of developing depression by 49%.

A recent meta-analysis involving 84 963 employees showed that an effort-reward imbalance is a strong predictor of the onset of depression in organisations.[48] It can also result in significant physical health compromise, including major hormonal imbalances. A 2019 study investigated the effects of two years of an effort-reward imbalance on cortisol production.[49] The study included 150 individuals with an average age of 42 years old and cortisol levels were measured at various points throughout the study period and beyond. The researchers found that the stress associated with an ongoing effort-reward imbalance was associated with blunted cortisol production. Producing too little cortisol can be extremely detrimental to health and symptoms include weakness, mental confusion, physical pain, rashes, allergies and even an abnormal heart rate.

An effort-reward imbalance can result in abnormal cortisol levels leading to physical and emotional compromise.

Yet this might be only the tip of the iceberg as cortisol is a critically important hormone that needs to be perfectly controlled in order for us to remain mentally, emotionally and physically healthy. It is common knowledge that chronic stress is associated with significantly raised cortisol. Research shows that raised cortisol can also manifest in internalising behaviours such as anxiety and depression as well as externalising behaviours that include aggression and attention issues.[50] What is less well understood is that long-term stress results in blunted cortisol production, which is known to further entrench the symptom set as a consequence by raised cortisol. In other words, both raised or blunted cortisol can cause significant emotional and mental health disorders.

Symptoms such as chronic fatigue, depression, anxiety, pain and allergies are hardly conducive conditions for the creation and the promotion of an inspired and productive workforce.

Today's employees are looking for more than a decent pay cheque, a pat on the back and a contrived smile and leaders and managers are therefore required to understand the entire effort-reward framework better.

The effort-reward model distinguishes between extrinsic situational components and intrinsic personal components. Research clearly shows that these components in combination determine health and performance outcomes in the workforce.[51] The external factors that contribute to this imbalance include job demands and assignment autonomy mismatched by remuneration, career-advancement opportunities and all-important appreciation. The intrinsic factors include excessive effort for the purpose of achieving approval and self-esteem. Simply stated – overcommitment.

The typical profile of overcommitted team members encompasses strong ambition combined with the need to control and gain esteem from others. These individuals have a difficult time withdrawing from work.

In many ways, we can all identify with overcommitment at some point in our career, or perhaps you are currently battling with it. Whether stemming from ambition and wanting to accelerate your career, or being driven by the need for approval by others, the stress and health effects are significant. Symptoms of long-term overcommitment include insomnia, poor self-rated health, emotional exhaustion and burnout.

Tackling overcommitment

There are ways leaders and managers can support employees who are experiencing (or are prone to) overcommitment in their professional lives. They have a role they can play in mitigating this organisational stress. While this stress often stems from life experiences, background and intrinsic personality, there are several action steps that decision makers can, and should, take to protect their star performers.

Step 1: Commit your teams to fewer projects

This is not easy when you have a team of star performers and are trying to grow the business as the knee-jerk response is to place the best people on all the important projects. However, as motivating and capable as these individuals are, they too have a finite capacity to manage workload.

Some time ago, a close friend of mine asked me to meet with one of his staff members who was suffering with various health concerns. His words to me were, 'Whatever it takes to help her, please do it. She is my best performer and I honestly can't function without her. Send me the invoice, have to go ... bye.'

A few days later I met the star performer and performed a range of assessments consisting of questionnaires, physical testing and some additional metabolic testing. During the initial screening/meeting she described her overwhelming experience of depression and anxiety, which was accompanied by ailing health. Because she was only in her late 20s, this came as a surprise. She was seeing a psychiatrist and was taking medication but stated that it only helped to a degree. She was burnt out, exhausted and she wasn't sleeping. She described her life as joyless with no purpose and as she unpacked her days, it was clear that she was overcommitted in a professional capacity in every respect, to the extent that breathing almost had to be scheduled in and bathroom breaks cut down.

Although there was a lot that could be done to improve her emotional and physical set through the proper application of dietary and nutritional interventions as well as environmental controls and selected therapies, unless she reduced her workload and the number of projects she was involved in, she was not going to appreciably change her current health landscape and steep decline in performance.

By committing your teams to only a handful of assignments, you are able to unlock greater productivity and engagement. Moreover, immersion in fewer projects will allow for more creative and innovative solutions and a greater probability of overall success.

Regular multitasking can lead to a decrease in IQ by 11%.

More than a decade of research has shown that multitasking negatively impacts memory and goal orientation.

A landmark study at York University[52] showed that multitasking was

Regular multitasking results in reduced brain volume.

responsible for reduced scores on a general comprehension test, at an average of 11%. In other words, regular multitasking can reduce your IQ. Surprisingly, the same study found that those individuals who worked in close proximity to multitaskers were also impacted with these bystanders showing a 17% reduction in general comprehension.

The impact of multitasking on cognition has puzzled scientists for some time and a team of researchers at University College in London were able to uncover this mechanism in the brain. Using advanced brain imagery, the scientists found that repeated exposure to multitasking causes atrophy in the anterior cingulate cortex of the brain.[53] This region is responsible for emotional regulation, attention allocation and impulse control.

Narrowing your team's task window will not only reduce organisational stress and profoundly enhance productivity, but it will also improve employee health and cognition.

Step 2: Clarify individual, team and organisational roles

The world is in a state of hyper vigilance and businesses are frantically looking to find new opportunities and rapidly create the 'new normal'.

It is imperative that time needs to be invested with the same caution and care as financial resources. Creating and communicating a shortlist of priorities will not only protect your teams from overcommitment, but will help to promote greater success. Leaders should endeavour to define individual and team roles and match these to the organisation's strategic objectives.

Overcommitment stress can be effectively reduced by better clarification of professional roles and better defined core priorities.

Much as the same as professional tennis, every player and their team have two objectives: to win a Grand Slam and reach Number 1 in the world. The effort required for a player to reach a final of a Grand Slam can be overlooked, almost as if the player has reached that point in the tournament based on talent alone. Yet, in reality, the journey to get there has been exhausting and has taken the time and effort of teams of highly committed professionals. At the top, support teams operate with military precision, working to create the perfect conditions for tennis excellence. Everyone has their designation and their roles are clearly defined with minimal time wastage.

For example, on game day, the role of the trainer is to help warm up the player for the pre-match practice, mix the recovery drinks, take towels to the court and take on the role of ball boy/girl during the session. Following the warm-up, the trainer will stretch the player, perform a light massage, mix a new batch of recovery drinks for the match, make sure there is a specific pre-game meal available and run errands such as fetching racquets, etc. Thirty minutes before the match, the trainer will take the player through another warm-up involving a range of match simulations, give the player a pep talk of sorts and head to the box, where their role transforms into that of a cheerleader for the next two to five hours. After the match, the trainer will help stretch the player, perform a recovery massage, set up the cold-plunging facilities, make sure there is a post-game meal available and help the player debrief from the match, whether they won or lost, with the rest of the team.

What makes this work is that each team member has a clearly defined role and is fully accountable for a specific outcome. Not only do these conditions limit the likelihood of over-commitment, but they also create the platform for success. Putting together a group of specialists, placed in their perfect role, working with other talent, can potentially create history. This model not only applies to sport at the highest level, but also to businesses – your business!

Step 3: Show more appreciation and care

Overcommitment often stems from the strong desire to feel valued and needed. To mitigate this stress, leaders and their management teams should set aside time every week to connect with their teams in a meaningful way. Having coffee or lunch together or just spending 30 minutes of your time talking to the person, as opposed to the employee, will make a profound difference.

Tackling the external factors

There are several converging factors that need to be constantly managed in order to reduce the stress of an effort-reward imbalance. The stress of job insecurity is arguably one of the more urgent challenges many businesses are facing. An integrated model that promotes skills development within the workforce, together with income-projection plans, transparent communications and strong support infrastructure, can go a long way in reducing this stress.

Carefully monitoring all the parts in this delicate balance can be well-served by using the assessment/checklist below. This list can be used to evaluate your teams, the entire workforce and yourself. Once the test is completed, areas that require action will become far more transparent.

- A score of 32 to 48 means there is a significant effort-reward imbalance and organisational stress is likely to be high. Identify two or three core areas that need improvement and put together a guiding coalition who will be responsible for bringing the new performance vision to fruition. Due to the level of importance, strong communication and urgency must accompany the change vision.
- A score of 20 to 31 means there is a good platform to work off but the level of stress is still likely to be high which means there is work to be done. Focusing on key areas will drive the new wellness and performance vision forward.
- A score of 12 to 19 means that the effort-reward balance is exemplary and organisational stress is likely to be low, employee health good and productivity high. Maintain this level of balance and continue with existing models.

Effort-reward balance	Strongly disagree	Disagree	Agree	Strongly agree
The current organisational work-load is very high	1	2	3	4
We are often required to work late and on weekends	1	2	3	4
The workdays are often interrupted and disturbed by meetings and administrative responsibilities	1	2	3	4
The physical and emotional demands of the job are visibly taking their toll on me and/or my team	1	2	3	4
Leadership and management always show proper respect for their teams	1	2	3	4
Our work environment promotes respect and support among colleagues	1	2	3	4
The organisation strives for fair-ness and justice	1	2	3	4
Career advancement, growth and succession planning are a central focus within the business	1	2	3	4
Professional roles echo educa-tion and training within the workforce	1	2	3	4
All employees are properly recognised for their efforts and achievements	1	2	3	4
Salaries and financial compensa-tion packages reflect efforts and achievements	1	2	3	4
Job security is a priority within the business	1	2	3	4
Total score				

The game plan

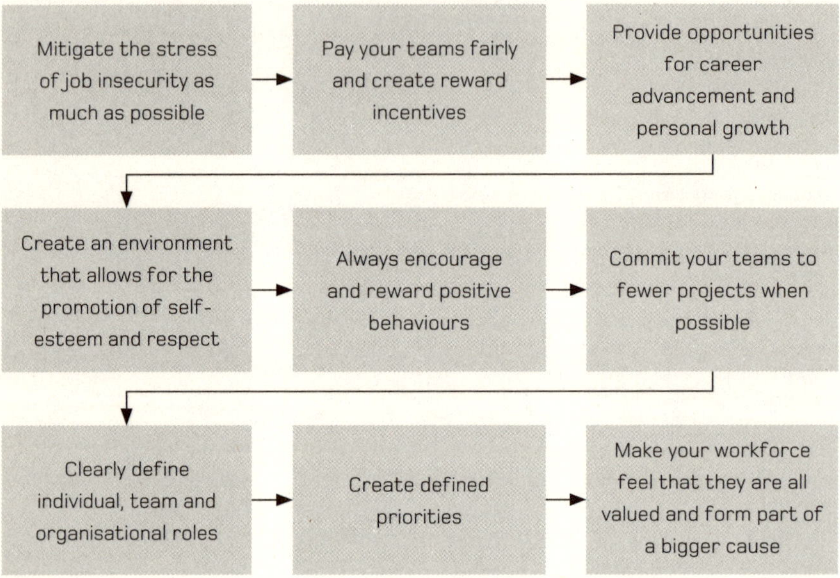

THE GAME PLAN

We are living in one of the most challenging and stressful times in human history. Recent media headlines tell us: 'The coronavirus pandemic is the worst crisis to face the world since World War II' – UN Secretary General

'The world should be prepared for the worst economic fallout since the Great Depression' – IMF

'1.6 billion workers in immediate danger of losing their livelihoods due to the coronavirus pandemic' – ILO

The world is grappling with unprecedented economic fallout, a growing education crisis and multiple converging health epidemics including stress and COVID-19, further fuelled by the rapid and exponential changes of the Fourth Industrial revolution.

Society's trust in NGOs, the media and government is at a low point, leaving businesses and their leadership to stem the tide.

Many businesses are in a colossal fight for their survival and it is blatantly obvious that with the collective set of conditions the world is operating under, an entirely new brand of leadership and organisational management is urgently needed.

The climate of fear and uncertainty demands that leaders and decision makers step out of their comfort zone and respond not only to business and industry issues, but political events, national challenges and employee health. Moreover, the role requires that they champion diversity and inclusion and fight environmental and social causes.

This new captaincy also commands exemplary self-management and personal awareness, as leaders will be expected to consistently radiate optimism and enthusiasm and show unwavering trust and belief in themselves and the people around them.

The modern leader needs to be mindful that the operating models that proved successful in the past, including risk aversion, conformity and refinement of existing practices, may need to be augmented or potentially even replaced by a creative vision, a fearless mindset, brave originality and vastly expanded thinking.

In order for businesses to thrive in these unpredictable and uncertain times, they will need to become considerably more productive and highly agile. This is no easy task, considering the current trends towards restructuring, downsizing, market changes and spend freezes. These efficiency-directed changes amplify employee stress, mental and physical health compromise and general unhappiness, all established productivity drains.

As daunting as it may seem, this is attainable with a clear vision, defined strategy and strong drive. Inspiring leadership, stress buffering and management, together with health promotion, are the fundamental building blocks for creating a successful culture where a shared purpose and shared values inspire each individual to reach their potential, culminating in a collective greatness.

Without sound individual and organisational health (especially mental health), talent cannot be fully realised, enthusiasm becomes faded, a business team cannot be innovative, it will not be able to deal with and anticipate change, it will struggle to display trust and engage in teamwork and ambitions will simply be unattainable. Through its influence on health and relationships, it is painfully obvious that stress has become one of the greatest barriers standing in the way of personal or professional success.

Fortunately, today's leaders, decision makers and management teams can draw on the wealth of scientific research into human health and organisational wellness and apply these learnings, with great speed and urgency. The four basic wellness pillars include: the strategic implementation of a health and wellness vision (ie creating a health orientated culture); the provision of health support tools; ongoing professional skills development and a shift in management practices that focus on inspiring the workforce and reducing organisational stress.

By combining and applying these interventions, lives can be positively changed, inequalities neutralised, potential unlocked, businesses protected and communities transformed, potentially setting in motion the much-needed socio-economic repair and healing.

Bringing a new performance vision to life is not without its challenges and therefore identifying the more common roadblocks and providing a road map to overcome them, is a key function. Circumnavigating personal and employee time limitations, budget restraints and how best to communicate this change vision to maximise its effectiveness are vital to success.

We all have to be part of this new generation of leaders in these stressful and uncertain times. Leadership is no longer about a title, but centres on actions and the impact we can have on the people around us. Because of this, we constantly need to strive towards being aspirational because relatable role models make us aim higher and, in essence, unlocks human potential. Leaders need to strive towards creating and promoting authentic connections, being empathetic and compassionate and endeavour to protect the well-being of those in their care. While we can't always control the events and circumstances that we are confronted with, we *can* control our responses and actions and this is important for our well-being and future success, and for the lives and health of those around us.

NOTES AND REFERENCES

All website references were live and correct during the research and writing process of this project.

1. The Conundrum

1 Konturek, Peter C., T. Brzozowski, and S. J. Konturek. 'Stress and the gut: pathophysiology, clinical consequences, diagnostic approach and treatment options'. *Journal of Physiology and Pharmacology* 62.6 (2011): 591–599.

2 Canavan, Caroline, Joe West, and Timothy Card. 'The epidemiology of irritable bowel syndrome'. *Clinical epidemiology* 6 (2014): 71.

3 Crohn's disease is an inflammatory bowel disease. It causes inflammation of your digestive tract, which can lead to abdominal pain, severe diarrhoea, fatigue, weight loss and malnutrition. Inflammation caused by Crohn's disease can involve different areas of the digestive tract in different people.

4 Ulcerative colitis is an inflammatory bowel disease that causes long-lasting inflammation and ulcers (sores) in your digestive tract. Ulcerative colitis affects the innermost lining of the large intestine (colon) and rectum.

5 Ng, Siew C., et al. 'Worldwide incidence and prevalence of inflammatory bowel disease in the 21st century: a systematic review of population-based studies'. *The Lancet* 390.10114 (2017): 2769–2778.

6 Dhabhar, Firdaus S., et al. 'Stress-induced redistribution of immune cells—From barracks to boulevards to battlefields: A tale of three hormones–Curt Richter Award Winner'. *Psychoneuroendocrinology* 37.9 (2012): 1345–1368.

7 Dhabhar, Firdaus S. 'The short-term stress response–Mother nature's mechanism for enhancing protection and performance under conditions of threat, challenge, and opportunity'. *Frontiers in Neuroendocrinology* 49 (2018): 175–192.

8 Fitzmaurice, Christina, et al. 'Global, regional, and national cancer incidence, mortality, years of life lost, years lived with disability, and disability-adjusted life-years for 29 cancer groups, 1990 to 2016: a systematic analysis for the global burden of disease study'. JAMA oncology 4.11 (2018): 1553–1568.

9 Cohen, Sheldon, et al. 'Chronic stress, glucocorticoid receptor resistance, inflammation, and disease risk'. *Proceedings of the National Academy of Sciences* 109.16 (2012): 5995–5999.

10 Song, Huan, et al. 'Association of stress-related disorders with subsequent autoimmune disease'. JAMA 319.23 (2018): 2388–2400.

11 Curran, Thomas, and Andrew P. Hill. 'Perfectionism is increasing over time: A meta-analysis of birth cohort differences from 1989 to 2016'. *Psychological Bulletin* 145.4 (2019): 410.

12 O'Donovan, Aoife, et al. 'Elevated risk for autoimmune disorders in Iraq and Afghanistan veterans with posttraumatic stress disorder'. *Biological Psychiatry* 77.4 (2015): 365–374.

13 These changes include reduced responsiveness of the immune system to the regulatory effects of cortisol, the increased expression of inflammatory cells through NF-κB, altered patterns of gene expression and methylation in immune cells and increased immune cell ageing.

14 https://www.who.int/whr/2001/media_centre/press_release/en/

15 Ansell, Emily B., et al. 'Cumulative adversity and smaller gray matter volume in medial prefrontal, anterior cingulate, and insula regions'. *Biological Psychiatry* 72.1 (2012): 57–64.

16 Koolschijn, P. Cédric MP, et al. 'Brain volume abnormalities in major depressive disorder: A meta-analysis of magnetic resonance imaging studies'. *Human brain mapping* 30.11 (2009): 3719–3735.

17 Chetty, Sundari, et al. 'Stress and glucocorticoids promote oligodendrogenesis in the adult hippocampus'. *Molecular psychiatry* 19.12 (2014): 1275.

18 Daniels, Judith K., et al. 'White matter integrity and its relationship to PTSD and childhood trauma—A systematic review and meta-analysis'. *Depression and anxiety* 30.3 (2013): 207–216.

19 Chao, Linda L., et al. 'Preliminary evidence of increased hippocampal myelin content in veterans with posttraumatic stress disorder'. *Frontiers in Behavioral Neuroscience* 9 (2015): 333.

2. Why Now?

1 https://ourworldindata.org/economic-growth.

2 The Maddison Project Database provides information on comparative economic growth and income levels over the long term.

3 https://ourworldindata.org/human-development-index.

4 Schwab, Klaus. The Fourth Industrial Revolution. Currency, 2017.

5 https://www.imf.org/external/datamapper/NGDP_RPCH@WEO/WEOWORLD.

6 https://www.weforum.org/reports/how-to-end-a-decade-of-lost-productivity-growth.

7 https://ourworldindata.org/hunger-and-undernourishment.

8 https://ourworldindata.org/hunger-and-undernourishment.

9 Methylation is a simple biochemical process and is the transfer of four atoms from one substance to another. It has a significant positive impact on many biochemical reactions in the body that regulate the activity of the cardiovascular, neurological, reproductive, and detoxification systems.

10 Neurotrophins are a family of proteins that induce the survival, development, and function of nerve cells in the body.

11 Glycogen synthase kinase 3 beta — or 'GSK3ß' for short — is an enzyme that has been linked to many important functions throughout the body and brain, including energy metabolism, neuronal cell development, and the regulation of the immune system.

12 Serotonin or 5-hydroxytryptamine is a monoamine neurotransmitter. It has a popular image as a contributor to feelings of well-being and happiness, though its actual biological function is complex and multifaceted, modulating cognition, reward, learning, memory, and numerous physiological processes such as vomiting and vasoconstriction.

13 Van den Broek, Thijs, and Maria Fleischmann. 'Prenatal famine exposure and mental health in later midlife'. Aging & mental health 23.2 (2019): 166–170.

14 Hoek, Hans W., et al. 'Schizoid personality disorder after prenatal exposure to famine'. *The American Journal of Psychiatry* 153.12 (1996): 1637. Neugebauer, Richard, Hans Wijbrand Hoek, and Ezra Susser. 'Prenatal exposure to wartime famine and development of antisocial personality disorder in early adulthood'. JAMA 282.5 (1999): 455–462. Hoek, Hans W., Alan S. Brown, and Ezra Susser. 'The Dutch famine and schizophrenia spectrum disorders.' Social psychiatry and psychiatric epidemiology 33.8 (1998): 373–379.

15 Wang, Chao, et al. 'Association between exposure to the Chinese famine in different stages of early life and decline in cognitive functioning in adulthood'. Frontiers in Behavioral Neuroscience 10 (2016): 146.

16 The Mini-Mental State Examination (MMSE) or Folstein test is a 30-point questionnaire that is used extensively in clinical and research settings to measure cognitive impairment.

17 The Montreal Cognitive Assessment (MoCA) is a widely used screening assessment for detecting cognitive impairment.

18 Stroop Color and Word Test provides a diagnosis of brain dysfunction, and the evaluation of stress, personality cognition and psychopathology.

19 Goh, J., et al. 'Workplace stressors & health outcomes: health policy for the workplace'. Behavioral Science & Policy 1.1 (2015):43–52.

20 https://www.mckinsey.com/industries/financial-services/our-insights/a-global-view-of-financial-life-during-covid-19.

21 Altmann, Erik M., J. Gregory Trafton, and David Z. Hambrick. 'Momentary interruptions can derail the train of thought'. *Journal of Experimental Psychology: General* 143.1 (2014): 215.

22 https://lifehacker.com/how-long-it-takes-to-get-back-on-track-after-a-distract-1720708353.

23 Adler, Gustavo, et al. and Marcos Poplawski-Ribeiro. 2017. 'Gone with the Headwinds: Global Productivity'. Staff Discussion Note 17/04, International Monetary Fund,

Washington, DC.
24 Goh, J., et al. 'Workplace stressors & health outcomes: health policy for the workplace'. Behavioral Science & Policy 1.1 (2015):43–52.
25 Kühn, Stefan. '1 Global employment and social trends.' *World Employment and Social Outlook* 2020.1 (2020): 15-38.
26 https://www.ilo.org/wcmsp5/groups/public/@dgreports/@dcomm/documents/briefingnote/wcms_749399.pdf.
27 Kühn, Stefan. '1 Global employment and social trends'. *World Employment and Social Outlook* 2019.1 (2019): 5–24.
28 Rugulies, Reiner, Birgit Aust, and Ida EH Madsen. 'Effort–reward imbalance at work and risk of depressive disorders. A systematic review and meta-analysis of prospective cohort studies'. *Scandinavian Journal of Work, Environment & Health* 43.4 (2017): 294–306.
29 Van Vegchel, Natasja, et al. 'Reviewing the effort-reward imbalance model: drawing up the balance of 45 empirical studies'. *Social science & medicine* 60.5 (2005): 1117–1131.
30 Chandola, Tarani, Alexandros Heraclides, and Meena Kumari. 'Psychophysiological biomarkers of workplace stressors'. Neuroscience & Biobehavioral Reviews 35.1 (2010): 51–57.
31 Lallukka, Tea, et al. '001-6 Changes in organisational injustice and subsequent changes in insomnia symptoms: using observational data as non-randomised pseudo-trials'. (2016): A2–A3.
32 Innosight is a management consulting firm advising enterprises on business strategy. Innosight was founded in 2000 by Harvard Business School professor Clayton M. Christensen and senior partner Mark W. Johnson.
33 https://www.innosight.com/wp-content/uploads/2017/11/Innosight-Corporate-Longevity-2018.pdf.
34 Frey, Carl Benedikt, and Michael A. Osborne. 'The Future of Employment: How susceptible are jobs to computerisation?' *Technological forecasting and social change* 114 (2017): 254–280.
35 https://www.lawgeex.com/resources/AIvsLawyer/.
36 https://www.iol.co.za/business-report/economy/unemployment-rate-drops-as-lockdown-prevents-job-search-44eee17d-8a9c-4a09-afe2-866851572ff5.
37 https://businesstech.co.za/news/business/332367/skills-vs-employment-in-south-africa-and-the-truth-about-getting-a-job/.
38 Gomis, Roger, Steven Kapsos, and Stefan Kuhn. 'World Employment and Social Outlook Trends 2020.' (2020).
39 World Economic Forum. 'The Future of Jobs Report 2018'. World Economic Forum, Geneva, Switzerland, 2018.
40 Goh, J., et al. 'Workplace stressors & health outcomes: health policy for the workplace'. Behavioral Science & Policy 1.1 (2015):43–52.
41 https://insight.jbs.cam.ac.uk/2020/economic-impact/?utm_source=MeltwaterPressRelease&utm_medium=Email&utm_campaign=COVID19&utm_content=GDPRisk_

CRS&mod=article_inline.
42 Frone, Michael R. 'What happened to the employed during the Great Recession? A US population study of net change in employee insecurity, health, and organizational commitment'. *Journal of Vocational Behavior* 107 (2018): 246–260.
43 Houdmont, Jonathan, Robert Kerr, and Ken Addley. 'Psychosocial factors and economic recession: the Stormont Study'. Occupational Medicine 62.2 (2012): 98–104.
44 Chou, Eileen Y., Bidhan L. Parmar, and Adam D. Galinsky. 'Economic insecurity increases physical pain'. *Psychological Science* 27.4 (2016): 443–454.
45 https://www.gallup.com/analytics/248909/gallup-2019-global-emotions-report-pdf.aspx.
46 Gaskin, Darrell J., and Patrick Richard. 'The economic costs of pain in the United States'. *The Journal of Pain* 13.8 (2012): 715–724.
47 Cheng, Grand H-L., and Darius K-S. Chan. 'Who suffers more from job insecurity? A meta-analytic review'. *Applied Psychology* 57.2 (2008): 272–303. Sverke, Magnus, and Johnny Hellgren. 'The nature of job insecurity: Understanding employment uncertainty on the brink of a new millennium'. Applied Psychology 51.1 (2002): 23–42.
48 Heine, Steven J., Travis Proulx, and Kathleen D. Vohs. 'The meaning maintenance model: On the coherence of social motivations'. *Personality and social psychology review* 10.2 (2006): 88–110.
49 Green, Francis. 'Health effects of job insecurity'. *IZA World of labor* (2015).
50 Green, Francis. 'Unpacking the misery multiplier: How employability modifies the impacts of unemployment and job insecurity on life satisfaction and mental health'. *Journal of Health Economics* 30.2 (2011): 265–276.
51 Sacks, Jonathan. *Morality: Restoring the Common Good in Divided Times*. Basic Books, 2020.
52 Junger, Sebastian. *Tribe: On homecoming and belonging*. Twelve, 2016.
53 Insulin-like growth factor 1 (IGF-1) also called somatomedin C, is a hormone similar in molecular structure to insulin, which plays an important role in childhood growth, and has anabolic effects in adults.
54 Uvnas-Moberg, Kerstin, and Maria Petersson. 'Oxytocin, a mediator of anti-stress, well-being, social interaction, growth and healing'. *Z Psychosom Med Psychother* 51.1 (2005): 57–80.
55 http://www3.weforum.org/docs/WEF_The_Promise_of_Platform_Work.pdf.
56 https://www.edelman.com/sites/g/files/aatuss191/files/2019-02/2019_Edelman_Trust_Barometer_Global_Report.pdf.
57 Manyika, James, et al. 'Independent work: Choice, necessity, and the gig economy'. *McKinsey Global Institute* 2016 (2016): 1–16.
58 https://www.imf.org/en/News/Articles/2020/04/07/sp040920-SMs2020-Curtain-Raiser.
59 Fairwork (2020) Gig Workers, Platforms and Government During Covid-19 in South Africa. Oxford, United Kingdom.
60 https://www.nature.com/articles/d41573-020-00073-5.
61 https://www.who.int/publications/m/item/

draft-landscape-of-covid-19-candidate-vaccines.
62 Amino acid fragments used to engineer the induction of highly targeted immune responses.
63 Viral vectors are tools commonly used by molecular biologists to deliver genetic material into cells. This process can be performed inside a living organism (in vivo) or in cell culture (in vitro). A chemically weakened virus is introduced to the body to transport pieces of the pathogen in order to stimulate an immune response.
64 Recombinant proteins are a manipulated form of proteins which are generated in various ways to produce large quantities of proteins or modify gene sequences. They are often synthetic peptides that contain only a fraction of the pathogenic organism.
65 Marmot, M.G., et al. 'Employment grade and coronary heart disease in British civil servants'. *Journal of Epidemiology and Community Health* 32.4 (1978):244–49. Marmot, M.G., et al. 'Health inequalities among British civil servants: the Whitehall II study'. *The Lancet* 337.8754 (1991):1387–93.
66 Gentes, Emily L., and Ayelet Meron Ruscio. 'A meta-analysis of the relation of intolerance of uncertainty to symptoms of generalized anxiety disorder, major depressive disorder, and obsessive–compulsive disorder'. *Clinical psychology* review 31.6 (2011): 923–933.
67 Rosser, Benjamin A. 'Intolerance of uncertainty as a transdiagnostic mechanism of psychological difficulties: A systematic review of evidence pertaining to causality and temporal precedence'. Cognitive Therapy and Research 43.2 (2019): 438–463.
68 Goh, J., et al. 'Workplace stressors & health outcomes: health policy for the workplace'. Behavioral Science & Policy 1.1 (2015):43–52.
69 https://www.cigna.com/static/www-cigna-com/docs/about-us/newsroom/studies-and-reports/combatting-loneliness/cigna-2020-loneliness-factsheet.pdf.
70 Leigh-Hunt, Nicholas, et al. 'An overview of systematic reviews on the public health consequences of social isolation and loneliness.' Public health 152 (2017): 157-171.
71 Wang, Jingyi, et al. 'Loneliness as a predictor of outcomes in mental disorders among people who have experienced a mental health crisis: a 4-month prospective study.' BMC psychiatry 20 (2020): 1-15.
72 https://www.hst.org.za/publications/South%20African%20Health%20Reviews/16%20SAHR_2019_Population%20ageing%20in%20South%20Africa.pdf.
73 https://ourworldindata.org/living-alone.

3. The Impact of the Giant Storm

1 https://www.stress.org/stress-research.
2 https://www.who.int/mental_health/evidence/burn-out/en/.
3 Rotenstein, Lisa S., et al. 'Prevalence of burnout among physicians: a systematic review'. JAMA 320.11 (2018): 1131–1150.
4 Jamieson, J.P., M.K. Nock, W.B. Mendes. 'Mind over matter: reappraising arousal

improves cardiovascular and cognitive responses to stress.' *Journal of Experimental Psychology: General* 141.3 (2012):417–22.

5 Zhang, L., et al. 'Effects of curcumin on chronic, unpredictable, mild, stress-induced depressive-like behaviour and structural plasticity in the lateral amygdala of rats'. *The International Journal of Neuropsychopharmacology* 17.5 (2014):793–806.

6 He, Hong-yi, et al. 'Association of brain-derived neurotrophic factor levels and depressive symptoms in young adults with acne vulgaris'. BMC psychiatry 19.1 (2019): 193.

7 Mahar, Ian, et al. 'Stress, serotonin, and hippocampal neurogenesis in relation to depression and antidepressant effects'. Neuroscience & Biobehavioral Reviews 38 (2014): 173–192.

8 https://ourworldindata.org/mental-health#prevalence-of-mental-health-and substance-use-disorders.

9 Brooks, Samantha K., et al. 'The psychological impact of quarantine and how to reduce it: rapid review of the evidence'. *The Lancet* (2020).

10 Sacks, Jonathan. *Morality: Restoring the Common Good in Divided Times.* Basic Books, 2020.

11 Wittchen, Hans-Ulrich, et al. 'The size and burden of mental disorders and other disorders of the brain in Europe 2010'. *European neuropsychopharmacology* 21.9 (2011): 655–679.

12 Insight, Matrix. 'Economic analysis of workplace mental health promotion and mental disorder prevention programmes and of their potential contribution to EU health, social and economic policy objectives'. *Rochester: Matrix Insight: Executive Agency for Health and Consumers* (2013).

13 https://ec.europa.eu/health/sites/health/files/mental_health/docs/compass_2017workplace_en.pdf.

14 Medibank. 'Sick at work: The cost of presenteeism to your business and the economy'. (2011).

15 Irastorza, X., M. Milczarek, and W. Cockburn. 'Second European Survey of Enterprises on New and Emerging Risks (ESENER-2)'. *Overview Report: Managing Safety and Health at Work. European Risk Observatory* (2016).

16 Beck, Arne, et al. 'Severity of depression and magnitude of productivity loss'. *Annals of Family Medicine* 9.4 (2011): 305–311.

17 https://tradingeconomics.com/european-union/labor-force-participation-rate.

18 https://medium.com/@muttalipolgun/what-is-the-real-cost-of-losing-an-employee-2df7e7e0da4b.

19 Oxford Economics. 'The cost of brain drain: understanding the financial impact of staff turnover.' Report, March. Retrieved April 18 (2014): 2018.

20 Melone, L. 'Calling it Quits'. (2006): 42.

21 https://www.consultancy.uk/news/23439/2019-saw-uk-retail-suffer-25-year-low.

22 https://www.bbc.com/news/business-51706225.

23 http://www.hse.gov.uk/statistics/causdis/stress.pdf.

24 Centre for Mental Health. Mental health at work: The business costs ten years on. (2017) https://www.centreformentalhealth.org.uk/publications/mental-health-work-business-costs-ten-years.
25 Stevenson, D., and P. Farmer. 'Thriving at work: the independent review of mental health and employers'. (2017).
26 THOR-GP is a reporting scheme that uses a research network of general practitioners with training in Occupational Medicine to determine the incidence of occupational disease, work-related ill health and sickness absence burden in the UK.
27 McManus, Sally, et al. Mental Health and Wellbeing in England: Adult Psychiatric Morbidity Survey 2014: A Survey Carried Out for NHS Digital by NatCen Social Research and the Department of Health Sciences, University of Leicester. NHS Digital, 2016.
28 https://happiness-report.s3.amazonaws.com/2020/WHR20.pdf.
29 https://news.gallup.com/poll/249098/americans-stress-worry-anger-intensified-2018.aspx?g_source=link_NEWSV9&g_medium=LEAD&g_campaign=item_&g_content=Americans%27%2520Stress%2c%2520Worry%2520and%2520Anger%2520Intensified%2520in%25202018.
30 https://www.apa.org/news/press/releases/stress/2014/stress-report.pdf.
31 https://www.apa.org/news/press/releases/stress/2017/state-nation.pdf. https://www.apa.org/news/press/releases/stress/2018/stress-gen-z.pdf.
32 https://www.apa.org/news/press/releases/stress/2020/stress-in-america-covid.pdf.
33 Goh, Joel, Jeffrey Pfeffer, and Stefanos A. Zenios. 'The relationship between workplace stressors and mortality and health costs in the United States'. Management Science 62.2 (2016): 608–628.
34 https://www.stress.org/42-worrying-workplace-stress-statistics.
35 https://www.wrike.com/blog/stress-epidemic-report-announcement/.
36 Evans-Lacko, Sara, and Martin Knapp. 'Global patterns of workplace productivity for people with depression: absenteeism and presenteeism costs across eight diverse countries'. *Social psychiatry and psychiatric epidemiology* 51.11 (2016): 1525–1537.
37 https://www.bloomberg.com/graphics/best-and-worst/#most-stressed-out-countries
38 http://www.statssa.gov.za/?p=12115.
39 https://data.worldbank.org/indicator/NY.GDP.MKTP.KD.ZG?end=2019&locations=ZA&start=1961&view=chart.
40 https://tradingeconomics.com/south-africa/gdp-growth-annual.
41 Strully, Kate W. 'Job loss and health in the US labor market'. *Demography* 46.2 (2009): 221–246.
42 Dooley, David, Ralph Catalano, and Georjeanna Wilson. 'Depression and unemployment: panel findings from the Epidemiologic Catchment Area study'. *American Journal of Community Psychology* 22.6 (1994): 745–765.
43 Eliason, Marcus, and Donald Storrie. 'Does job loss shorten life?' *The Journal of Human Resources* 44.2 (2009): 277–302.

44 Sullivan, Daniel, and Till Von Wachter. 'Job displacement and mortality: An analysis using administrative data'. *Quarterly Journal of Economics* 124.3 (2009): 1265–1306.

45 Kivimäki, Mika, et al. 'Long working hours and risk of coronary heart disease and stroke: a systematic review and meta-analysis of published and unpublished data for 603 838 individuals'. *The Lancet* 386.10005 (2015): 1739–1746.

46 Virtanen, Marianna, et al. 'Long working hours and depressive symptoms: systematic review and meta-analysis of published studies and unpublished individual participant data'. *Scandinavian Journal of Work Environment & Health* 44.3 (2018): 239–250.

47 https://profmed.co.za/wp-content/uploads/2019/01/New-Profmed-infographic2018-final.pdf.

48 https://www.ipsos.com/en/what-worries-world-may-2020.

49 Stander, Marthinus Petrus, et al. 'Depression and the Impact on Productivity in the Workplace: Findings from a South African Survey on Depression in the Workplace'. *International Journal of Depression and Anxiety*. S 2 (2016): 1–8.

50 Henderson, Max, et al. 'Work and common psychiatric disorders'. *Journal of the Royal Society of Medicine* 104.5 (2011): 198–207.

4. The Action Plan

1 https://www.edelman.com/sites/g/files/aatuss191/files/2020-01/2020%20Edelman%20Trust%20Barometer%20Global%20Report.pdf.

2 https://businesstech.co.za/news/lifestyle/334357/heres-how-many-skilled-professionals-are-leaving-south-africa-every-day/.

3 https://www.forbes.com/sites/williamarruda/2016/11/15/9-differences-between-being-a-leader-and-a-manager/#38efb7694609.

4 Mankins, Michael. 'Great companies obsess over productivity, not efficiency'. Harvard Business Review 3 (2017).

5 http://www3.weforum.org/docs/WEF_TheGlobalCompetitivenessReport2019.pdf.

6 Goh, Joel, Jeffrey Pfeffer, and Stefanos Zenios. 'Exposure To Harmful Workplace Practices Could Account For Inequality In Life Spans Across Different Demographic Groups'. *Health Affairs* 34.10 (2015): 1761–1768.

7 Omotoso, Kehinde O., and Steven F. Koch. 'Assessing changes in social determinants of health inequalities in South Africa: a decomposition analysis'. *International Journal for Equity in Health* 17.1 (2018): 181.

8 Olshansky, S. Jay, et al. 'Differences in life expectancy due to race and educational differences are widening, and many may not catch up'. *Health Affairs* 31.8 (2012): 1803–1813.

9 https://ourworldindata.org/life-expectancy.

10 Marmot, Michael G., et al. 'Health inequalities among British civil servants: the Whitehall II study'. *The Lancet* 337.8754 (1991): 1387–1393.

11 https://www.ceicdata.com/en/indicator/south-africa/labour-productivity-growth.

12 Bloom, David E., et al. *The global economic burden of noncommunicable diseases*. No. 8712. Program on the Global Demography of Aging, 2012.
13 Trautmann, Sebastian, Jürgen Rehm, and Hans–Ulrich Wittchen. 'The economic costs of mental disorders: Do our societies react appropriately to the burden of mental disorders?.' EMBO reports 17.9 (2016): 1245–1249.
14 Evans-Lacko, Sara, and Martin Knapp. 'Global patterns of workplace productivity for people with depression: absenteeism and presenteeism costs across eight diverse countries'. *Social psychiatry and psychiatric epidemiology* 51.11 (2016): 1525–1537.
15 Song, Zirui, and Katherine Baicker. 'Effect of a workplace wellness program on employee health and economic outcomes: a randomized clinical trial'. JAMA 321.15 (2019): 1491–1501.
16 Chapman, Larry. 'Meta-evaluation of worksite health promotion economic return studies'. *J Health Promot* 248 (2003): 682–707.
17 Lechner, Lilian, and Hein de Vries. 'Effects of an employee fitness program on reduced absenteeism'. *Journal of Occupational and Environmental Medicine* 39.9 (1997): 827–831.
18 Bowne, Donald W., et al. 'Reduced disability and health care costs in an industrial fitness program'. *Journal of Occupational Medicine: official publication of the Industrial Medical Association* 26.11 (1984): 809–816.
19 Baicker, Katherine, David Cutler, and Zirui Song. 'Workplace wellness programs can generate savings'. *Health Affairs* 29.2 (2010): 304–311.
20 Mattke, Soeren, et al. 'Workplace wellness programs study'. *Rand Health quarterly* 3.2 (2013).
21 Goh, Joel, Jeffrey Pfeffer, and Stefanos A. Zenios. 'The relationship between workplace stressors and mortality and health costs in the United States'. *Management Science* 62.2 (2016): 608–628.
22 Pfeffer, Jeffrey. *Dying for a Paycheck: How Modern Management Harms Employee Health and Company Performance – and What We Can Do About It.* HarperCollins, 2018.
23 Takala, Jukka, et al. 'Global estimates of the burden of injury and illness at work in 2012'. *Journal of Occupational and Environmental Hygiene* 11.5 (2014): 326–337.
24 LaMontagne, Anthony D., et al. 'A systematic review of the job-stress intervention evaluation literature, 1990–2005'. *International Journal of Occupational and Environmental Health* 13.3 (2007): 268–280.
25 https://www.barralinstitute.com.
26 Grant, Adam M. *Originals: How Non-Conformists Move the World.* Penguin, 2017.
27 Kotter, John P. *Leading Change.* Harvard Business Review Press, 2012.
28 Mankins, Michael C., and Eric Garton. Time, Talent, Energy: Overcome Organizational Drag and Unleash Your Team's Productive Power. Harvard Business Review Press, 2017.
29 Mathieu, Michael, Kevin J. Eschleman, and Danqiao Cheng. 'Meta-analytic and multiwave comparison of emotional support and instrumental support in the workplace'. *Journal of Occupational Health Psychology* 24.3 (2019): 387.
30 Lazarus, Richard S. 'Progress on a cognitive-motivational-relational theory of emotion'.

American Psychologist 46.8 (1991): 819.

31 Watson, David, et al. 'The two general activation systems of affect: Structural findings, evolutionary considerations, and psychobiological evidence'. *Journal of Personality and Social Psychology* 76.5 (1999): 820.

32 Shah, Naimatullah, Sadia Anwar, and Zahir Irani. 'The Impact of Organisational Justice on Ethical Behaviour'. (2017).

33 Goh, J., et al. 'Workplace stressors & health outcomes: health policy for the workplace'. *Behavioral Science & Policy* 1.1 (2015):43–52.

34 Colquitt, Jason A., et al. 'Justice at the millennium, a decade later: A meta-analytic test of social exchange and affect-based perspectives'. *Journal of Applied Psychology* 98.2 (2013): 199.

35 Barsky, Adam, and Seth A. Kaplan. 'If you feel bad, it's unfair: A quantitative synthesis of affect and organizational justice perceptions'. *Journal of Applied Psychology* 92.1 (2007): 286.

36 Hunt, Vivian, et al. 'Delivering through diversity'. McKinsey & Company. Retrieved April 3 (2018): 2018.

37 Derven, Marjorie. 'Diversity and inclusion by design: best practices from six global companies'. *Industrial and Commercial Training* (2014).

38 Economic profit margin is the difference between accounting profit and opportunity cost the business has forgone as the business has invested in its existing project.

39 https://www.mckinsey.com/featured-insights/gender-equality/taking-the-lead-for-inclusion.

40 https://hbr.org/2020/01/5-strategies-for-creating-an-inclusive-workplace.

41 Nielsen, Morten Birkeland, Stig Berge Matthiesen, and Ståle Einarsen. 'The impact of methodological moderators on prevalence rates of workplace bullying. A meta-analysis'. *Journal of Occupational and Organizational Psychology* 83.4 (2010): 955–979.

42 Van de Vliert, Evert, Ståle Einarsen, and Morten Birkeland Nielsen. 'Are national levels of employee harassment cultural covariations of climato-economic conditions? *Work & Stress* 27.1 (2013): 106–122.

43 Van den Brande, Whitney, et al. 'The role of work stressors, coping strategies and coping resources in the process of workplace bullying: A systematic review and development of a comprehensive model'. *Aggression and Violent Behavior* 29 (2016): 61–71.

44 Nielsen, Morten Birkeland, and Ståle Valvatne Einarsen. 'What we know, what we do not know, and what we should and could have known about workplace bullying: an overview of the literature and agenda for future research'. *Aggression and violent behavior* 42 (2018): 71–83.

45 Nielsen, Morten Birkeland, Anne-Marthe Rustad Indregard, and Simon Øverland. 'Workplace bullying and sickness absence: a systematic review and meta-analysis of the research literature'. *Scandinavian Journal of Work, Environment & Health* (2016): 359–370.

46 Xu, Tianwei, et al. 'Workplace bullying and violence as risk factors for type 2 diabetes: a multicohort study and meta-analysis'. *Diabetologia* 61.1 (2018): 75–83.

47 Namie, Gary, and Ruth Namie. *Bully at work: What you can do to stop the hurt and reclaim your dignity on the job*. Sourcebooks, Inc., 2009.

48 Rugulies, Reiner, Birgit Aust, and Ida EH Madsen. 'Effort–reward imbalance at work and risk of depressive disorders. A systematic review and meta-analysis of prospective cohort studies'. *Scandinavian Journal of Work, Environment & Health* (2017): 294–306.

49 Penz, Marlene, et al. 'Effort-reward imbalance at work is associated with hair cortisol concentrations: Prospective evidence from the Dresden Burnout Study'. *Psychoneuroendocrinology* 109 (2019): 104399.

50 Ruttle, Paula L., et al. 'Disentangling psychobiological mechanisms underlying internalizing and externalizing behaviors in youth: Longitudinal and concurrent associations with cortisol'. *Hormones and behavior* 59.1 (2011): 123–132.

51 Hamilton, John E. 'Cash or kudos: Addressing the effort-reward imbalance for academic employees'. *International Journal of Stress Management* 26.2 (2019): 193.

52 Sana, Faria, Tina Weston, and Nicholas J. Cepeda. 'Laptop multitasking hinders classroom learning for both users and nearby peers'. *Computers & Education* 62 (2013): 24–31.

53 Loh, Kep Kee, and Ryota Kanai. 'Higher media multi-tasking activity is associated with smaller gray-matter density in the anterior cingulate cortex'. *Plos one* 9.9 (2014).

ACKNOWLEDGEMENTS

To the team at Pan Macmillan, I cannot begin to express my gratitude for your belief in me, for your support, valued advice and input.

And to Jane, who brought the book and its message to life.

THE STRESS CODE APP

The genesis of The Stress Code app was wanting to create a simplified and accessible version of my book, *The Stress Code*, an in-depth look at stress that provides the skills, tools and resources required to thrive during challenging and difficult times in our lives.

The app was originally constructed to complement the book, but as the two-year development process, and its numerous iterations, unfolded and evolved, it emerged as a tool with vastly expanded functionality, specifically relating to health promotion and leadership.

On an individual level, the app offers the user the ability to assess their stress and resilience levels and check in on their mood experiences. It provides an objective rating system, comparatives and an all-important strategy, but most importantly it gives the user an understanding as to what stresses are having the greatest impact on their mental, physical and emotional health.

Following a one-year pilot study with a US-based professional services company, I was better able to understand the existing relationship between stress and resilience scores within the context of creativity and productivity and realisation of potential. For example, if a person's stress was too low or too high, their potential would be undermined, indicating an ideal performance range or 'sweet spot'. By the same token, if during challenging times resilience dipped below a certain threshold, individual potential would also not be fully realised at a time when it was needed most. This motivated me to create the novel 'Potential Index', now a central feature of the app.

In late April 2020, during the height of the global lockdown, I included a 'Burnout Barometer'. The motivation behind this new feature was that despite working from home, many professionals were (and continue to be) working longer hours and are unable to properly differentiate between their personal and professional lives. The 'Burnout Barometer' allows users to monitor and successfully manage their burnout.

At its inception, the app was designed to tackle key stress topics, such as mindset, support, connection, exercise, diet and nutrition, but due to the complexity of chronic stress and the broad symptom set, I decided to create an additional 'Health Hacks' feature. This tool covers the most common symptoms of stress, such as worry, anger, frustration and fatigue, and ways in which to successfully manage these conditions through targeted lifestyle interventions.

The technology's strongest feature is that it is able to create a powerful organisational overview using anonymised data inputs. A detailed dashboard provides leadership and human resources a real-time view of their team's stress and resilience levels together with an all-important mood profile. The technology is designed to help identify those stresses that are having the greatest impact on the business, and calculate the human and economic cost.

This knowledge and understanding can be extremely valuable in establishing the relative contribution of the different organisational stresses in compromised health and business performance and where the wellness focus needs to be placed.

Finally, the app gives leaders and their teams an opportunity to measure and even quantify resilience. Resilience is the capacity and dynamic process of being able to successfully overcome stress and life's challenges, while maintaining normal psychological and physical functioning. In simple terms, resilience defines our ability to thrive in adversity and is central in the realisation of our potential.

The anonymised data provides a clear insight of the resilience landscape, through quantification, comparatives and identification of strengths and existing hurdles. Psychological resilience is comprised of several converging characteristics that include health, social support, optimism, persistence, self-worth, personal values, adaptability and emotional regulation. Being able to identify group strengths can help businesses to better leverage off their teams' intrinsic abilities. At the same time, by identifying roadblocks, intervention steps can be taken to improve overall team and organisational performance.

The Stress Code app is a tool for individuals and leaders alike and provides invaluable data to equip users with the steps to fully actualise their potential.

ANDROID APP ON Google play

Download on the App Store